Finance and Financial Intermediation

Finance and Financial Intermediation

A Modern Treatment of Money, Credit, and Banking

HAROLD L. COLE

OXFORD
UNIVERSITY PRESS

Oxford University Press is a department of the University of Oxford.
It furthers the University's objective of excellence in research, scholarship,
and education by publishing worldwide. Oxford is a registered trade mark of
Oxford University Press in the UK and certain other countries.

Published in the United States of America by Oxford University Press
198 Madison Avenue, New York, NY 10016, United States of America.

© Oxford University Press 2019

Library of Congress Cataloging-in-Publication Data

Names: Cole, Harold Linh, 1957– author.
Title: Finance and financial intermediation : a modern treatment of money,
credit, and banking / Harold Cole.
Description: New York, NY : Oxford University Press, [2019] | Includes index.
Identifiers: LCCN 2018042498 | ISBN 9780190941703 (hardcover : alk. paper) |
ISBN 9780190941697 (pbk. : alk. paper)
Subjects: LCSH: Finance. | Intermediation (Finance)
Classification: LCC HG173 .C663 2019 | DDC 332—dc23 LC record available at
https://lccn.loc.gov/2018042498

CONTENTS

Preface ix

PART ONE Assets and the Structure of Financial Markets

1. Overview of the Financial System 3
   1. Financial System 3
   2. Lending and Insurance 4
   3. Penalties 7
   4. Financial Markets 10

2. Market Operation 14
   1. Securities Markets 14
   2. Treasury Auctions 17

PART TWO Asset Pricing

3. Asset Pricing I: Risk-Neutral Pricing 23
   1. Asset Pricing Methodology 23
   2. Information over Time and Probability Theory 24
   3. Risk-Neutral Pricing 25
   4. Bubbles 39
   5. The Efficient Markets Hypothesis 43

4. Asset Pricing with Growth 45
   1. Simple Growth 1 45
   2. Simple Growth 2 47
   3. Problems 49

5. Asset Pricing II 56
   1. Problems with the Simple Risk Neutral Model 56

2. Nominal Rates 58
3. Liquidity Benefit 59
4. Risk Aversion and the Pricing of Risk 60
5. Asset Pricing and Growth Revisited 65
6. Better but Far from Problem Free 68
7. Problems 69

6. Asset Pricing III: Arbitrage-Based Pricing 72
   1. Arbitrage Model 73
   2. Implications of Arbitrage-Based Pricing 74
   3. Asset Pricing Super Problem 79
   4. Factor Models 83
   5. Problems 84

7. Derivatives 85
   1. Derivative Pricing 89

PART THREE Firm Behavior in Light of Asset Pricing Theory

8. Investment and Capital Structure of the Firm 97
   1. Optimal Decisions under Certainty 97
   2. Optimal Decisions under Uncertainty 101
   3. Capital Structure 106
   4. Problems 110

PART FOUR Money, Exchange Rates, and Payments

9. Money 115
   1. Velocity Model 116
   2. Inventory (Baumol-Tobin) Model of Money 117
   3. Search Model of Money 119
   4. Standard Money Demand Functions 124
   5. Problems 124

10. Exchange Rates and Nominal Interest Rates 126
    1. Exchange Rates 127
    2. Interest Rate Parity 132

11. Moving Away from Money 136
    1. Electronic Payment Methods 136
    2. Credit Card Transactions and the Internet 138

3. Cryptocurrencies and Bitcoin 139
4. Everything Starts with Keeping Secrets 143

PART FIVE Financial Intermediation

12. Lending and the Development of Banks 155
    1. A Bit of Financial History 155
    2. A Simple Model of Lending 157
    3. Auditing and Debt: Townsend's Costly State Verification Model 162
    4. The Rise of Financial Intermediaries 165

13. More on Banks and Banking 168
    1. Banking in the U.S. 168
    2. Diamond and Dybvig's Model 170
    3. Savings and Loan Associations and the Crisis of the 1980s 179
    4. More Recent Trends in Banking 180
    5. The Demand for Safe Assets and Securitization 183
    6. Problems 186

14. The Financial Meltdown and the Great Recession 188
    1. Housing and Finance 188
    2. The Macroeconomy 193
    3. The Aftermath 194

PART SIX Deficits, Debt, Inflation, and Default

15. Debt, Spending, and Inflation 199
    1. A Bit of Public Finance History and Facts 199
    2. Fiscal Facts for the U.S. 201

16. Modeling Government Debt and Inflation 204
    1. Experiment 1 205
    2. Experiment 2 207
    3. Experiment 3 210
    4. Experiment 4 211
    5. The Barro-Gordon Model of Inflation 212
    6. Barro-Gordon and Debt 215

17. Debt, Default, and Interest Rates 217
    1. Latin American Debt Crises 217
    2. The EU Crisis 222

3. Modeling Default 225
4. Model of Sovereign Borrowing and Default 226

PART SEVEN Reviews

18. Math Reviews 241
    1. Optimization Review 241
    2. Probability Theory Review 245

Index 249

PREFACE

These notes grew out of lecture material that I developed while teaching a Money, Credit, and Banking course at the University of Pennsylvania. Traditionally, this has been a fairly low-brow institutionally oriented course. But finance has been at the heart of most major economic downturns, including the Great Depression, the more recent Great Recession, and the even more recent EU debt crisis. Looking at these sorts of events, I felt that there was a substantial amount of material on the macroeconomic aspects of finance and its interaction with the overall economy that a modern economist needs to know. This led me to teach a very different style of course, and in doing so, I needed to construct a very different style of text.

The text focuses on achieving a theoretical understanding of the material. While there is much to like in the philosopher George Santayana's famous quote that "those who cannot remember the past are doomed to repeat it," there is also something fundamentally missing from it. History repeats itself in many respects but often there are important differences. This is why economic theory is important, since it allows us to adapt our understanding to different circumstances. For this reason, I have tried to put the material being taught into some historical context while, at the same time, emphasizing the theory we use to think through past, current, and future events. Understanding the theory allows one to adapt our thinking to the novel aspects of current circumstances.

Several examples of technological progress have made creating this text possible. The first is Latex, which was invented in the 1980s. It has made creating a text with math and figures much easier than before. The second is Google, Google Scholar, and Wikipedia, all of which showed up in the 2000s. Finding information on a myriad of subjects was much harder before their creation. The third and final input is FRED, the online database of the Federal Reserve Bank of St. Louis, which made collecting data and developing figures much easier. I thank all of their creators.

PART ONE

Assets and the Structure of Financial Markets

We start with a brief overview of financial markets. We are interested in knowing something about what sorts of assets are out there, how they are traded, and where we can find data on them. We then try to sort out how these assets are priced. Since asset pricing is an extremely interesting topic, we delve pretty deeply into it.

Overview of the Financial System

This chapter gives an overview of the financial system and its basic taxonomy.

1. FINANCIAL SYSTEM

A *financial system* is a densely interconnected network of financial intermediaries, facilitators, and markets that serves three major purposes: *allocating capital, sharing risks*, and *facilitating intertemporal trade*.

(1) Individuals with valuable projects may need additional funding to undertake them. At the same time, individuals with funds but no good projects seek investment opportunities. *Allocating capital* allows individuals to specialize in being savers or investors.

(2) *Sharing risks* enables individuals to invest in their own project as well as in others to diversify risk. At the same time, it may be efficient to have them specialize in terms of the project they work on. Diversifying using financial claims enables risk sharing without also work or project sharing.

(3) *Intertemporal trades* occur between those who want to consume more than their income today with those who want to consume less. For example, students borrowing for college today trade with middle-aged people who want to save for their retirement.

Financial markets admit an incredibly diverse set of participants. *Borrowers* include inventors, entrepreneurs, and other economic agents (such as domestic households, governments, established businesses, and foreigners), with potentially profitable business ideas (positive net present value projects) but limited financial resources (expenditures greater than revenues). *Lenders* or savers include domestic households, businesses, governments, and foreigners with excess funds (i.e., revenues greater than expenditures). The financial system also helps to link risk-averse entities called *hedgers* to risk-taking entities known as *speculators*.

1.1. Internal vs. External Finance

When a firm funds investments out of current and past profits, this is called *internal finance*. When a firm has to seek additional funds from outsiders, this is called *external finance*. Without a financial system, all entrepreneurs would have to self-fund their projects out of their own savings, that is, internal finance only. It is often argued that financial frictions and a poorly developed financial system force firms to overly rely on internal finance and that this hinders their ability to grow.

2. LENDING AND INSURANCE

2.1. Direct Lending

One way to make loans is for individuals to simply match up and enter into contracts. This is called peer-to-peer lending (P2P) or "crowd lending." Businesses that provide these lending services typically do so online. As a result, they have lower overhead costs, which can lead to lower interest rates for borrowers and high returns to lenders, at least in principle. (These loans are typically unsecured; see more on this below.)

Peer Lending Network is an online peer lending marketplace that connects people looking for a loan with real people willing to make loans (http://www.peerlendingnetwork.com/index.html).

Step 1. People looking for a loan post a listing for a loan with the amount they need at a rate they can afford.
Step 2. Lenders bid the amount they are willing to lend the borrower and the rate at which they are willing to lend.
Step 3. When the listing is complete, the qualified bids are combined into a single loan for the borrower. Each month, the borrower pays the new loan amount to the lenders until the loan is repaid.

Several issues may come up with respect to participating in this market:

- Evaluating loan prospects may require specialized knowledge and the ability to gather information about the loan candidate.
- Enforcing your claims may also involve legal costs and there can be big economies of scale here. For example, you might have a department that specializes in claims collection that starts at the lowest cost means-of-collecting and gradually escalates up the cost chain.
- For reports of problems, see http://www.businessweek.com/investor/ content/apr2009/pi2009043_811816.htm.

2.2. Secured and Unsecured Loans

Secured loans are loans for which some asset, commonly referred to as *collateral*, has been pledged in case the debtor does not repay the loan. Failure to repay leads to a transfer of the ownership of this asset from the debtor to the creditor. Unsecured loans are simply loans for which no collateral was pledged. Examples of secured loans include

- mortgages, for which the house is pledged
- business loans, for which some physical or financial asset is pledged

Examples of unsecured loans include

- credit card debt
- commercial paper

Secured loans can involve lower transactions fees since in the event of a failure to repay, the creditor simply gets the collateral. Also, because the holder of a secured loan has been assured that he/she is first in line for a claim on a specific asset in the case of failure to honor the loan contract, these loans are generally considered safer than unsecured credit. As a result, they typically command a lower rate of interest.

Mortgages are an important example of secured loans. Mortgages date back to the Middle Ages. They can involve either residential property, in which case a home-buyer borrows to finance the purchase of his house while pledging it as collateral, or commercial property, in which case a business makes a similar arrangement.

Secured loans are often *over-collateralized* with a common margin being 10–20%. For example, home buyers typically put down at least 20% of the price of the home and borrow the remainder. Note that since they are pledging their house as well, the loan is over-collateralized by 20%. We will examine why this is the case later on.

2.3. Good Projects vs. Bad Projects

In a world with certainty, this is relatively straightforward to define. A good project is a profitable project, while a bad one is not. By *profitable* we mean that after all the investments are made and the receipts are collected,

(1) there is a positive net amount of money left, and
(2) the net is greater than we would have gotten from simply investing the money in another available project of comparable risk.

This is referred to as a *positive net present value project.*

Even in a world with certainty, a profitable project is not simply one that has a net positive amount of money left. To see why, note that one could always invest in a savings account and earn interest, and so, on net, have a positive amount of money left. Hence, one inherently needs to take account of the opportunity cost of investing in this project versus another.

2.4. Risky Projects

Once we allow for uncertainty, evaluating projects, investments, and assets becomes much trickier. Our notion of what is a good project or investment must also take into account risk; otherwise, someone who wins at roulette would be claiming that this was a good investment. So, it's not going to be enough to look at a single ex post outcome and declare whether a project was good or bad. Somehow, we need to take into account the full range of potential outcomes. One standard approach is to simply look at the expected return on the project. But, as we see later, this often does a poor job of explaining asset prices, because individuals often care about the circumstances in which the investment project pays off. Filling in all the details in a coherent way is going to require a lot of structure, but we will get there.

2.5. Information Frictions

A key problem in financial contracts is that the borrower may have better information about his project than the lender. This situation can arise for a variety of reasons:

- Evaluating a project may require specialized knowledge or experience. The borrower may naturally be better equipped to undertake this evaluation, since he/she has to run the project.
- The borrower may have obtained some confidential information, e.g., examining core samples from prior drilling at the proposed drilling or lease site.

Of course the borrower could just pass on his information, but credibility may be a problem. This is especially true if the borrower has limited liability or bankruptcy protection. This creates a situation in which, if the project does well, both lender and borrower win, but the borrower wins big. On the other hand, if the project goes bad, both the lender and the borrower lose but the lender loses big. With these kinds of payoffs, the borrower can have an incentive to go ahead even though the project is not very good.

2.5.1. UNDERWRITING AND LLOYD'S OF LONDON

Underwriting is a process that a financial entity undertakes to assess whether a customer is a good bet for their product. This involves assessing the risks that that customer poses. Examples include the risks of repayment for a mortgage borrower, property damage risks for someone buying property insurance, and so on. The term arose from the practice at Lloyd's of London.

Lloyd's began in the coffee house owned by Edward Lloyd in the 17th century. Lloyd's is an insurance market (not a company) and it acts to regulate the market. So-called *Names* were rich individuals who joined Lloyd's for a year at a time and backed policies written at Lloyd's with all of their personal wealth (unlimited liability). (This unlimited liability policy has changed more recently.) Names who wanted to take part in insuring some risk (originally the risks associated with sea voyages) would write their names down under the information that was written on a Lloyd's slip about this venture—hence the term *underwriting*.

3. PENALTIES

Historically and even across countries and states, there can be big differences in credit remedies and borrower penalties. These differences can have big effects on people's incentive to borrow money, and can, in turn, affect the extent of investment, especially risky investment, being undertaken.

European bankruptcy laws tend to be harsher than U.S. ones in that companies typically end up in liquidation. The various countries also treat creditors quite differently.

3.1. Harsh Penalties for Failure to Repay

Historically penalties imposed on borrowers who failed to repay their debts were much more severe than they are today:

- Debt bondage was common in ancient Mediterranean societies, including Greek city-states.
- Under the early Roman Republic, a person could pledge himself as collateral for a loan, in a type of contract called a Nexum. If he failed to pay, he was liable to become his creditor's slave.
- During Europe's Middle Ages, debtors, both men and women, were locked up together in a single large cell until their families paid their debt. Some debt prisoners were released to become serfs or indentured servants (debt bondage) until they paid off their debt in labor.
- Prior to the mid-19th century, debtors' prisons were a common way to deal with unpaid debt.

With very harsh penalties, borrowers have a strong incentive to borrow only if they can repay the loan. Hence, there is not much need for information gathering by lender.

3.2. Modest Penalties under Modern Bankruptcy

Bankruptcy laws have reduced the penalties from becoming insolvent. From the U.S. Courts website (http://www.uscourts.gov/services-forms/bankruptcy):

> Bankruptcy laws help people who can no longer pay their creditors get a fresh start—by liquidating assets to pay their debts or by creating a repayment plan. Bankruptcy laws also protect troubled businesses and provide for orderly distributions to business creditors through reorganization or liquidation.
>
> Most cases are filed under the three main chapters of the Bankruptcy Code—Chapter 7, Chapter 11, and Chapter 13. Federal courts have exclusive jurisdiction over bankruptcy cases. This means that a bankruptcy case cannot be filed in a state court.

The goal here is not just to make the lender whole while making the insolvent borrower suffer. Instead, we also want to help the borrower to recover from his adverse outcome.

3.3. Efficient Penalties

- With harsh penalties:
  - A borrower who was not confident of his ability to repay would not borrow.
  - The borrower will take care to maintain his ability to repay.
  - As a result, the lender does not need to gather a lot of information on the borrower and how his project is doing.
- With modest penalties:
  - A borrower may borrow even when he may not be able to repay (i.e. take risks). The borrower may also exaggerate his likelihood of repayment. Moreover, the borrowers with the most risky projects and who are thus those less likely to repay, may be the most eager to borrow and therefore willing to pay the highest interest rates. This is called *adverse selection* because the pool of people who take up the loan offer or contract are worse than those in the overall pool.
  - The borrower may not have as much incentive to make his project pay off once he has contracted a debt obligation. If we cannot monitor his efforts, then he may slack off. This is called *moral hazard.*
  - So lenders need to gather information to evaluate borrowers and to monitor their post-loan behavior.

How to gauge which sort of penalties are right?

Project outcomes may be inherently random: How much grain does a plot of land produce? How many fish does a fishing boat catch? How many hats does a hat store sell? Given such randomness, harsh penalties may make individuals too reluctant to undertake projects if outside funding is required.

Gathering information about or monitoring a borrower is costly. Given the need to gather information, the lender must demand a higher return on the loan to cover his costs. These higher returns make the loan more expensive. Hence, modest penalties may make it much harder for individuals to secure outside funding for projects.

This suggests that efficient punishment is neither too harsh nor too lenient.

The need to gather information in the modern environment of modest penalties can have some interesting implications about what form financial institutions will take. Information gathering is thought to exhibit economies of scale:

- There are fixed costs of setting up an information network or learning how to gather information.

- Lenders may need a variety of specialized information for evaluating each project.

These economies of scale may help to explain why financial institutions tend to be larger these days than they used to be.

3.4. Building and Loan (B&L) Associations

One way around information frictions and weak enforcement was through ethnic B&L associations. These first arose in the early 1800s among ethnic Americans. One of their main purposes was to promote homeownership. These associations helped overcome the information frictions associated with different ethnic communities interacting with the established society. Because these communities were tightly knit, social sanctions added additional penalties for improper behavior or bad outcomes. One of their main purposes was to promote homeownership. See http://www.thebhc.org/publications/BEHonline/2004/Mason.pdf

4. FINANCIAL MARKETS

4.1. Types of Markets

There are a wide variety of different financial markets due to the wide array of different financial instruments. Here is a basic taxonomy.

4.1.1. PRIMARY VS. SECONDARY MARKETS
Primary markets are markets in which newly created (issued) instruments are sold for the first time. An important example is new issues of Treasury bonds and bills.

4.1.2. CENTRALIZED VS. DECENTRALIZED
Centralized markets work through a main or central exchange. Orders are routed to this exchange and buy orders are matched up with sell orders. In centralized exchanges the *quoted price*, which is the price in the most recent transaction, is available to the participants, as is the history of quoted prices. Classical examples of centralized exchanges are the New York Stock Exchange and the Chicago Board of Trade, where futures and options are traded. Originally these markets worked through *open outcry* on an exchange floor.

Decentralized markets work through a variety of locations, typically connected by some sort of electronic network. Trading is done directly between the two parties to the trade without the sort of rules that many exchanges impose. In many cases the heart of a decentralized market is a connected set of brokers who both trade among themselves as well as with the general public. A classic example of a decentralized market is the mortgage market in which borrowers go around to various banks and other lending institutions seeking a loan. Many derivatives are traded in decentralized markets.

4.1.3. SHORT TERM VS. LONG TERM

Money markets are used to trade instruments with less than a year to maturity (repayment of principal). Examples include the markets for T-bills (Treasury bills or short-term government bonds), commercial paper (short-term corporate bonds), banker's acceptances (guaranteed bank funds, such as a cashier's check), negotiable certificates of deposit (large-denomination negotiable CDs, called NCDs), fed funds (overnight loans of reserves between banks), call loans (overnight loans on the collateral of stock), repurchase agreements (short-term loans on the collateral of T-bills), and foreign exchange (currencies of other countries).

Securities with a year or more to maturity trade in *capital markets*. Examples include longer term government debt, called Treasury Bonds, corporate bonds, commercial and consumer loans.

- Some capital market instruments, called perpetuities, never mature or fall due. Equities (ownership claims on the assets and income of corporations) and perpetual interest-only loans are prime examples.
- Most bonds or IOUs have maturities of 30 years or less.
- Interest-only loans mature in 15 or 30 years with a so-called balloon payment, in which the principal falls due all at once at the end of the loan.
- Consols is the common name for perpetual bonds issued by the Bank of England. These bonds were redeemable at the option of the government (which means that the government could retire the bond by paying the principal at a time of its choosing). Consols were first issued in the 1750s and paid an interest rate of around 3%. The last consol bonds were redeemed in 2015.

4.1.4. DERIVATIVES

A derivative is a financial instrument whose value is dependent upon an underlying asset. Derivatives are broadly categorized by the relationship between the underlying asset and the derivative (e.g., forward, option, swap); the type of underlying asset (e.g., equity derivatives, foreign exchange derivatives, interest rate derivatives, commodity derivatives, or credit derivatives); the market in which they trade (e.g., exchange-traded or over-the-counter); and their pay-off profile. Derivatives can be used for speculating purposes or to hedge risk.

There are three major classes of derivatives:

(1) *Futures/Forwards* are contracts to buy or sell an asset on or before a future date at a price specified today. Futures contracts are standardized contracts traded through an exchange. A forward contract is a non-standardized contract written by the parties themselves.

(2) *Options* are contracts that give the owner the right, but not the obligation, to buy (in the case of a call option) or sell (in the case of a put option) an asset. The contract fixes the strike price (the price at which the sale takes place), and the maturity. With a European option the owner has the right to require the sale to take place on the maturity date. With an American option the owner can require the sale to take place at any time up to the maturity date. If the owner of the contract exercises this right, the counterparty has the obligation to carry out the transaction.

(3) *Swaps* are contracts to exchange cash (flows) on or before a specified future date based on the underlying value of currencies/exchange rates, bonds/interest rates, commodities, stocks, or other assets.

4.1.5. FINANCIAL INSTITUTIONS

Finance obtained through financial institutions is commonly called indirect finance as opposed to direct finance through financial markets. They are commonly categorized according to the nature of the asset transformation they undertake:

(1) Depository institutions issue short-term deposits and either buy long-term securities or make long-term loans. They include commercial banks, savings banks, and credit unions.

(2) Insurance companies, including health, property or casualty insurance companies.

(3) Investment companies: pension and government retirement funds, which transform corporate bonds and stocks into annuities; mutual funds, which transform portfolios of stocks and bonds into negotiable "shares" that can be easily redeemed; money market mutual funds, which preform the same function for money market instruments.

4.2. Regulation

Markets are regulated by a number of entities, whose functions may overlap:

- The Securities and Exchange Commission (SEC) oversees exchanges and OTC markets.
- The New York Stock Exchange (NYSE), which oversees itself
- The Commodities Futures Trading Commission (CFTC) oversees futures market exchanges.
- The Office of the Comptroller of the Currency oversees federally chartered commercial banks
- The Federal Deposit Insurance Corporation (FDIC) oversees almost all depositories
- State banking and insurance commissions oversee state banks and insurance companies
- The Federal Reserve System conducts monetary policy; supervises and regulates banking institutions; maintains the stability of the financial system; and provides financial services to depository institutions, the U.S. government, and foreign official institutions.

Regulators serve four major functions:

(1) Reducing asymmetric information by encouraging transparency. That usually means requiring both financial markets and intermediaries to disclose accurate information to investors in a clear and timely manner.
(2) Protecting consumers from scammers, shysters, and assorted other grifters.
(3) Promoting financial system competition and efficiency.
(4) Ensuring the soundness of the financial system by acting as a lender of last resort, mandating deposit insurance, and limiting competition through restrictions on entry and interest rates.

Note that (3) and (4) are in conflict with each other. This becomes particularly true when regulators are reluctant to allow large financial institutions to fail. Limiting competition is generally supported by existing firms.

2

Market Operation

1. SECURITIES MARKETS

Individuals trade securities through brokers, dealers, or broker-dealers. A *broker* (B) is someone who buys or sells a security on behalf of the investor and charges a commission. A *dealer* (D) is someone who maintains an inventory of the security in which he is a "market maker" and buys and sells to the investor out of his inventory. A *broker-dealer* (BD) combines both of these functions. In this case the BD chooses whether to try to execute the investor's order as a broker or a dealer. Since executing the order as a dealer raises the possibility that the dealer will seek to exploit the investor, a BD must notify the investor if he is acting as a dealer.

Securities are exchanged either through organized exchanges or privately through so-called over-the-counter markets. When securities trades are carried out through an exchange, these trades include the benefits offered by the exchange, such as various rules designed to protect investors, centralized information production and communication, and default or counterparty protection. Private trades of securities are typically carried out through a network of traders often centered around a small number of dealers.

Trading on an exchange has changed quite a bit. It used to be that the exchanges enforced fairly high fixed commissions on all of the traders operating at the exchange. On the New York Stock Exchange, for example, these ranged from $3 plus 2% on small trades under $400, down to $39 plus 0.1% on trades over $500. This made it expensive, especially for small investors, to buy securities. In

1975 the SEC changed the rules, requiring that the brokerage business deregulate and do away with fixed fees for trading stocks. This led to a sharp drop in these fees and opened the door to the discount brokerage business that we see today. Interestingly, the bid-ask spread, the difference between dealers' buying and selling price, did not systematically fall over the 20th century. [1]

In order to execute a trade, investors typically select a broker, a dealer, or a broker-dealer to execute the trade. Then they place an order with this agent. This order comes in three basic forms:

(1) A *market order* directs the agent to buy or sell the security at the prevailing price as soon as possible.

(2) A *limit order* specifies the minimum price at which the investor is willing to sell or the maximum price at which he is willing to buy. The agent is supposed to seek to execute the order under these terms, but there is no guarantee as to when or if the order will be executed.

(3) A *stop order* is an order that becomes a market order once the target price has been reached, which triggers the execution of the order.

Limit orders and stop orders typically come with either an expiration date/time or a "good until canceled" stipulation.

If the agent is a broker-dealer then the agent has to decide how he is going to execute the trade. If he decides to execute the trade internally out of his own inventory, the rules of the exchange generally stipulate that the BD inform the investor of this and execute the trade at a "best price." In executing the trade internally, the BD is acting as a dealer. The profit the BD earns comes through the bid-ask price spread. If the agent decides to execute the trade externally, he seeks to trade with another BD and generally receives a commission for doing so. BDs working within an exchange have reporting requirements for their trades. Clearing and settlement are typically handled either through the exchange or through some third party.

Securities dealers need to hold the security in which they are seeking to make a market, and this leads to a need to finance their holdings of this security. They typically do this using a collateralized loan contract called a repurchase agreement or repo. In a standard repo, the lender gives a cash loan to the borrower, who sells the lender a bundle of securities that the borrower agrees to buy back at a future date and price. If the borrower defaults on the buyback agreement, then the lender gets to keep the bundle of securities. A repo from the perspective

1. See Charles Jones, "A Century of Stock Market Liquidity and Trading Costs," Columbia University research paper, 2002.

of the borrower is a reverse repo from the perspective of the lender. Securities dealers use both repos and reverse repos to manage their balance sheets while maintaining a sufficient inventory of the securities in which they are making a market.

There are two main components of the repo market based on how the exchanges are handled or settled. The triparty repo market is one in which a third party, typically a clearing bank, helps support and implement the trade by entering it onto its books and making sure that the terms of the agreement are met. Major third parties in the repo market include JPMorgan Chase and Company, and the Bank of New York. The other component of the repo market is the bilateral market, where the agreement and exchange are handled directly by the parties to the repo.

A bilateral repo agreement contains: (i) the principal, or amount of cash to be given to the borrower; (ii) the interest rate earned by the buying and selling of the collateral at the agreed terms; (iii) the type of securities to be delivered; (iv) the haircut, or extent to which the market value of the collateral exceeds the principal; and (v) the date/time when the repo matures and reverse transactions are to be executed. In bilateral repos, a dealer who receives securities from a reverse repo can repledge these securities.[2]

Banks in the form of dealer banks play an important role in financial markets. They act as dealers in securities markets and provide brokerage services. They make loans to market participants, thereby providing liquidity to these markets. These dealer banks make use of collateral, some of which they own and some of which they have received as part of prior agreements, in order to finance their activities as cheaply as possible.

For example, a dealer bank may help finance a broker-dealer by agreeing to a repo with the BD in which the dealer bank makes a loan taking in an asset owned by the BD as collateral. The dealer bank can then engage in a reverse repo with another investor who wants to go long on the asset the dealer bank got in the first transaction—in other words, agreeing to give the asset in exchange for cash today, with an agreement to buy back the asset in the future. Note here that the dealer bank has reused or repledged the asset it got in the first repo. At the same time, the cash that the dealer bank got from the reverse repo undoes the loss in liquidity it suffered when it made the initial loan under the initial repo agreement. This restores its cash balances, enabling the dealer bank to engage in further transactions.

2. For more on repos see Biktoria Baklanova, Adam Copeland, and Rebecca McCaughrin, "Reference Guide to U.S. Repo and Securities Lending Markets," Staff Report #70, Federal Reserve Bank of New York, September 2015.

In this way the dealer bank is building up an interconnected structure of financial transactions that allow it to very efficiently finance its activities. However, this interconnected structure is also a source of vulnerability, if one of the parties to this transaction defaults on its obligations. For example, if asset prices fell, this could reduce the value of the asset held by the BD, which is likely to make the BD default on his loan. At the same time, the asset the BD gave as collateral for the loan is also likely to have fallen in value. This may lead the second investor, who made a loan to the dealer bank in exchange for this asset as collateral, to want to undo the loan or ask for more collateral, in turn putting financial pressure on the dealer bank. Things get even more complicated if the maturities of the original repo and the reverse repo are not the same, since this can leave the dealer bank needing to find an offset repo/reverse repo to undo the impact of whichever instrument matures first. [3]

2. TREASURY AUCTIONS

The U.S. Treasury holds regular auctions on a pre-announced schedule to sell government debt obligations in order to finance the operations of the U.S. government. At these auctions a variety of securities are sold, including bills, notes, and bonds. The Treasury also sells Treasury inflation protected securities (TIPS), whose payoff is indexed to the rate of inflation.

Investors can buy these securities directly from the government through TreasuryDirect at https://www.treasurydirect.gov/tdhome.htm. Here one can see the schedule for the upcoming auctions. Treasury bills are currently being offered in 4-week, 13-week, 26-week, 52-week, and 123-day forms. Treasury notes are currently being offered in 2-year, 3-year, 5-year, 7-year, and 10-year forms. The bond being offered is the standard 30-year bond.

Investors can bid at these auctions in two ways. The first is called "competitive bidding" and is limited to a maximum of 35% of the security being offered. This is done to prevent cornering or manipulating the market. With a competitive bid, bidders specify the yield at which they are willing to buy. The Treasury then ranks the competitive bids from lowest yield (highest implicit price) to highest yield (lowest implicit price), and accepts bids up until the competitive bids are exhausted or the maximum share is reached. All accepted bids are priced at the highest accepted yield. The second is called "non-competitive bidding"; bidders

3. For more on dealer banks see Adam Kirk, James McAndrews, Parinitha Sastry, and Philp Weed, "Matching Collateral Supply and Financing Demands in Dealer Banks," *FRBNY Economic Policy Review*, December 2014.

are guaranteed to receive the bills they want at the yield determined at the auction. This yield is the highest accepted yield on the competitive bids.

This type of auction is called a "uniform price" auction since all of the bidders end up paying the same price. The Treasury used to run auctions under the discriminating price protocol in which accepted bids paid the price implied by the yield they had bid. The uniform, or "Dutch," auction protocol was first introduced in 1974 on long-term securities. It was felt that this format would encourage smaller and less informed bidders to participate more in Treasury auctions relative to a discriminating price auction in which the bid price or yield played such a key role. Non-competitive bidding was introduced in 1947, and before the switch to uniform price auctions, non-competitive bidders received the average of the competitive bids. Initially, bids were made in terms of the price that a bidder was willing to pay for the security, but in 1974 the Treasury switched to bidding in terms of the yield.[4]

Discriminating price auctions are those in which the accepted bids pay the price they bid, not the lowest price that was accepted. To starkly compare the two auction protocols, imagine bidders bid according to Table 2.1. If the lowest accepted price was $90 in a uniform price auction, the sellers would collect 90 * (10 + 15), while in a discriminating price auction they would collect 100 * 10 + 90 * 15. Thus, given the bids, a discriminating price auction will always yield weakly more than a uniform price auction. However, the bidders know that they have the potential to buy the asset at a much higher price than the lowest accepted price, which becomes essentially the market price of the asset. Thus they face the possibility of large losses from aggressive bidding and tend to shade their bids down as a result. Given this, which bidding protocol is better is an open question. There are results in auction theory that show under certain circumstances that the expected revenue from a variety of different types of auctions is the same, but they rely on risk neutrality and independent valuations of the good being auctioned.[5]

Table 2.1. BIDS AT THE AUCTION

Bid Price	Bid Quantity
100	10
90	15
80	10

4. https://www.treasurydirect.gov/indiv/products/prod_auctions_glance.htm.

5. See for example Riley, John G., and William F. Samuelson. "Optimal auctions." The American Economic Review 71.3 (1981): 381–392.

Many governments auction their debt using discriminating price auctions. For example, in Germany the accepted competitive bids are accepted at their bid price, while the non-competitive bids pay the average price among the competitive bids, just as we use to do in the U.S. In addition, only financial institutions that are members of the Bund Issue Auction Group can participate in the auction. All other investors must acquire these securities from the participants.[6] Around the world, discriminating price auctions are slightly more common than uniform price auctions.[7]

6. For more information, see http://www.deutsche-finanzagentur.de/en/institutional-investors/ primary-market/tender-process/ and http://www.deutsche-finanzagentur.de/en/institutional-investors/primary-market/bund-issues-auction-group/c647.

7. See Leonardo Bartolini, and Carlo Cottarelli, "Designing Effective Auctions for Treasury Securities." *Handbook of Fiscal Policy* 98 (2001): 1287.

PART TWO

Asset Pricing

We start with the risk-neutral asset pricing model. After developing this model, we discuss its strengthens and weakness. This leads us to try to extend the model in a variety of ways, but the most important is with respect to risk. In our first attempt, we develop the consumption-based asset pricing model. While that model has better risk pricing predictions, it still falls short of what is needed. For that reason we turn to an arbitrage-based stochastic discount factor model. Fortunately, the main insights from each model carries over to the next, and the material cumulates as well.

3

Asset Pricing I: Risk-Neutral Pricing

Asset prices play a crucial role in economic activity. They are the mechanism through which we "price" intertemporal activities. We use these prices in order to evaluate the overall benefit of expenditures at certain points in time and receipts at other points in time. This sort of cost-benefit analysis covers everything from firm investment projects to whether or not college is financially worthwhile. We also use these prices to evaluate the consequences of risk. A risky project has different possible payoffs at a given point in time, and how those outcomes are distributed can influence its value today. In this way we are using asset prices to tell us about "good" and "bad" gambles. In both their intertemporal and risk evaluation roles, asset prices are a major determinant of any kind of activity in which inputs and outputs are not simultaneous. Since this covers almost everything, it's hard to overstate their importance.

1. ASSET PRICING METHODOLOGY

We want to construct a model within which we can think about asset pricing and compare our model's predictions to the data. If we posit a representative agent, then this activity is very simple to do because we can think in terms of a single agent's decision problem. The equilibrium prices are then the ones that clear the market, and market clearing is very simple, since the representative agent consumes per capita output and holds his per capita share of all assets. This nice feature is also the major drawback of our methodology; we ignore all distributional effects of shocks. It also means that we are ignoring asset markets' most fundamental function: sharing risk among different agents. Despite this, we will plow ahead because of this methodology's ease.

We use the portfolio allocation rules of our representative agent to price assets in the following way: First, we derive the agent's optimal allocation rules. To do this, we pose the individual's decision problem and then use first-order conditions to determine the solution to his/her problem. This solution implies his/her optimal portfolio. Then we determine the pricing relationships that would allow the assets we consider to be held in proportion to their supply. We then take these prices to be the predictions of our model.

A more complicated methodology involves heterogeneous agents, and in this case, we have to solve for prices as equilibrium objects. This more advanced methodology is beyond the scope of our tool set, so we will work within the range of the possible.

2. INFORMATION OVER TIME AND PROBABILITY THEORY

We're going to need to develop some formal theory in order to think precisely about what we're talking about. Assume that in each period t a state s_t is chosen from a set of possible states S. The information that someone has as of date t, denoted by I_t. I_t, can be thought of as having all kinds of different bits of information in it. The most obvious and simplest thing is to have it include the history of states through t, which is given by

$$I_t = s^t = (s_1, ..., s_t).$$

(Note that we are using superscripts here to denote the history of shocks through our current period t.) In what follows, we will typically focus on s^t as the information set.

A simple example of the sort of event tree we have in mind is given in Figure 3.1. In this tree there is a single node for the state at time t and two possible outcomes in each successor date. The information state is the history of realizations s^{t+2}.

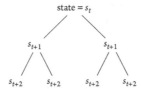

Figure 3.1 Event Tree.

The realization of any exogenous random variable at date t, like x_t, simply depends upon the state at time t, or $x_t(s^t)$. Endogenous variables like the individual's wealth at date t, w_t, will, in general, depend upon the history through date t, or $w_t(s^t)$. This creates a natural history dependence within our model.

The realization that we will see of the entire history through date T (the end of history for us) depends upon the underlying *state of the world*, which we denote by ω. In other words, $s^T(\omega)$. There is a set of possible states of the world Ω. Note that we are making an important distinction between the current "state" which will determine the current realization of any exogenous random variables, and the "state of the world" which will determine the entire sequence of realizations of these random variable through the end of time.

As we see more of the history, we can rule out some states of the world and not others. Let $A = \{\omega \text{ such that } s^t(\omega) = \bar{s}^t\}$, where $\bar{s}^t$ is some fixed realization of the history through t. Then,

$$\Pr\{\omega|\bar{s}^t\} = \frac{\Pr\{\omega\}}{\Pr\{A\}} \text{ if } \omega \in A \text{ and } 0 \text{ otherwise.}$$

Thus, given an initial probability distribution over $\omega \in \Omega$, we can construct all of the probabilities of a history realization, $\Pr\{A\} = \Pr\{\omega \in \Omega : s^t(\omega) = \bar{s}^t\}$, as well as the conditional probabilities. This is why this "state of the world" specification is attractive.

3. RISK-NEUTRAL PRICING

We start with a fairly general specification of the portfolio investment problem of a risk-neutral investor. Being risk neutral means that his flow utility from consumption is linear. As a result, the value of any random amount of consumption is equal to the value of expected consumption. Hence, the investor has a neutral attitude toward risk - he neither dislikes nor likes it.

Consider the portfolio choices of a risk-neutral investor who has the following investment problem

$$\max_{a_1} c_1 + E_1\beta \left\{\max_{a_2} c_2 + E_2\beta \left\{\max_{a_3} c_3 + E_3\beta \left\{\max_{a_4} c_4 + ...\right\}\right\}\right\},$$

where his flow budget constraint is given by

$$y_t + a_{t-1}Q_t - p_t a_t = c_t,$$

and where:

- c_t is his period t consumption
- E_t is his period t forecast of the future
- y_t is his period t income
- a_t is the amount of the asset held between t and $t + 1$
- Q_t is the total payout in period t on the asset per unit invested
- p_t is the price of the asset in period t.

To reduce the complexity, we assume that there is only a single asset. Later, we can generalize this if we want to.

This is a complicated maximization problem. At date 1 the agent is picking a_1 while looking ahead to the fact that at date $t = 2$ the agent will pick a_2, and so forth. Hence, he is forecasting the future, both in terms of exogenous outcomes and his own actions. In the formal notation:

- There is the forecast of $t = 2$ coming through E_1.
- There is the forecast of the forecast of $t = 3$ coming through $E_1 \{E_2\}$, and so forth.

But at future dates the agent may have more information about the future and Q_t in particular. How to think about your future actions, when in the future you will know more, is tricky. To figure out how to deal with this, we start by positing a decision rule for the agent.

3.1. Forming the Payoff

Let $a_t(s^t)$ denote the optimal asset choice at date t based upon the information at time t, s^t. Then from the budget constraint,

$$c_t = y_t + a_{t-1}Q_t - p_t a_t(s^t).$$

The value of this optimal solution is given by

$$y_1 + a_0 Q_1 - p_1 a_1 + \sum_{t=2}^{T} \beta^{t-1} E_1 ... E_t \{y_t + a_{t-1}Q_t - p_t a_t(s^t)\}.$$

We can use this construction to examine the gains and losses of small changes $a_t(s^t)$.

3.2. Perturbing the Payoff and Optimal Portfolios

If this choice is optimal then simple changes cannot improve things. How about increasing a_1 and increasing c_2 by an offsetting amount so a_2 is unchanged?

$$\frac{d}{da_1} \left[y_1 + a_0 Q_1 - p_1 a_1 + E_1 \beta \left\{ y_2 + a_1 Q_2 - p_2 a_2 + E_2 \beta \{...\} \right\} \right]$$

$$= -p_1 + E_1 \beta \{Q_2\}$$

$$= 0.$$

This gain must be zero or we didn't have an optimal initial choice. Since we have a linear condition, it follows that

$$p_1 = \beta E_1 \{Q_2\},$$

otherwise the agent would demand either $+$ or $-$ infinity of the asset.

3.3. First Pricing Rule

How about changing a_t and lowering c_{t+1} to offset its impact? If we evaluate this change from the date t information s^t, it looks like

$$-p_t + \beta E_t \{Q_{t+1}\} = 0$$

since the time t agent is behaving optimally.

This then implies that

$$p_t = \beta E_t \{Q_{t+1}\}.$$

The price of the asset in period t is the expected one-period-ahead payout discounted by β.

3.4. Interest Rates

An interest rate contract is one that pays a fixed rate of interest $R_t = 1 + r_t$ in each period for each unit you invest. (We will try to consistently use lower case for the net interest rate r_t and upper case for the gross interest rate R_t). To determine the

one-period rate of interest, assume you bought one unit of such a contract, held
it for one period; then as a result, the payoff change is

$$-1 + \beta E_1 \{1 + r_1\} = -1 + \beta (1 + r_1).$$

So, it must be the case that the one-period-ahead interest rate is

$$1 = \beta (1 + r_1),$$
$$r_1 = \beta^{-1} - 1.$$

Note that the expectation, E_1, is just equal to the actual because there is no
uncertainty with respect to the return in period 1.

What about the interest rate between $t = 1$ and $t = 2$? Because this is occurring
over two periods, whatever interest rate we agree to at $t = 1$ you get twice, so the
payout is $(1 + r_2)^2$. Hence, we get that

$$1 = \beta E_1 \beta E_2 (1 + r_2)^2 = \beta^2 (1 + r_2)^2$$

because there is no uncertainty. This then leads to

$$1 = \beta^2 (1 + r_2)^2 = \beta^2 (1 + 2r_2 + r_2 r_2)$$
$$r_2 = \beta^{-1} - 1.$$

Note that $r_2 r_2$ represents the impact of compounding, and that $r_1 = r_2$ because
the discount factor is the same.

So, if we want the *real risk-free* interest rate to vary over time here, then we need
the discount rate β to vary, something like $\beta(t)$. This suggests that time variation
in discount rates may play an important role.

3.5. Compounding

To avoid confusion when talking about interest rates we standardized on the
length of time. Hence, we speak of annual rates. But what happens when our time
period is shorter than a year? If the interest rate is an annual rate and the length of
time is one year then we need to pay you $(1 + r)$. But what should we pay you if
only $1/2$ a year has passed? If we pay you 1, that seems too low, but paying $1 + r$
seems too high. We need an interest factor that we can apply once after 6 months
and twice after a year. This leads to compounding.

Compounding has to do with the number of times the interest rate factor is
applied within the time period. If the annual interest rate is r, the compounding
rate per year is n, and the number of years is t, then the interest rate factor is

$$\left(1 + \frac{r}{n}\right)^{nt}.$$

If $n = 2$ and $t = 1$, then this becomes

$$\left(1 + \frac{r}{2}\right)^2 = 1 + 2\frac{r}{2} + \left(\frac{r}{2}\right)^2,$$

and in general the amount of compounding rises with n. If $n = \infty$, then this becomes

$$e^{rt}.$$

Note here that you need to know not only the annual rate but also the rate of compounding in order to evaluate the implied payoff. To standardize everything, rates are normally quoted in annual continuously compounded form. We will normally ignore compounding and annual rates and simply work with one-period rates.

3.6. Bond Contracts

3.6.1. PRICING A PURE DISCOUNT BOND

A pure discount bond is the simplest type of security. It is a claim to a one-time payment at some future date. We are interested in the price at which the bond sells for today.

Example: A claim to 100 units next period.

$$p_t = \beta E_t\{100\} = \beta * 100$$

Example: A claim to 100 units in 10 periods.
In this case the change in the payoff is

$$-p_t + \beta^{10} E_t\{E_{t+1}\{...E_{t+10}\{100\}\}\} = -p_t + \beta^{10} * 100.$$

So

$$p_t = \beta^{10} * 100.$$

3.6.2. PRICING A COUPON BOND

A *coupon bond* is a bond that pays a coupon for some period of time and then, in the final period, pays a larger lump sum called the *principal*. The origin of the term comes from the fact that the original bonds had coupons that were detached and traded in for the coupon payment.

Example: Consider a bond that pays a coupon of 10 for the next 9 periods and in the 10th period pays 100.

In this case the change in the payoff is

$$- p_t + \beta E_t \{10 + \beta E_{t+1} \{10 + \beta E_{t+2} \{...E_{t+10} \{100\}\}\}\}$$

$$= -p_t + \sum_{j=1}^{9} \beta^j * 10 + \beta^{10} * 100.$$

So

$$p_t = \sum_{j=1}^{9} \beta^j * 10 + \beta^{10} * 100.$$

Bonds at Par:

The coupon is often chosen so that the bond trades at the value of the principal payment. This is called *trading at par*.

Consider a coupon bond that promises to pay a coupon C in every future period up to and including the redemption period, when it also pays the principal P. Assume that the gross risk-free rate is R. Then the value of the bond is

$$V = \sum_{t=1}^{T} \frac{C}{R^t} + \frac{P}{R^T}.$$

If the bond sells at par, then $V = P$ and

$$P \left[1 - \frac{1}{R^T} \right] = \sum_{t=1}^{T} \frac{C}{R^t} = \frac{C}{R} \left[1 + \frac{1}{R} + \left(\frac{1}{R} \right)^2 + ... + \left(\frac{1}{R} \right)^{T-1} \right].$$

Define the infinite series by

$$Z = \left[1 + \frac{1}{R} + \left(\frac{1}{R} \right)^2 + ... \right],$$

then note that

$$\left[1 + \frac{1}{R} + \left(\frac{1}{R} \right)^2 + ... + \left(\frac{1}{R} \right)^{T-1} \right] = Z \left[1 - \frac{1}{R^T} \right].$$

So, our bond expression becomes

$$P = \frac{C}{R}Z$$

and note that the horizon T has now dropped out. To value Z, note that

$$Z\left[1 - \frac{1}{R}\right] = 1$$

by cancellations. Hence,

$$Z = \frac{1}{1 - \frac{1}{R}} = \frac{R}{R-1}.$$

This then leads to the conclusion that the bond will sell at par if

$$rP = C.$$

In other words, so long as the coupon is equal to the net interest due on the principal, a risk-free bond will sell at par.

Other Types of Coupon Bonds:
Coupon bonds can be a bit more exotic than the simple bonds we have considered so far. The coupon can be deferred (not paid) for several years. Unsurprisingly these are called *deferred coupon bonds*. The coupon can change over time and can even be indexed in some fashion; perhaps to current interest rates.

An interesting early bond was issued by King William III (William of Orange) to finance his war against France and King Louis XIV. King William issued bonds in 100 pound notes in 1693. The notes promised a coupon payment of 7 pounds for each note. However, the original owner of the bond could only receive a payment while alive. Once some of the original owners died, their coupons would be distributed among the remaining original bond owners. These notes were called "King William's Tontine," and the last remaining original owner lived to be 100 years old, at which time she was earning thousands of pounds per year. This kind of bond, which combines an annuity with a coupon bond, was quite popular for a while in Europe. However, they were eventually outlawed in many countries because of the fear that the bond owners would have too strong an incentive to kill each other once their numbers were pared down.

3.6.3. THE YIELD

Investors wanted a way to compare the return offered by different debt contracts. These contracts could differ in terms of their coupons, their principals, and even the length of time to maturity. They came up with the yield as a way of doing so. The *yield* of a security is the implicit interest rate implied by the price. The interest rate is taken to be constant in part because there are many different time-varying interest rates that can be consistent with the same price for a sufficiently rich debt contract, that is, one that paid a coupon over time. The yield is restricted to debt contracts and focuses on their promised return because one can have many different views on stochastic events.

> **Example:** Consider a bond that pays a coupon of 10 for the next 9 periods and in the 10th period pays 100, and has a price p.

The yield R is a solution to

$$p = \sum_{j=1}^{9} \left(\frac{1}{1+R}\right)^j * 10 + \left(\frac{1}{1+R}\right)^{10} * 100.$$

So the yield on this bond is
$$R = \beta^{-1} - 1.$$

3.6.4. HOW CAN YIELDS VARY WITH MATURITY?

Imagine that the discount varies over time. Then the payout is

$$y_1 + a_0 Q_1 - p_1 a_1 + \sum_{t=1}^{T} \left[\prod_{j=1}^{t} \beta(j)\right] E_1 ... E_t \left\{y_t + a_{t-1} Q_t - p_t a_t(s^t)\right\},$$

and the impact of acquiring a two-period bond is

$$-p_1 + \beta(1)\beta(2),$$

hence
$$R_2 = [\beta(1)\beta(2)]^{-1/2} - 1.$$

More generally

$$1 + R_t = \left[\prod_{j=1}^{t} \beta(j)\right]^{-1/t}.$$

3.6.5. The Yield Curve and Short-Term Rates

Our result that

$$R_t = \left[\prod_{j=1}^{t} \beta(j) \right]^{-1/t}$$

also implies that the yield for a t period bond is such that

$$1 + R_t = \left[\left(1 + R_1^2\right) \cdots \left(1 + R_t^{t+1}\right) \right]^{1/t},$$

where R_j^{j+1} is the one-period interest rate between period j and period $j + 1$.

So, an upward sloping yield curve implies higher future short-term rates.

3.7. Forward Contracts

What if we allowed people to make agreements to trade this asset at date 1?

A *forward contract* would be an agreement to trade the asset at a price p_1^t at date t.

What would be the change in my payoff from buying one unit of this contract and consuming the benefit at $t + 1$?

$$-p_1^t \beta^t + \beta^{t+1} E_1 \left\{ E_2 \left\{ \ldots E_t \left\{ Q_{t+1} \right\} \right\} \right\}.$$

What would be my payoff from selling one unit of this contract?

$$+p_1^t \beta^t - \beta^t E_1 \left\{ E_2 \left\{ \ldots E_{t-1} \left\{ p_t \right\} \right\} \right\}$$

3.7.1. Iterated Expectations

What is the expectation of my future expectation?

Imagine that I thought that the future value would be 10, but I also thought that my future expectation of the future value would be 11. Imagine also that my future self was both rational and had at least as much information as I had. Something seems very wrong here. Shouldn't I follow the lead of my wiser future self and change my beliefs to 11? If I'm rational too that sounds right.

Fortunately,

$$E_1 \left\{ E_2 \left\{ \ldots E_t \left\{ Q_{t+1} \right\} \right\} \right\} = E_1 \left\{ Q_{t+1} \right\}.$$

This is called the *law of iterated expectations*.

Remark 1. To see why this holds, assume that the payoff in period 3 is given by $Q(s^3)$. Then, my expectation at time $t = 2$, given that I know s^2, is given by

$$E_2 Q = \sum_{s^3} Q(s^3) \Pr(s^3|s^2),$$

where $\Pr(s^3|s^2)$ is the conditional probability of s^3 given s^2. The expectation in period $t = 1$ is given by

$$\sum_{s^3} Q(s^3) \Pr(s^3|s^1) = \sum_{s^3} \left\{ Q(s^3) \sum_{s^2} \Pr(s^3|s^2) \Pr(s^2|s^1) \right\}.$$

Here we have made use of how conditional probabilities work and the law of total probability. It then follows that

$$\sum_{s^3} Q(s^3) \Pr(s^3|s^1) = \sum_{s^3} \sum_{s^2} Q(s^3) \Pr(s^3|s^2) \Pr(s^2|s^1).$$

We can interchange the order of summation so long as the absolute value of the sums is bounded. Hence

$$\sum_{s^3} Q(s^3) \Pr(s^3|s^1) = \sum_{s^2} \sum_{s^3} Q(s^3) \Pr(s^3|s^2) \Pr(s^2|s^1)$$

$$= \sum_{s^2} E_2 \left[Q(s^3)|s^2 \right] \Pr(s^2|s^1).$$

Thus our current expectation is just a weighted average of our future expectations where the weights are the conditional probabilities of our having those future beliefs. See Wikipedia (https://en.wikipedia.org/wiki/Law_of _total_expectation) for more.

In light of the law of iterated expectations, we get that

$$-p_1^t \beta^t + \beta^{t+1} E_1 \{E_2 \{...E_t \{Q_{t+1}\}\}\}$$
$$= -p_1^t \beta^t + \beta^{t+1} E_1 \{Q_{t+1}\}.$$

and that

$$+p_1^t \beta^t - \beta^t E_1 \{E_2 \{...E_{t-1} \{p_t\}\}\}$$
$$= +p_1^t \beta^t - \beta^t E_1 \{p_t\}.$$

Hence

$$p_1^t = E_1\{p_t\} = \beta E_1\{Q_{t+1}\}.$$

So the forward price is just the expectation of the future price, which is consistent with the discounted expected payoff.

3.8. Pricing Risky Securities

Consider a security whose payout is a random variable. Let $d_t(s_t)$ denote the payout in period t in state s_t.

Consider buying a unit of this security at date 1 and selling it at date 2. Then the change in your payoff is

$$-p_1 + \beta E\{d_2 + p_2\},$$

which implies that

$$p_1 = \beta E\{d_2 + p_2\}$$

and

$$\frac{d_2 + p_2}{p_1}$$

is the realized return.

What if you held the security for two periods starting at date 1? Then the change in your payoff is

$$-p_1 + \beta E_1\{d_2 + \beta E_2\{d_3 + p_3\}\}.$$

Hence (using the law of iterated expectations)

$$p_1 = \beta E_1\{d_2 + \beta(d_3 + p_3)\}$$

and by extension

$$p_1 = E_1\left\{\sum_{t=2}^{T} \beta^{t-1} d_t + \beta^{T-1} p_T\right\}.$$

3.8.1. RISKY EQUITIES

If we interpret d_t as the dividend on the equity and p as its price, then we have the standard risk-neutral equity pricing formulas

$$p_1 = \beta E \{d_2 + p_2\}$$

and

$$p_1 = E_1 \left\{ \sum_{t=2}^{T} \beta^{t-1} d_t + \beta^{T-1} p_T \right\}.$$

3.8.2. RISKY BONDS

Assume that there is a chance π that the bond will default in each period. If the bond does not default prior to period t then

$$d_t = Q \text{ for } t < T$$

and

$$d_T = P.$$

If the bond defaults in period τ, then

$$d_t = 0 \text{ for all } t \geq \tau.$$

What is the change in the agent's expected payoff from buying some of this bond?

$$-p_1 + (1 - \pi) \{\beta Q + (1 - \pi)\beta \{Q + (1 - \pi)\beta \{...\}\}\},$$

so

$$p_1 = \sum_{t=2}^{T-1} [(1 - \pi)\beta]^{t-1} Q + [(1 - \pi)\beta]^T P. \tag{1}$$

Note that the yield on this bond is

$$R = [(1 - \pi)\beta]^{-1} - 1,$$

so the higher the default probability, the higher the yield.

3.8.3. PRICING SECURED DEBT

Many debt securities come with collateral. An obvious example is a mortgage that is secured by the home being purchased. Here we want to think about how the presence of collateral can affect the interest rate that a lender is going to charge on a loan. We will again assume that the probability that the borrower may default in each period is π. If the borrower does not default, then he/she pays the coupon Q

in each period $t < T$, and in the final period he/she pays the principal P. We will assume that the borrower secures the loan with some collateral. Start by assuming that the collateral is riskless and that it has value K in any period in which it is liquidated. Note that its value to the borrower may be higher than K.

This is a lot like the problem we just did for risky debt, except now when the borrower defaults, the lender gets K. In this case the value of the loan looks like

$$
\begin{aligned}
p_1 &= \sum_{t=2}^{T-1} [(1-\pi)\beta]^{t-1} Q + [(1-\pi)\beta]^T P \\
&\quad + \pi\beta K + (1-\pi)\pi\beta^2 K + (1-\pi)^2\pi\beta^3 K + ... + (1-\pi)^{T-1}\beta^T \pi K \\
&= \sum_{t=2}^{T-1} [(1-\pi)\beta]^{t-1} Q + [(1-\pi)\beta]^T P + \sum_{t=0}^{T-1} (1-\pi)^t \beta^{t+1} \pi K.
\end{aligned}
\tag{2}
$$

So the security on this loan raises its value in proportion to the overall default risk and the value of the collateral.

But what happens if the collateral itself is risky? That turns out to depend a lot on the nature of the risk. Assume that the value of the collateral is either K^h with probablity Π or 0 with probability $1 - \Pi$. Assume that $\Pi K^h = K$. Then our answer is unchanged if this risk is *independent* of the default actions of the borrower.

This independence assumption is a big one. Often, when things go bad for the borrower, it also means that things are going bad for his collateral. Let's make an extreme assumption and assume that when the borrower defaults, his collateral is going to be worthless because of this high degree of correlation in the risk. In this case, the value of the loan reverts to (1). Note that this result is independent of the size of K.

For a more realistic case, let's assume that the average value of the collateral is K but the expected value of the collateral is $K/2$ conditional on the borrower going into default. In this case we just replace K with $K/2$ in (2). This example illustrate why one might need to offer more than \$100 worth of collateral to secure (make riskless) a \$100 loan. It all depends upon the correlation of the risks in the collateral and the default behavior of the borrower.

Remark 2. Collateral usage has become increasingly sophisticated. While initially it generally took the form of physical property, such as a house or other building or a piece of equipment, it has become common to use financial assets as collateral. The most common forms of collateral are cash and government securities because evaluating these assets is particularly straightfoward since default risk is low and government debt markets tend to be thick. Collateralization of dividend exposure is now very common. Also, collateral tends to play a large role in the over-the-counter market. Collateral calls occur when a lender demands more collateral in order to continue a loan or roll over an outstanding loan. As we saw in the simple example, with a lack of independence in the collateral securing risky investments, an increase in the riskiness of the investment can necessitate a large increase in the collateral the lender demands. The lender can also move to seize the collateral if the lender suspects that the assets the collateral is securing have fallen sharply in value. These outcomes can have a major impact on a venture.

During the financial crises associated with the Great Recession of 2006-2010, collateral events played a crucial role. At its height, securitized banking was a $12 trillion business. The major players included investment banks like Bear Stearns, Lehman Brothers, Morgan Stanley, and Merrill Lynch. It also included some major commercial banks like Citigroup, J.P. Morgan, and Bank of America. The assets being traded in this market included various sorts of collateralized debt obligations (CDOs). Originally, these CDOs included various corporate debt obligations, but they came to include assets like mortgage-backed-securities (MBS) in a big way. The participants often held very large positions, which they financed through collateralized borrowing or repurchase agreements. In these repurchase agreements or repos, an investor like Bear would sell some assets to a buyer, while at the same time agreeing in advance on the price that they would repurchase the asset. In this way, the asset sale was really just a collateralized loan where the buyer could keep the asset if things went bad. The percentage earned by the buyer is in effect the interest rate they earn on their loan and is called the repo rate.

The investment bank Bear Stearns was a large issuer of asset-backed securities, particularly MBS. Two of Bear's hedge funds found themselves in financial difficulty in June 2007. The funds had large positions in CDOs, which were thinly traded. When the value of these assets was thought to have fallen, one of the lenders to these funds, Merrill Lynch, seized $850 million worth of collateral pledged to secure these loans. Bear Stearns felt that it needed to prop up its hedge funds to maintain its reputation. So Bear pledged $3.2 billion as security on a loan to bail out one of these hedge funds. At about this time, Bear had almost $400 billion in assets being supported by only $11 billion in net worth. So, its leverage ratio was an eye-popping 36+ to one. Bear ended up being bailed out by the Federal Reserve and was sold to J.P. Morgan Chase.[1]

J.P. Morgan served as the clearing bank for another investment bank, Lehman Brothers, which also ran into difficulties during the crisis. In its role as a clearing bank, Morgan advanced Lehman up to $100 billion as part

---

1. See https://en.wikipedia.org/wiki/Bear_Stearns.

of the various overnight repurchase agreements Lehman was entering into. Morgan held on to the collateral Lehman offered on these loans. However, this collateral included some fairly speculative securities that later turned out to have fairly low value. As a result, J.P. Morgan claimed that some $25 billion of the amount it had advanced Lehman was unpaid. Morgan responded to this by seizing $8.6 billion worth of collateral that Lehman Bros.'s holding company had offered as additional collateral right before the firm went into bankruptcy. [2]

3.9. Average Returns

With a stochastic asset the realized return can be high or low. For that reason it is useful to focus on the average return. Normally one would construct such a return from a long time series realization for the asset or from a pool of realizations for this type of asset. However, within our theoretical structure we can ask what our pricing model implies.

What is the realized average return on a risk security? It is the implicit interest rate $1 + r$ such that

$$p_1 = E\left\{ \sum_{t=2}^{T} \left(\frac{1}{1+r} \right)^{t-1} d_t \right\}.$$

Hence the average return is

$$r = \beta^{-1} - 1$$

for all of our risky securities.

This is a very stark result. It follows from the fact that all risk is priced by the expected value; hence, risk is not priced. It is also grossly counterfactual, at least for certain important types of risk. We will return to this point in the next chapter when we evaluate our model and seek to correct its deficiencies.

4. BUBBLES

4.1. Pure Gambles and Bubbles

Bubbles is a term one frequently hears thrown about. In discussing the Great Recession, one commonly hears about the housing bubble. A natural question

---

2. See http://www.wsj.com/articles/lehman-brothers-j-p-morgan-lawsuit-over-repo-market-resumes-1413572011

to ask of our pricing model is whether it can have bubbles, and if so, what do they look like.

Consider buying into a gamble in which you would give up q today in order to get X tomorrow with probability π and zero otherwise. Then in order for our agent to be just willing to hold this gamble, it must be the case that

$$q = \beta \pi X.$$

Now, let's relabel things a bit and assume that you were thinking about holding a stochastic security whose future price would be q_{t+1} with probability π and zero otherwise. Then this same logic would say that

$$q_t = \beta \pi q_{t+1}.$$

If we rearrange things we get that

$$q_t = (\beta \pi)^{-t+1} q_1.$$

This is a pure bubble security that pays no dividend ever.

- Note that if $q_1 = 0$, then this security just has a zero price forever.
- Then, for any $q_1 > 0$, the price must grow at an exponential rate (assuming the bubble has not burst) forever.
- Next, note that the exponential rate is increasing in the probability that the bubble bursts: $1 - \pi$.
- Finally, note that this is a pure gamble and it only works because we don't know for sure when the bubble burst. However, it bursts in finite time with probability one.

Now consider a security whose price was determined by its dividend flow, and that price was given by

$$p_t = E_t \sum_{j=t+1}^{\infty} \beta^{j-t} d_j.$$

What happens if we add our pure bubble security to this security? That is, what if you buy the combination of the two? Arbitrage would imply that the price of the combination should be the sum of the two prices, or

$$q_t + p_t = E_t \sum_{j=t+1}^{\infty} \beta^{j-t} d_j + (\beta \pi)^{-t+1} q_1$$

if the bubble has not burst yet, and

$$p_t = E_t \sum_{j=t+1}^{\infty} \beta^{j-t} d_j$$

if it has.

4.2. Bubbles: Are They Everywhere or Nowhere?

This suggests that we can always construct a bubble on any security and simply have the price behave according to

$$\tilde{p}_t = \begin{cases} E_t \sum_{j=t+1}^{\infty} \beta^{j-t} d_j + (\beta\pi)^{-t+1} q_1 & \text{if it has not burst} \\ E_t \sum_{j=t+1}^{\infty} \beta^{j-t} d_j & \text{if it has burst.} \end{cases}$$

How plausible is this model of pricing?

- The bubble has to potentially go on forever and the price has an exponential growth component so eventually the bubble part will swamp the fundamental part coming through the dividends.
- If there was a group that could become convinced that prices must rise forever (call them idiots), then perhaps they could be counted on to end up holding the security once it came near any ceiling where it must burst.

4.3. Bubbles in History

The Dutch Tulip-Bulb bubble arose in the 1600s in Holland. Tulips had been popular and rare in Holland for some time after originally being imported from Turkey during the 1500s. A non-fatal virus arose that produced novel color patterns. These bulbs were highly valued and their supply was limited by the fact that tulips grow from bulbs which are produced by the original plant, not from seeds. As the prices of the bulbs with the virus continued rising, people increasingly saw them as sound investments. At the bubble's peak, in early 1637, a single rare bulb sold for the same amount as a castle. Eventually, the speculators tried to liquidate their holdings and prices fell dramatically, with many bulbs becoming almost worthless.

The South Sea bubble arose in the early 1700s. In 1711, the South Sea Company helped restore faith in the British government's creditworthiness by purchasing 10 million pounds of government bonds. As a reward, the company was given a monopoly over all trade to the South Seas. It was commonly believed that this trade would be very profitable. The stock price exploded in 1720, going from around 160 pounds a share up to almost 10,000 pounds, before collapsing back to 200 pounds by the end of the year.

The U.S. stock market boomed after World War I only to crash in 1929. The 1920s were a very dynamic period featuring big advances in mass production of the automobile and the radio, along with mass electrification. The gross national product (GNP) grew rapidly and the stock market boomed. Growth peaked in 1929: industrial production peaked in July of 1929 and declined sharply by the end of the year. The stock market peaked in September of 1929, then went through a period of great instability before crashing. The crash started on October 24 (Black Thursday) in heavy trading and the market continued downward thereafter.

An important factor in the crash was widespread involvement in the market through margin buying. With the start of the crash, bankers called in these margin accounts.

While each of these incidents is commonly referred to as a bubble, were they true bubbles in the sense illustrated by our model? Or were they instances in which there were substantial uncertainties about the future and a very real prospect of high returns that would justify the high prices at the peak? With the tulip bubble, the initially very limited supply and the slow increase in that supply coming from the original bulbs could offer a long period of high gains. However, as the supply of a variety eventually increased, one might expect the price to fall. An additional factor is that a new flower, the hyacinth, replaced the tulip in popularity. In a similar vein, what did the future hold at the dawn of 1929? The rapid rate of technological progress during the 1920s and the "war to end all wars" might well be taken to indicate that the future was extremely bright. Fundamental

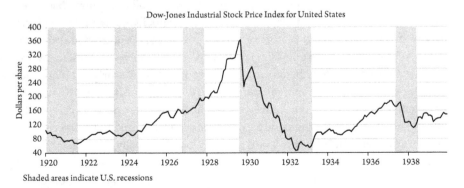

Figure 3.2 Stock Prices in the 1920s and 1930s.
SOURCE: FRED. Data Source: National Bureau of Economic Research.

uncertainty seems to have been an important element of the major bubbles in history, and suggests that the true story here may not be so simple.

5. THE EFFICIENT MARKETS HYPOTHESIS

A standard assertion is that financial markets are "informationally efficient." Do bubbles contradict this hypothesis?

Strong Form: The markets get prices right given all publicly available information. This form seems to be contradicted by the existence of bubbles (though it seems to require a model).

Weak Form: There are no arbitrage profits based on trading on publicly available information. Rational bubbles do not admit arbitrage profits by design. So, because there are no trading gains by construction, our model of a bubble does not contradict this form of efficiency:

The current price, if the bubble has not burst, is

$$p_t = E_t \sum_{j=t+1}^{\infty} \beta^{j-t} d_j + q_t$$

and the expected payout is

$$E\{Q_{t+1}\} = \pi \left\{ E_t \sum_{j=t+1}^{\infty} \beta^{j-t} d_j + q_t (\beta\pi)^{-1} \right\}$$
$$+ (1-\pi) \left\{ E_t \sum_{j=t+1}^{\infty} \beta^{j-t} d_j \right\},$$

so

$$\frac{E\{Q_{t+1}\}}{p_t} = \beta^{-1}$$

and there are no arbitrage profits.

5.1. Further Evidence of the Efficient Markets Hypothesis

We thus conclude the following about efficient markets:

- Studies have found that when a firm publishes its latest earnings or makes a dividend change, the major part of the adjustment to its stock price occurs within 5 to 10 minutes.

- Professionally managed funds typically fail to recoup their manager's fees.
- Insiders do better on their trades.

The first result implies that markets add new information very rapidly. The second suggests that one cannot make trading gains based on publicly available information. The third result suggests that having more information does help.

4

Asset Pricing with Growth

We live in a growing world and we need a model of asset pricing to account for this. When we look at the plot of real output in Figure 4.1, it appears to be growing exponentially. The absolute increases are getting bigger, but the proportionate changes look roughly constant over time. Another clue is that the log of real output seems to be roughly linear with respect to time. We're going to want to take account of this in modeling growth.

1. SIMPLE GROWTH 1

We start with a simple deterministic growth model which we can use to understand some basic features of the relationship between growth and prices. It will prove convenient to assume that time is infinite here. Also assume that the long-run growth rate is g, and for now take it to be deterministic. Given this, expected dividends over time look like

$$E\{D_t\} = (1 + g)^t D_0,$$

and the initial price would satisfy our simple pricing relationship

$$P_0 = \frac{D_1 + P_1}{1 + r},$$

where $(1+r)^{-1}$ is some appropriate discount rate; in other words, r is the net interest rate. Recursively substituting leads to

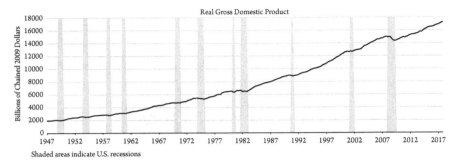

Figure 4.1 GDP

SOURCE: FRED. Data Source: U.S. Bureau of Economic Analysis.

$$E_0 \sum_{t=1}^{\infty} (1+r)^{-t} D_t = \sum_{t=1}^{\infty} \left[\frac{1+g}{1+r} \right]^t D_0.$$

For the price to be finite, we need $r > g$.

Then, the price would be given by

$$P_0 = \left[\frac{1+g}{1+r} \right] \frac{1}{1 - \left[\frac{1+g}{1+r} \right]} D_0$$

$$= \frac{1+g}{r-g} D_0.$$

From this expression, we can see that the price will rise deterministically with the dividends, or

$$P_t = \frac{1+g}{r-g} D_t = \frac{1+g}{r-g} D_0 (1+g)^t.$$

But this implies that the price-dividend (or price-earnings) ratio would be

$$\frac{P_0}{D_0} = \frac{1+g}{r-g}.$$

Hence, the ratio of prices to dividends is constant despite the fact that both are growing. This implies that the price-dividend ratio is a natural statistic by which to examine the market's expectations with respect to g. From this expression we can see that increases in future growth raise the price-dividend ratio today. Having examined the implications of the deterministic model, we turn next to the stochastic model.

2. SIMPLE GROWTH 2

Now we want to take account of the fact that growth is not deterministic in order to understand the implications of growth shocks form our model. To do this, assume that there are two possible growth rates g^h and g^l, where $g^h > g^l$. We will assume that the probabilities of these two realizations tomorrow depends both on the growth rate outcome tomorrow and the current growth rate you had today. This is a natural way of allowing for things like persistence in the growth rates. So, assume that the probability of high growth is π^h if the current growth rate is high, while it is π^l if the growth rate is low. If $\pi^h > \pi^l$, then a high growth rate today will make it more likely we will have a high growth rate tomorrow.

This simple growth process leads to a transition matrix of the form

$$\Pi = \left[\begin{array}{cc} \pi^h & 1 - \pi^h \\ \pi^l & 1 - \pi^l \end{array} \right].$$

To understand this matrix, let π_0 be the current probability that we are in the high growth state today. Then, our state is the vector $[\pi_0, 1 - \pi_0]$. Normally, we will start out knowing where we are, so say $\pi = 1$. Then, the probabilities tomorrow are given by

$$[\pi_0, 1 - \pi_0]\, \Pi = \left[\pi_0 \pi^h + (1 - \pi_0)\pi^l, \pi_0(1 - \pi^h) + (1 - \pi_0)(1 - \pi^l) \right],$$

which gives us the probabilities of being in the high and low growth rate state tomorrow, given the probabilities today. Continuing in this fashion, we get that in two periods these probabilities are given by

$$[\pi_0, 1 - \pi_0]\, \Pi^2,$$

and so forth. In the limit these probabilities will settle down for any starting values for π (assuming that π_h and π_l are also between zero and one). At this limiting value, $\bar{\pi}$, it will turn out that

$$\bar{\pi} = \bar{\pi}\Pi.$$

To try to determine the prices in our model, we are going to need to use the guess-and-verify method. So, conjecture that there are two prices that depend upon the realized total growth factor

$$Z_t = \prod_{j=0}^{t} (1 + g_j),$$

and that

$$P_t^h = Z_t P^h,$$
$$P_t^l = Z_t P^l,$$

where P_t^h is the price of the equity if the growth rate between $t-1$ and t was high, and P_t^l if it was low.

Next, we need to see if our guess works. Given our assumptions, our prices would be the solution to

$$P_t^h = Z_t P^h = \frac{1}{1+r} \left\{ \begin{array}{l} \pi^h \left(P^h + D_0\right)(1+g^h)Z_t \\ +(1-\pi^h)\left(P^l + D_0\right)(1+g^l)Z_t \end{array} \right\}$$

and

$$P_t^l = Z_t P^l = \frac{1}{1+r} \left\{ \begin{array}{l} \pi^l \left(P^h + D_0\right)(1+g^h)Z_t \\ +(1-\pi^l)\left(P^l + D_0\right)(1+g^l)Z_t \end{array} \right\}.$$

These equations verify our conjecture (since Z_t will drop out) and show that we need different prices only because $\pi^h \neq \pi^l$. Also, as the two probabilities get closer together, so too will the prices (but that may be a bit harder to see). Next, note that these expressions also imply that prices and dividends will be growing because both are changing with Z_t.

What about the price-dividend ratio?

$$\frac{P_t^h}{D_t} = \frac{P^h}{D_0} = \frac{\frac{1}{1+r}\left\{ \begin{array}{l} \pi^h \left(P^h + D_0\right)(1+g^h) \\ +(1-\pi^h)\left(P^l + D_0\right)(1+g^l) \end{array} \right\}}{D_0}$$

and

$$\frac{P_t^l}{D_t} = \frac{P^l}{D_0} = \frac{\frac{1}{1+r}\left\{ \begin{array}{l} \pi^l \left(P^h + D_0\right)(1+g^h) \\ +(1-\pi^l)\left(P^l + D_0\right)(1+g^l) \end{array} \right\}}{D_0}.$$

So, the price-dividend ratio will be high (low) in the high (low) state because future growth is expected to be high (low).

2.1. Price-Dividend Ratios in the Data

In Figure 4.2 I have plotted both the price-dividend ratio and the more conventional price-earnings ratio for the S&P 500 over a long historical period.[1] The data

---

1. The price earnings ratio is more commonly used because firms may choose to move around or smooth the timing at which they pay out their earnings, something we have ignored in our analysis.

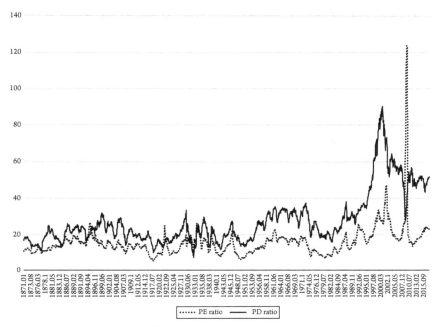

Figure 4.2 Price Earnings and Price Dividend Ratio Over Time.
SOURCE: Robert Schiller.

are from Robert Shiller's online database and were used in his well known book entitled *Irrational Exuberance.*

The behavior of the price-dividend ratio is roughly consistent with our theory. Periods of high anticipated growth seem to be associated with high price dividend ratios. After the growth boom of the 1920s and the mass production of the car, P/E ratio had risen to 20.2 in September of 1929, while the P/D was also high at 33.3. Both ratios fell dramatically during the Great Depression, bottoming out at 9.3 and 7.2, respectively, in June 1932. One feature that really stands out in the figure is how very high these ratios were at the height of the tech boom, reaching 46.4 for the price-dividend ratio and 72.7 for the price-earnings ratio in December of 2001, before crashing.[2]

3. PROBLEMS

Problem 1. Consider the following forecasting problem. Assume that the random variable x_t takes on a value of either 1 or 0 with equal probability each period. Assume that time runs for three periods, and an outcome will be a triplet of zeros and ones.

2. The price-earnings ratio skyrockets briefly during the Great Recession due to a very sharp fall in earnings. Between the middle of 2008 and the beginning of 2009, earnings fall by a factor of about 5, before recovering by the end of 2009. Dividends are much smoother during this period, as firms often smooth dividends relative to earnings.

(1) How many possible three-period histories (or outcomes) are there? What is the probability of each outcome? What is the expected value of the sum of the x's, or

$$E\left\{\sum_{t=1}^{3} x_t\right\}?$$

(2) After we have seen the outcome in the first period, how many histories have positive probability and how many have zero probability? Assuming that $x_1 = 1$, what is the conditional forecast of the sum of the x's

$$E\left\{\sum_{t=1}^{3} x_t \mid x_1 = 1\right\}?$$

(3) After we have seen the outcomes in both the first and the second periods, how many outcomes have positive probability? Assume that $x_1 = 1$ and $x_2 = 0$. What is the conditional forecast now, or

$$E\left\{\sum_{t=1}^{3} x_t \mid x_1 = 1 \,\&\, x_2 = 0\right\}?$$

Problem 2. Now consider the following forecasting-the-forecasts of others exercise where we still assume that x_t is as described in Problem 1. In period one, I know that $x_1 = 1$ and I can work out the forecasts that the new me in period 2 will make. Figure out what those possible forecasts can be, and the likelihood of each of those forecasts. Then, compare my expectation of my future expectation

$$E_1 E_2 \left\{\sum_{t=1}^{3} x_t \mid x_1 = 1\right\}$$

to my forecast

$$E_1 \left\{\sum_{t=1}^{3} x_t \mid x_1 = 1\right\}.$$

Problem 3. Assume that in period 3 the value of the asset can take four different values $Q(1), ..., Q(4)$. Assume that between date 1 and date 2, I find out whether $\{Q(1), Q(2)\}$ will be realized or $\{Q(3), Q4)\}$ will be realized. Assume that the probability of the first case is π_1 and the second case is $1 - \pi_1$. Assume that the lower index in the set will occur with probability π_2, while the higher index will occur with probability $1 - \pi_2$. Draw out the event tree with the appropriately labeled transition probabilities. Assign some values to $Q(1), ..., Q(4)$, and the probabilities π_1 and π_2. Compute the expected value at the two nodes in date 2 and the expected value as of date 1. Verify that the expected value as of date 1 is the average of your next period expectations. Discuss which of the two probabilities you used in this average and why.

Problem 4. Use our simple asset pricing model

$$p_t = \beta E_t \{Q_{t+1}\}$$

to compute the one-period-ahead interest rates

(1) Assume that $\beta = .95$ and $\beta = .90$.
(2) If we think that real rates of interest are roughly 1%, and if we think that a period in our model is roughly a quarter, what is the discount rate that will generate this annual interest rate? (Assume that compounding is done every quarter.)

Problem 5. Assume that discount rates vary over time and are given by $\beta(t)$. Assume that the individual's preferences are given by

$$c_1 + \beta(1)E_1 \{c_2 + \beta(2)E_2 \{c_3 + \beta(3)E_3 \{...\}\}\}.$$

Write down the individual's portfolio problem, and derive the individual's optimality condition. Use that condition to derive the pricing rule, and then use that pricing rule to say how short term interest rates will change over time, and how the one-period rate will be different from the two-period rate.

Problem 6. Deferred coupon bonds are similar to standard coupon bonds except that the coupon payments do not start for a while, typically several years. Consider the following two bonds:

(1) A standard coupon bond that pays a coupon in each of the next nine years before finally paying the principal at the end of the 10th year.
(2) A deferred coupon bond in which the coupon does not begin until three years have passed (so you don't get a coupon in the first two years). The coupon is paid each year up until and including the 9th year. In the 10th year the principal is repaid.

Assume that $\beta = .95$, and that the coupon is 5 and the principal is 100. Discuss how the prices of these two bonds would differ. Assume that you could buy a contract that was going to pay you 5 in year 1 and year 2. What can you say about the price of this contract and its relationship to the two bond prices? Assume now that the coupon is paid in the 10th year along with the principal for both of our two bonds. How much would this change the price of the bond?

Problem 7. Are the yields on the two bonds we considered in problem 6 the same? Please explain your answer. Could time-varying discount rates–i.e., $\beta(t)$–change your answer?

Problem 8. Assume that the yield on a one-period bond is 3%, on a two-period bond is 4%, and a three-period bond is 5%. Construct the expected future one-period interest rates that are consistent with this yield curve. Are these short-term rates rising or falling?

Problem 9. The yield on a 5-year German bond was about 3%, while that on a Italian bond was about 7%. Assume that these were pure discount bonds and that this yield difference was entirely due to default risk. Assume that this default risk is the same in every period, and if the Italians default, the bond will only pay off 1/2 its contracted amount. What is the per-period probability of default that accounts for this difference in returns? Does this probability seem large or small to you based on your reading of the newspapers reports or description of the EU crisis? How might you explain the difference between your probability of a default and the size of the yield premium?

Problem 10. Consider a simple futures contract on a security with a stochastic payoff structure. Assume that the payoff of the security depends upon the history of realizations of a simple up-down process. The set of possible histories, their probabilities, and the payoffs of the asset are given in the following table.

States	Payoff Q	Probabilities
(u,u)	115	$\frac{1}{2} * a$
(u,d)	105	$\frac{1}{2} * (1 - a)$
(d,u)	95	$\frac{1}{2} * (1 - a)$
(d,d)	85	$\frac{1}{2} * a$

(1) How does the expected value of Q change with a in the first period? For both $a = 1/3$ and $a = 2/3$, compute the expected payoffs in period 2 when only the first realization has been seen (i.e., either u or d).

(2) Assume that $\beta = 1$ and our representative price is risk-neutral, so that the price of the security is just equal to the conditional expectation

of Q. What is the price in the first period and what are the possible prices in the second period for your two different values of a?

(3) Imagine you had purchased the option of buying the security at a price of 100 in the second period. This is a European option since it has a fixed exercise date. Under what conditions (i.e., $s = u$ or d) would you want to exercise that option, and how much would you expect to make on this option from the perspective of period 1? Do this again for both values of a. Finally, what would you expect to pay for this option in the first period?

(4) Imagine this was an American option and you could exercise the option in either period 2 or period 1. Assume that you saw a value of $s = u$ in the first period. Would you want to exercise your option or wait? Does your answer depend upon a? How would you expect the period 1 value of the American option to be relative to the value of the European option.

Problem 11. We are going to think about how repayment risk affects the interest rate charged on a mortgage. Assume that the short-term interest rate takes on a value of 2% with probability π and 4% with probability $1 - \pi$.

(1) Consider the decision of a mortgage lender who must decide whether to issue a two-period mortgage at rate R prior to knowing the short-term interest rate. If he issues the mortgage, he will earn R next period and $1 + R$ the period after that for every dollar of the mortgage he sells. If he invests in the short-term money market, his expected return is

$$[1.02]^2 * \pi^2 + 2[1.02 * 1.04] * \pi * (1 - \pi) + [1 - \pi]^2 * (1.04)^2.$$

Compute the mortgage rate R that will lead him to just break even if we assume that $\pi = 0, 1/2$ or 1.

(2) Now assume that instead of paying R for sure in the next period, the borrower will repay $1 + R$ (and thereby completely repay his mortgage) if the short-term interest rate is 2%, while if the interest rate is 4% he will pay R next period and $1 + R$ two periods later. In the case where the interest rate is 2%, assume that the lender just invests his funds in the short-term market. Compute again the mortgage rate that will enable him to break even. Explain why the rate has changed.

Problem 12. In *Dow 36,000*, a book written at the end of the 1990s, Glassman and Hassett made the following calculation to predict the Dow Jones Index.

Note this corresponds to the peak of the internet bubble. At that point the Dow Jones was at 9,000 and the dividend yield was at 2%, so $D = .02 *$ $9000 = 180$. They assumed that the long-run growth rate of the economy was 2.5% and that the discount rate was $r = 3\%$ (which was the current yield on Treasury bills at the time). With these assumptions,

$$P = \frac{180}{.03 - .025} = \frac{180}{.005} = 36000.$$

This led them to predict that the Dow was not overvalued and would rise to 36,000 in the next few years. See https://en.wikipedia.org/wiki/Dow_36,000.

But by the beginning of 2000, the Dow was roughly at 11,000, and by 2015, it stood at roughly 18,000. So what went wrong? One standard response is that the discount rate the authors used is too low, since firms face higher borrowing costs on payouts that are risky. Explore the impact of changing r and show how it can affect your prediction for the Dow.

Problem 13. Consider an equity security that pays a dividend of 1 in bad times and a dividend of 1.5 in good times. Assume that $\beta = .95$. Assume that the transition probability for good and bad states is

$$\Pi = \begin{bmatrix} .75 & .25 \\ .25 & .75 \end{bmatrix},$$

where state 1 is the good state and state 2 is the bad state. Then if the price vector is

$$P = \begin{bmatrix} P^G \\ P^B \end{bmatrix},$$

where P^G is the good state price and P^B is the bad state price, it must satisfy

$$P = \beta \Pi \begin{bmatrix} P^G + 1.5 \\ P^B + 1 \end{bmatrix}.$$

(1) Try to solve for the price vector.
(2) Starting from the fundamental price in step (1), assume that there was a bubble on this security. Assume that the probability of collapse is 10%. Construct the path of the security for 10 periods.

Problem 14. Consider a special version of our growth economy. Output grows at either the high or the low rate up until time T. Then, from time T onward, it grows at the realized rate in time T. This means that conditional on being at time T, future growth is now deterministic. Try to solve for the price that will prevail at time T depending upon the realized growth rate and the accumulated history of growth. Note that you should be able to derive a simple analytic expression as we did in the completely deterministic case. Hopefully this gives you some more intuition as to why our guess worked.

Problem 15. Many large loans are collateralized. For example, imagine someone getting a loan to buy a $100 million hotel. If one thinks that the most that the hotel could fall in value is $10 million over the 5 years of loan, then posting $10 million in risk-free bonds would make the loan pretty close to risk-free, since the lender can keep the collateral and recover the property in the event of bankruptcy by the borrower. However, if the loan was for the purchase of financial assets, whose value could fall in half, and if the collateral itself were similar financial assets whose payoffs were likely to be correlated, then the lender could face a situation in which both the assets purchased and the collateral had fallen sharply in value. Discuss how this would change the amount of collateral that the lender would require in order for the loan to be essentially risk-free. Then read and discuss this article on collateral management practices and how the financial collapse of the Great Recession changed behavior: http://www.wallstreetandtech.com/operations/wall-street-taking-a-closer-look-at-collateral-management/d/d-id/1260721?

5

Asset Pricing II

1. PROBLEMS WITH THE SIMPLE RISK NEUTRAL MODEL

This has been fun, but now for some bad news about the asset pricing model we have developed.

1. Interest rates move around quite a bit. In Figure 5.1 I have plotted the yield for a 3-month Treasury bill based upon the secondary market price; clearly the rates change a lot. Of course, these are nominal rates.

The height of nominal interest rates was during the late 1970s and early 1980s. These years were a period of high inflation, which suggests that bringing inflation into our model and seeing how it affects interest rates may help resolve this linkage. It's also interesting to note that in the post-2008 period we had some of the lowest interest rates since the Great Depression in the 1930s.

2. The yield curve, which shows the different yields by maturity at a point in time, typically slopes upward, but short-term rates are not on average rising over time.

Figure 5.2 illustrates this fairly starkly. The 1-year T-bond rate is almost always below the 5-Year T-bond rate, which is almost always below the 10-year rate. Despite this, interest rate fell fairly systematically during the entire period of the figure (1982–2018). There are periods when the short-term rate is above the long-term rate. This is called an inverted yield curve in the literature. If you look

Figure 5.1 U.S. Treasury Yields Over Time.
SOURCE: FRED. Data Source: Board of Governors of the Federal Reserve System (U.S.).

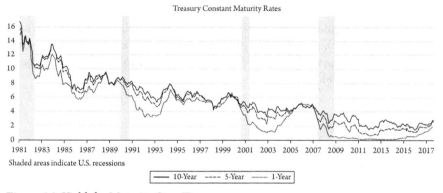

Figure 5.2 Yields by Maturity Over Time.
SOURCE: FRED. Data Source: Board of Governors of the Federal Reserve System (U.S.).

closely, most of the time when the yield curve inverts the economy goes into a recession.

3. The average return on equities is higher than that on bonds in Table 5.1. This is commonly called the *equity premium*. The return on 3-month T-Bills is less than that on 1 year Government Bonds, which is less that on the return on a portfolio of stocks (Table 5.1). This period includes the Great Depression when stock returns were very negative.

Table 5.1. ANNUAL RATES OF RETURN ON INVESTMENTS IN T-BILL, BONDS, AND STOCKS

Period	T-Bills	Bonds	Stocks
1928–2010	3.66%	5.01%	9.32%

SOURCE: http://pages.stern.nyu.edu/~adamodar/New_Home_Page/
datafile/histret.html (geometric average)

So, to summarize some problems we have observed with our basic model:

(1) Interest rates move around quite a bit. Of course these are nominal rates.
(2) The yield curve is typically upward sloping, but short-term rates are not on average rising over time.
(3) The average return on equities is about 6% higher than that on bonds.
(4) Assets whose payouts are highly correlated with the average payout of the market earn higher average returns.
(5) The average return on risky securities is countercyclical, falling during boom times and rising during downturns.

The first problem suggests that short-term securities provide some other service (possibly a liquidity service) which can explain their lower rate of return. The others suggest that we need to price risk more seriously. (In the risk-neutral model risk was not priced since only the expected value mattered.) We move on to a series of fixes which can help with these problems.!

2. NOMINAL RATES

Money rules the world, so let's allow it in. To do that, we will augment our basic model to allow for nominal prices. To keep things simple, we will have only our single consumption good, so only its price will determine the overall price level.

Consider the portfolio choices of a risk neutral investor who has the following investment problem:

$$\max_{a_1} c_1 + E_1\beta \left\{ \max_{a_2} c_2 + E_2\beta \left\{ \max_{a_3} c_3 + E_3\beta \left\{ \max_{a_4} c_4 + ... \right\} \right\} \right\},$$

where his flow budget constraint is given by

$$P_t y_t + a_{t-1} Q_t - p_t a_t = P_t c_t.$$

Here P_t is the price of the consumption good in period t, and p_t and Q_t are the nominal price and nominal payout of the asset.

Now, let's consider lowering c_t by 1 and raising c_{t+1} by the accumulated savings

$$P_t \triangle c_t = -p_t \triangle a_t$$
$$E_t \{\triangle c_{t+1}\} = E_t \left\{ \frac{Q_{t+1}}{P_{t+1}} \right\} \triangle a_t.$$

So,

$$\triangle c_t + \beta E\{\triangle c_{t+1}\} =$$
$$-\frac{p_t}{P_t}\triangle a_t + \beta E_t\left\{\frac{Q_{t+1}}{P_{t+1}}\right\}\triangle a_t = 0$$

for no gain, and

$$p_t = E_t\beta\left\{\frac{P_t}{P_{t+1}}Q_{t+1}\right\}.$$

This leads to a nominal interest rate

$$(1 + R_t)E_t\left\{\frac{P_t}{P_{t+1}}\right\} = \beta^{-1}.$$

Now, movements in the change in prices lead to changes in the nominal interest rate. If the price level is expected to rise, then the nominal interest rate will rise to offset its effect on the total real return. Note that the only uncertainty is with respect to (hereafter, w.r.t.) P_{t+1}. Because of *Jensen's inequality*, $E_t\{1/P_{t+1}\} \neq 1/E_t\{P_{t+1}\}$. (See Wikipedia for more information.)

3. LIQUIDITY BENEFIT

Some assets can more readily be used as collateral or more quickly sold. These assets are said to have higher liquidity. This liquidity benefit can affect the equilibrium price of the security. Assets that are highly liquid tend to be very standardized, trade on thick markets, and have very low risk. Examples include short-term Treasury bills at time of issue and gold. Examples of non-liquid assets include houses and race horses.

3.1. The Impact of Liquidity on Yields

Consider a one-period bond that also gives a liquidity benefit of L, and a 10-period coupon bond that does not. The change in payoffs is

$$-p_1^1 + \beta\{100 + L\}$$

and

$$-p_1^{10} + \sum_{t=2}^{T-1}\beta^t Q + \beta^T P,$$

where Q is the coupon and P is the principal. Trivially, the yield on the coupon bond is $\beta^{-1} - 1$, while that on the one-period bond is lower since the price is higher. Factors like the size of the money supply, the supply of short-term debt, and the overall perceived level of risk could effect the liquidity benefit from short-term debt.

With time-varying discount factors $\beta(t)$ and a liquidity benefit $L(t)$ for short-term debt, we can have a generally upward sloping yield curve without rising short-term rates. However, a particularly steep yield curve does suggest rising short-term rates while a particularly flat or negative yield curve does suggest falling short-term rates. We can also have time variation in the yield curve and the implied short-term interest rates.

4. RISK AVERSION AND THE PRICING OF RISK

4.1. Risk Aversion

Assume that the individual has a concave utility function over flow consumption

$$u(c), \text{ where } u'(c) > 0 \text{ and } u''(c) < 0.$$

Assume that the individual cares about his expected utility in each period and not his expected consumption

$$E\{u(c)\}.$$

Assume that his overall payoff is his discounted expected utility

$$E_1\left\{\sum_{t=1}^{T}\beta^t u(c_t)\right\}.$$

With concave preferences the more you are consuming the less you benefit from more consumption:

$$u'(c)\triangle c.$$

With concave preferences,

$$u(E\{c\}) > E\{u(c)\}$$
$$\cong u(E\{c\}) + u'(E\{c\}) E\{c - E\{c\}\}\}$$
$$+ u''(E\{c\}) \frac{E\{[c - E\{c\}]^2\}}{2}$$
$$= u(E\{c\}) + u''(E\{c\}) \frac{E\{[c - E\{c\}]^2\}}{2},$$

because the benefit of an increase in consumption is less than the loss from a decrease.

4.2. Evaluating a Lottery

Assume we had a consumption lottery where you get consumption level c with probability $\Pr(c)$. Then your payoff is

$$\sum_c u(c)\Pr(c).$$

Let $\bar{c} = \sum_c c\Pr\{c\}$, then

$$u(c) \simeq u(\bar{c}) + u''(\bar{c})\frac{(c-\bar{c})^2}{2},$$

and

$$\sum_c u(c)\Pr(c) \simeq u(\bar{c}) + u''(\bar{c})\frac{var(c)}{2}.$$

With standard preferences in which $u' > 0$ and $u'' < 0$, the payoff from the lottery is less than that of consuming the expected value of consumption and the size of the penalty is roughly linear in the variance of consumption, with the penalty coefficient being determined by the curvature of utility as captured by u''.

Example 1. To take a concrete example, assume that preferences were quadratic, so

$$u(c) = Ac - \frac{B}{2}c^2$$

with the understanding that c is never so big it gets above the bliss point (the point at which $A - Bc^* = 0$). Then, the payoff looks like

$$A\bar{c} - B\frac{var(c)}{2}.$$

Example 2. To take another concrete example, consider a power function of the form

$$u(c) = \begin{cases} \frac{c^{1-\alpha}-1}{1-\alpha} & \text{for } \alpha \geq 0 \text{ and not equal to 1} \\ \log(c) \text{ for } \alpha = 1. \end{cases}$$

(it can be shown that as $\alpha \to 1$, the first payoff in example 2 converges to the second payoff in the example; i.e., $\log(c)$) In this case the payoff from the lottery looks like

$$u(\bar{c}) + u''(\bar{c})\frac{var(c)}{2} = \frac{\bar{c}^{1-\alpha} - 1}{1 - \alpha} - \alpha\bar{c}^{-\alpha-1}\frac{var(c)}{2}$$

$$= \frac{\bar{c}^{1-\alpha} - 1}{1 - \alpha} - \alpha\bar{c}^{1-\alpha}\frac{var(\frac{c}{c})}{2}$$

$$= \bar{c}^{1-\alpha}\left[\frac{1}{1 - \alpha} - \alpha\frac{var(\frac{c}{c})}{2}\right] - \frac{1}{1 - \alpha}.$$

Here, the expected level of consumption is being rescaled by a factor α times the % variation in consumption $var(\frac{c}{c})$. So with these preferences we care about the risk relative to expected consumption. That seems like a very attractive formulation. After all, if you have \$1000, losing \$100 seems like a big deal. But if you have \$1 million, it doesn't. These preferences are called constant-relative-risk-aversion (CRRA) and this is one reason why we like them.

4.3. Portfolio Decisions and Asset Prices

The individual's overall payoff is given by

$$E\left\{\sum_{t=1}^{T}\beta^{t-1}u(c_t)\right\},$$

where

$$c_t = y_t + a_{t-1}Q_t - p_t a_t(s^t).$$

Consider buying a unit of this security at date 1 and selling it at date 2. Then the change in your payoff is

$$-u'(c_1)p_1 + \beta E\left\{u'(c_2)\left[d_2 + p_2\right]\right\}.$$

Next we impose our equilibrium condition that the marginal gain from holding the asset in the correct supply is 0. This implies that

$$p_1 = \beta\frac{E\left\{u'(c_2)\left[d_2 + p_2\right]\right\}}{u'(c_1)}$$

$$= \frac{\beta}{u'(c_1)}\left(E\left\{u'(c_2)\right\}E\left\{d_2 + p_2\right\} + cov\left[u'(c_2), \left[d_2 + p_2\right]\right]\right),$$

since

$$cov(a, b) = E\left\{(a - E(a))(b - E(b))\right\}$$

$$= E\left\{ab - E(a)b - aE(b) + E(a)E(b)\right\}$$

$$= E\left\{ab\right\} - E(a)E(b).$$

This is a very different theory of risk pricing:

$$p_1 = \frac{\beta}{u'(c_1)} \left(E\{u'(c_2)\} E\{d_2 + p_2\} + cov\left[u'(c_2), [d_2 + p_2]\right]\right),$$

where the value of an asset depends upon a combination of its expected return and its covariance with consumption:

(1) To the extent that consumption is growing then $E\{u'(c_2)\} < u'(c_1)$, and as a result the discount rate will be lower.
(2) If the covariance with consumption $= 0$, then it will work just like risk-neutral pricing model.
(3) If the covariance is *positive*, then the covariance with u' will be negative and the price will be *lower*.

Our *discount factor* in the risk neutral world was simply β, and all of our asset pricing was given by

$$p_t = \beta E\{Q_{t+1}\} \text{ or } 1 = \beta E\{R_{t+1}\},$$

where $R_{t+1} = Q_{t+1}/p_t$ is the return. With risk aversion, our *stochastic* discount factor, m_{t+1}, is given by

$$m_{t+1} = \beta \frac{u'(c_2)}{u'(c_1)},$$

and our asset pricing rule is given by

$$p_t = E\{m_{t+1}Q_{t+1}\} \text{ or } 1 = E\{m_{t+1}R_{t+1}\}.$$

4.4. CAPM

There is a special version of our risk-averse asset pricing model that is widely known, called the *capital asset pricing model* or CAPM. We want to briefly lay out this version of the model in this section. In the model, we assume that investors live for 2 periods and have quadratic preferences over consumption

$$u(c_t) + \beta u(c_{t+1}) = E \sum_{t=1}^{2} \beta^{t-1} \left[c_t - \frac{1}{2}(c_t - c^*)^2 \right].$$

To understand this preference assumption note that there is a linear term with respect to consumption, just as in our risk-neutral model, but there is also a quadratic penalty for the extent to which consumption deviates from its bliss point c^*. This bliss point is supposed to be too high for the household to actually achieve, so more is always preferred to less.

We assume that these investors have no labor income and that they have some initial wealth, W, which they can allocate among a variety of assets indexed by i. This allocation is subject to a first-period budget constraint, and we will also have a second-period budget constraint that determines second-period consumption. These constraints are given by

$$\sum_i \omega_i + c_1 = W \text{ and } \sum_i \omega_i R_i = c_2.$$

Here W is wealth. The price of each asset has been normalized to one, so we can just focus on returns, R_i, on each asset and asset positions ω_i.

The first-order condition for the optimal choice of ω_i is determined by substituting these budget constraints into our preferences

$$u\left(W - \sum_i \omega_i\right) + \beta u\left(\sum_i \omega_i R_i\right)$$

and differentiating with respect to the asset position ω_i to get

$$-u'(c_1) + \beta E u'(c_2) R_i = 0.$$

This condition can be written out in terms of our specific preferences as

$$-[1 - (c_1 - c^*)] + \beta E\{[1 - (c_2 - c^*)] R_i\} = 0.$$

This in turn can be rewritten as

$$1 - c_1 + c^* = \beta [1 - E(c_2) + c^*] E(R_i) \\ - \beta cov(c_2, R_i).$$

In this last expression, the first term on the left-hand side (l.h.s.) is the risk-neutral assessment and the second is a risk adjustment.

In equilibrium, the price of the assessment must be low enough, so that the return is high enough, so that supply equals demand. This requirement will end up determining the return on the security through its prices, since $R_i = Q_i/P_i$, where Q_i is the total payout and P_i is the price. In equilibrium, since supply must equal demand, the representative investor must end up holding the market. Hence, ω_i will equal the relative value shares of security in terms of the total supply of investment assets.

Taking as given the market portfolio and the equilibrium returns, we can define the return on wealth as $R^W = \sum_i \omega_i R_i / \sum_i \omega_i$. Then, note that since this is the return the investor earns on his savings,

$$
\begin{aligned}
m_{t+1} &= \beta \frac{u'(c_2)}{u'(c_1)} = \beta \frac{[1 - (c_2 - c^*)]}{[1 - (c_1 - c^*)]} = \beta \frac{1 + c^* - R^W(W - c_1)}{1 + c^* - c_1}, \\
&= \frac{\beta(1 + c^*)}{1 + c^* - c_1} - \frac{\beta(W - c_1)}{1 + c^* - c_1} R^W, \\
&= a_t - b_t R^W
\end{aligned}
$$

This stochastic discount factor has a constant term and a stochastic part coming from how the return on wealth alters consumption.

The (gross) risk-free rate will satisfy

$$
1 = E\{m_{t+1}\} R^f \Rightarrow R^f = 1/E\{m_{t+1}\} = 1/\left[a_t - b_t E\{R^W\}\right].
$$

Any return will satisfy

$$
\begin{aligned}
1 &= E\{m_{t+1} R_i\} = E\{m_{t+1}\} E\{R_i\} + cov(m_{t+1}, R_i) \\
&= \frac{E\{R_i\}}{R^f} - b cov(R^W, R_i).
\end{aligned}
$$

Thus, expected returns will be higher if the covariance is positive to offset the second term being negative. The negative term comes from the fact that high R^W implies high c_2 which implies low $u'(c_2)$.

5. ASSET PRICING AND GROWTH REVISITED

We return now to asset pricing and consider how having curvature in our preferences affects our prior results. To do that, we consider two cases. Consider the following asset pricing problem in a growing economy. Assume that our consumer has risk averse preferences

$$
u(c_1) + \beta E_1\{u(c_2) + \beta E_2\{u(c_3) + \beta E_3\{\cdots\}\}\},
$$

where

$$
u(c) = \frac{c^{1-\alpha}}{1 - \alpha}.
$$

Note that this implies

$$u'(c) = c^{-\alpha}.$$

The household's budget constraint is given by

$$y_t + (d_t + p_t)\,a_{t-1} - p_t a_t = c_t.$$

Assume that income y_t and dividend d_t on our security grow at a constant rate g, so

$$y_{t+1} = y_t(1 + g) \text{ and}$$
$$d_{t+1} = d_t(1 + g).$$

Starting from an optimal solution, $\{a_t\}_{t=1}^T$, we can derive our optimal asset pricing relationship by considering a small deviation in asset purchases at time t. This implies that

$$-u'(c_t)p_t + \beta u'(c_{t+1})\left[d_{t+1} + p_{t+1}\right] = 0.$$

Assume that growth implies that consumption also grows at a constant rate, so

$$c_{t+1} = c_t(1 + g).$$

Conjecture that the price also grows at a constant rate, $p_{t+1} = (1 + g)p_t$. This leads to

$$p_t = \beta(1 + g)^{-\alpha}\left[d_t + p_t\right](1 + g),$$

and hence to

$$p_t = \beta(1 + g)^{1-\alpha}\frac{d_t}{1 - \beta(1 + g)^{1-\alpha}}.$$

From this expression we can see our prices will grow at rate $(1 + g)$ since this is the rate that d_t will be growing over time. We can also see the impact of curvature on the pricing of our dividend series. With power preferences (or constant relative risk aversion, CRRA) it works like a modification of the discount rate: $\tilde{\beta} = \beta(1 + g)^{1-\alpha}$. This will lead to greater discounting if $\alpha < 1$, where $(1+g)^{-\alpha}$ is the greater discounting coming from consumption growth, and $(1 + g)$ is capturing the offsetting growth in dividends.

Finally, note that this expression implies that the price-dividend ratio will be

$$\frac{\beta(1 + g)^{1-\alpha}}{1 - \beta(1 + g)^{1-\alpha}}.$$

Thus it will be constant over time, just as before. The ratio will depend upon β, with a small β making it smaller. Finally, note that if we have a lot of curvature in our preferences and $\alpha > 1$, the ratio will be smaller the larger is g.

Now consider a simple stochastic version of our growth model in which there are two states, h and l drawn independently each period, where each state has probability $1/2$. In the high state,

$$c_t^h = (1+g)^t c_h \text{ and } c_t^l = (1+g)^t c_l,$$
$$d_t^h = (1+g)^t d_h \text{ and } d_t^l = (1+g)^t d_l.$$

If we go to our pricing relationship and take account of uncertainty, we get that

$$-u'(c_t)p_t + \beta E\{u'(c_{t+1})[d_{t+1} + p_{t+1}]\} = 0.$$

Next note that this second term will take the form

$$\beta E\{u'(c_{t+1})[d_{t+1} + p_{t+1}]\} = \beta \frac{1}{2}\left[(c_{t+1}^h)^{-\alpha}(d_{t+1}^h + p_{t+1}^h) + (c_{t+1}^l)^{-\alpha}(d_{t+1}^l + p_{t+1}^l)\right].$$

So, because of our independent and identically distributed (i.i.d.) assumption, the future looks the same regardless of which state we're in today. Guess that this implies there are two state-contingent prices, p_t^h and p_t^l, and that they both grow at rate g. This implies that

$$p_t^i = \frac{X_t(1+g)^{1-\alpha}}{(c_t^i)^{-\alpha}} \text{ for } i = h, l$$

where

$$X_t = \beta \frac{1}{2}\left[(c_t^h)^{-\alpha}(d_t^h + p_t^h) + (c_t^l)^{-\alpha}(d_t^l + p_t^l)\right].$$

Note the ratio

$$\frac{X_t}{(c_t^i)^{-\alpha}}$$

will grow at rate $(1+g)$ because growth coming through consumption will cancel out and we will just have price and dividend growth driving the ratio. Then, note that we have two equations in two unknowns, p_h and p_l, which verifies the second part of our conjecture. Finally, note that the only reason these equations will differ is that the denominators are different. This implies that $p_l > p_h$ because the cost of consumption is higher when consumption is lower.

6. BETTER BUT FAR FROM PROBLEM FREE

This revised theory of asset pricing moves the model's predictions in the right direction. However, it struggles along several key dimensions. Primarily, this is because the variation in aggregate consumption is fairly small; hence, even with a fairly high degrees of curvature, the variation in $u'(c)$ is also not large. This makes the covariance term for stocks small and hence implies too low a risk premium. It also makes the time variation in the pricing of risk low, so it's hard to match the cyclical variation in returns. Starting from our prior pricing relationship

$$p_1 = \frac{\beta}{u'(c_1)} \left(E\{u'(c_2)\} E\{d_2 + p_2\} + cov\left[u'(c_2), [d_2 + p_2]\right]\right),$$

assume that preferences are CRRA, so

$$u(c) = \frac{c^{1-\alpha} - 1}{1 - \alpha}$$

and hence

$$p_1 = E\left\{\beta\left(\frac{c_2}{c_1}\right)^{-\alpha}\right\} E\{d_2 + p_2\} + cov\left[\beta\left(\frac{c_2}{c_1}\right)^{-\alpha}, (d_2 + p_2)\right].$$

The first component is the "risk-neutral" part, with our discount rate of $E\left\{\beta\left(\frac{c_2}{c_1}\right)^{-\alpha}\right\} = 1/(1 + R^f)$. The second term is the risk adjustment and it can be rewritten as

$$cov\left[\beta\left(\frac{c_2}{c_1}\right)^{-\alpha}, (d_2 + p_2)\right] = corr\left[\beta\left(\frac{c_2}{c_1}\right)^{-\alpha}, (d_2 + p_2)\right] *$$

$$std\left(\beta\left(\frac{c_2}{c_1}\right)^{-\alpha}\right) * std(d_2 + p_2)$$

$$= \beta * corr\left[\left(\frac{c_2}{c_1}\right)^{-\alpha}, (d_2 + p_2)\right] * std\left(\left(\frac{c_2}{c_1}\right)^{-\alpha}\right) * std(d_2 + p_2)$$

using the definition of a correlation (the covariance divided by the two standard deviations). Any correlation is bounded between -1 and 1, so there is a clear limit on what this term can contribute. So consider the lowest price case where the correlation is -1 indicating that the payout of the asset moves exactly opposite to the marginal utility of consumption. Since the marginal utility of consumption moves negatively with consumption, another way of saying this is that the asset payout is perfectly correlated with consumption in the form of c_2^α. In this case, the risk penalty looks like

$$-\beta * std\left(\left(\frac{c_2}{c_1}\right)^{-\alpha}\right) * std\left(d_2 + p_2\right).$$

One can see from this that the penalty for risk is equal to the amount of risk, as captured by the standard deviation of the payout, times a term that depends on the standard deviation of the growth rate of aggregate consumption which is quite low. This low volatility of consumption growth limits the risk adjustment even with very high degrees of curvature coming from a high value of α.

Moreover, having a high degree of risk aversion suggests that people should be willing to pay a lot for a small amount of insurance against all of the individual risks they face. These risks, which are quite large at the level of the individual but average out in the aggregate, include medical expenses and health risk, fire- and weather-related risk, and so on. People do not seem to be that sensitive to these risks, so it seems implausible (within the context of this model) that they are that sensitive to aggregate consumption risk.

7. PROBLEMS

Problem 16. The U.S. Treasury periodically auctions bonds and bills. (For an example of the current schedule see https://www.treasury.gov/resource-center / data-chart-center / quarterly-refunding / Documents / auctions.pdf.) Once a bill or bond has aged relative to its auction date, it is called "on the run." On-the-run bills and bonds generally trade at a slight discount relative to when they were newly issued. A lot of trading of bills and bonds takes place around the date of issue (including just before). Discuss why the fact that an on-the-run bond is now less common—i.e., a 30-day bill becomes in succession a 29-, 28-day, etc. bill—would reduce its liquidity benefit. How might you use this to explain why the on-the-run bonds offer a slight yield premium?

Problem 17. Assume that you have a concave utility function $u(c)$, where $u'(c) > 0$ and $u''(c) < 0$. Make a graph to illustrate how the marginal utility of consumption will change with the level of consumption. Next, consider the payoff to an individual who buys tickets in a lottery. Assume that the individual gives up p units of sure consumption for each ticket in order to get either $h > p$ units with probability π and $l < p$ units with probability $1 - \pi$.

The payoff to an individual is given by

$$\pi u(Y - pa + ha) + (1 - \pi)u(Y - pa + la),$$

where a is the number of lottery tickets that he buys.

(1) How does his payoff change with the number of tickets he buys? What condition would indicate the optimum number of tickets?
(2) An actuarially fair lottery is one in which the cost is just equal to the expected winnings. Write down an expression for this condition. Would our individual want to buy any tickets in an actuarially fair lottery? Try to prove your answer.

Problem 18. Assume that the preferences of our representative consumer exhibit constant relative risk aversion and are given by

$$u(c) = \frac{c^{1-\gamma} - 1}{1 - \gamma}.$$

This implies that the marginal utility of consumption is given by

$$u'(c) = c^{-\gamma}.$$

The percentage standard deviations of output and consumption (i.e. s.d./mean) are 1.72 and 1.27, respectively. Assume that there are two states of the world, *high* and *low*, which occur with equal probability. Assume that the expected values of c and y are one. We want to construct their percentage deviations in the high and low states to hit the %s.d. This implies that we are solving for the deviation from the mean, α, such that

$$\sqrt{\frac{1}{2}\left([1 + \alpha - 1]^2 + [1 - \alpha - 1]^2\right)} = \sqrt{\alpha^2} = \alpha$$

is equal to our standard deviation target, which is .0172 and .0127, respectively.

Given these values, we can now seek to price a claim to output. From our dividend formula, this is going to be

$$P = E\left\{\sum_{t=1}^{\infty} \beta^t u'(c_t)y_t\right\} = \sum_{t=1}^{\infty} \beta^t \frac{\left[(1 + \alpha_c)^{-\gamma}(1 + \alpha_y) + (1 - \alpha_c)^{-\gamma}(1 - \alpha_y)\right]}{2}.$$

Use what you learned about infinite discounted sums to construct an analytic formula for this sum. Then, compute the price for $\gamma = 2, 5, 10$ when we take $\beta^{-1} = 1.01$ (that is, a 1% real return, which is roughly right). Note that $\gamma = 10$ is a lot of curvature but your return differences are pretty small.

Problem 19. Discuss why as the risk premium on the equities of a sector of the economy are likely to become higher as the sector becomes more important. Do so using the simple CAPM model where investors have quadratic preferences over consumption.

6

Asset Pricing III: Arbitrage-Based Pricing

We are going to discuss an alternative approach to pricing risk. This model doesn't really try to account for the pricing of risk, but rather tries simply to quantify it and examine its implications. This approach assumes that there is a sufficiently rich set of securities so that we can price any event. It also assumes that arbitrage forces all prices to be *consistent*. What we mean by that is if there are two equivalent ways to generate the same payoffs, then they must cost the same. Otherwise, we could simply short the more expensive way and go long on the cheaper way and earn positive arbitrage profits. All of these assumptions held in our prior models; however we will be putting much less structure on these prices. We will see that many of the basic results we have derived will carry over to this more general model.

Our risk-averse pricing model gave us a state-contingent discount factor which we need in order to account for why some payoffs are valued less than others at a given point in time. This is the only way we can explain why average returns are not equal, and why we see some securities, like equities, systematically offer higher returns. In the risk averse pricing model the state-contingent discount rates,

$$\beta \frac{u'(c_{t+1})}{u'(c_t)}$$

moved in the right direction, being low when future consumption, c_{t+1}, was high relative to current consumption, c_t. But it did not move nearly enough because aggregate consumption was not volatile enough. So, in order to get much action we needed to have insanely high risk aversion. But if people were really that risk averse, no one would get out of bed in the morning, and our ancestors would never have gone out and hunted woolly mammoths when there were saber-tooth tigers around. So, what we're going to do is think directly in terms of the sort of state-contingent discount rates we need to account for asset prices.

1. ARBITRAGE MODEL

Let's think about things in terms of states today, s, and states tomorrow, s'. Assume that the structure of assets is rich enough that we can essentially make contingent trades that promise a unit in state s' tomorrow. Denote $\rho(s'|s)$ as the price of such a unit delivery contract agreed to in state s, which pays out in state s'. Arbitrage implies that if $Q(s')$ is the payout of a security tomorrow, then it better be the case that

$$p = \sum \rho(s'|s)Q(s').$$

If not, we could either short the quantity $Q(s')$ of these state-contingent contracts and buy the security that pays out $Q(s')$, or the reverse.

Given this arbitrage result, if we define the *stochastic discount factor* as

$$m(s'|s) = \frac{\rho(s'|s)}{\pi(s'|s)},$$

the price of any security that pays out Q is

$$p = E(mQ)$$

and the return R earned by any security has to satisfy

$$1 = E(mR).$$

The quest in asset pricing can be thought of as trying to find a good model of m.

1.1. Where Do We Get Our State Contingent Prices?

We can get them from various contingent delivery contracts if they are rich enough. Assume that we have a collection of assets indexed by i, and that for each asset we have its payoff in state s' tomorrow $Q_i(s'|s)$. Then, fixing the state today, s, let A be a matrix of payoffs of dimension $I \times \#s'$ (So $A(i,j)$ gives the payout of asset i in state j tomorrow.) Then, we seek a weighting vector such that

$$w(s') * A = [0, ..., 1, 0, ..., 0],$$

where the 1 is in column s' and 0 otherwise. Given this, the price of a unit-contingent bond $\rho(s'|s)$ is simply

$$w(s') * p_i(s),$$

where $p_i(s)$ is a price vector for each of the securities in state s.

2. IMPLICATIONS OF ARBITRAGE-BASED PRICING

There are four implications:

1. The value is additive:

$$E(m(a+b)) = E(ma) + E(mb).$$

2. If R^f is the risk-free rate, then since

$$1 = E(mR^f),$$

   it must be that
$$\frac{1}{R^f} = E(m).$$

3. Using the definition of covariance

$$cov(m, x) = E\{[m - E(m)][x - E(x)]\} = E(mx) - 2E(m)E(x)$$
$$+ E(m)E(x)$$
$$= E(mx) - E(m)E(x),$$

   we get that

$$p = E(m)E(x) + cov(m, x)$$
$$= \frac{E(x)}{R^f} + cov(m, x).$$

4. Idiosyncratic risk is not priced: if $cov(m, x) = 0$, then

$$p = E(m)E(x) + cov(m, x)$$
$$= E(m)E(x)$$
$$= \frac{E(x)}{R^f}.$$

(So idiosyncratic risk is priced the same way overall risk was priced in the risk-neutral model.)

Example 3. Idiosyncratic Risk Pricing: Assume that there were two aggregate states $s' = \{h, l\}$ and the payoff of our security was $x = x(s') + \varepsilon$, where ε is i.i.d. noise. Then

$$p = \sum_{s'=\{h,l\}} \sum_{\varepsilon} m(s'|s)\,(x(s') + \varepsilon)\,\Pr(\varepsilon)\,\Pr(s'|s),$$

$$= \sum_{s'=\{h,l\}} m(s'|s) \left\{ \sum_{\varepsilon} (x(s') + \varepsilon)\,\Pr(\varepsilon) \right\} \Pr(s'|s)$$

but since $\sum_{\varepsilon} \varepsilon \Pr(\varepsilon) = 0$ (because it is i.i.d. noise), it follows that

$$p = \sum_{s'=\{h,l\}} m(s'|s)x(s')\,\Pr(s'|s).$$

2.1. Statistical Aside

Let $x(s)$ and $m(s)$ be random variables where s indexes states of the world and $\Pr(s)$ gives the probability of s. If we wanted to project x on m, then we would be seeking to

$$\min_{\alpha} E\left\{[x - \alpha m]^2\right\},$$

which leads to

$$E\left\{[x - \alpha m]\,m\right\} = 0,$$

or

$$\alpha = \frac{E(xm)}{E(m^2)}.$$

Then note that the forecast error is orthogonal to m since

$$E\left\{[x - \alpha m]\,m\right\} = E\left\{xm - \frac{E(xm)}{E(m^2)}m^2\right\} = E\left\{xm - E(xm)\right\} = 0.$$

2.2. More Implications of Arbitrage-Based Pricing

5. Aggregate or systemic risk is priced. To see this, consider the following statistical exercise. Consider regressing x on m

$$x = proj(x|m) + \varepsilon$$

where ε is the uncorrelated or a noise component. Then

$$proj(x|m) = \frac{E(mx)}{E(m^2)} m.$$

Then the price of x is

$$E(mx) = E\left(\left[proj(x|m) + \varepsilon\right]m\right) = E\left(proj(x|m)m\right),$$

so only the aggregate risk in the $proj(x|m)$ is priced.

2.3. Statistical Aside Take Two

If we wanted to forecast x using m, then we would want to solve

$$\min_{\alpha,\beta} E\left\{[x - \alpha - \beta m]^2\right\},$$

which leads to

$$E\{x - \alpha - \beta m\} = 0 \Rightarrow \alpha = E\{x - \beta m\}$$

and

$$E\{[x - \alpha - \beta m]\, m\} = 0 = cov\,(x - \alpha - \beta m, m) + E(x - \alpha - \beta m)E(m)$$
$$= cov(x, m) - \beta cov(m, m)$$

since

$$cov(a + b, c) = E\{[a + b - E(a) - E(b)]\,[c - E(c)]\}$$
$$= E\{[a - E(a)]\,[c - E(c)]\} + E\{[b - E(b)]\,[c - E(c)]\}$$
$$= cov(a, c) + cov(b, c).$$

Here's the statistical punchline:

$$\beta = \frac{cov(x, m)}{var(m)}.$$

Moreover,

$$E\{[x - \alpha - \beta m] \, m\} = 0,$$

so here too the forecast error is orthogonal because we have used up all of the information in m to forecast x.

2.4. Expected Return-Beta Representation

Start from our return expression

$$1 = E(mR) = E(m)E(R) + cov(m, R)$$
$$\Rightarrow E(R) - R^f = -R^f cov(m, R).$$

Then, note that

$$E(R) = R^f + \left(\frac{cov(m, R)}{var(m)}\right)\left(-\frac{var(m)}{E(m)}\right).$$

Then

$$\beta = \frac{cov(m, R)}{var(m)}$$

is the regression coefficient of R on m, and

$$\lambda = -\frac{var(m)}{E(m)}$$

is called the *market price of risk* in part because it is the same for all returns.

2.5. Mean-Variance Frontier

Start from the return for asset i:

$$1 = E(mR^i) = E(m)E(R^i) + \frac{cov(m, R^i)}{\sigma(m)\sigma(R^i)}\sigma(m)\sigma(R^i),$$

where $\sigma(\cdot)$ is the standard deviation, and note that $cov(m, R^i)/\left[\sigma(m)\sigma(R^i)\right]$ is the correlation of m and R^i and therefore lies between -1 and 1.

Hence

$$|E(R^i) - R^f| \leq \frac{\sigma(m)}{E(m)}\sigma(R^i).$$

This implies that the set of possible means and variances is limited by $\sigma(m)/E(m)$.

The *Sharpe ratio,* which is a measure of excess returns per unit of risk, is

$$\frac{E(R^i) - R^f}{\sigma(R^i)}.$$

If we use the standard consumption-based asset pricing model, then $m = \beta u'(c')/u'(c)$, and our prior result becomes

$$\left|\frac{E(R^i) - R^f}{\sigma(R^i)}\right| \leq \frac{\sigma(m)}{E(m)} \simeq \gamma\sigma(\triangle \ln(c)),$$

where γ is the degree of risk aversion. The problem is that the standard deviation of the growth rate of consumption is pretty small, and so γ has to be huge to explain the equity premium.

When thinking about the Sharpe ratio or any sort of similar statistic, it is interesting to think of it both unconditionally and conditionally. For example, we could look at a long time series of returns on a given security. We could compute the mean and standard deviation of the return in order to determine the unconditional Sharpe ratio. But we may also be interested in asking the question: What does the risk-return trade-off look like in recessions vs. expansions?

To sort out what we mean here and clarify our thinking, assume that there were two events we might see, say A and B, and that associated with each of these events was a set of states. So we can talk about the overall set of states as the union of A and B. Thus, initially, the expected return would be computed on the total set of states, or

$$ER = \sum_s R(s)Pr(s).$$

But conditional on s being in A, then the conditional expectation is given by

$$E\{R|A\} = \sum_{s \in A} R(s)Pr(s).$$

Given this, we can define the conditional variance as

$$\sum_{s \in A} (R(s) - E\{R|A\})^2 Pr(s)/Pr(A)$$

Using these objects, we can define the conditional Sharpe ratio. Remember in doing so that we need the standard deviation, which is the square root of the variance.

The conditional Sharpe ratio is highly volatile for a couple of reasons. First, the conditional variance is often much lower than the unconditional variance. Second, we often get some time series variation in the standard deviation. Often, we find that the standard deviation is higher in bad times than in good. This holds for many asset returns as well as for labor income.

3. ASSET PRICING SUPER PROBLEM

We will try here to construct a simple arbitrage-based pricing example based on roughly plausible numbers. We will then use this simple example to understand much of what we have gone over. We will assume that there are two possible states, g and b. That makes four possible transitions. We will try to calibrate our payoffs to roughly match the actual data. The good state is observed roughly $2/3$ of the time and the bad roughly $1/3$ of the time, and the transition probabilities seem to be roughly independent of the current state. So our transition probabilities are

$$\begin{bmatrix} 2/3 & 1/3 \\ 2/3 & 1/3 \end{bmatrix},$$

where state 1 is g and this is an i.i.d. model. This is roughly in line with the fact that positive annual growth rates of GDP are observed more frequently than negative annual growth rates.

Starting from our fundamental pricing relationship

$$E\{mR\} = 1,$$

we want to come up with some plausible return numbers. The risk-free rate is fairly constant at about 2% on an annual basis. The equity premium varies quite a bit from a low of 2% in the good state to a high of 8%. This implies an average return of 4% in the good state and 10% in the bad state. These returns are in line with the fact that returns are countercyclical and vary a lot over the business cycle. We are going to ask our model to reproduce these numbers.

Starting with the risk-free rate, this gives us our risk-free return equations

$$\left[m(g|s)\frac{2}{3} + m(b|s)\frac{1}{3} \right] R^f = 1,$$

where $R^f = 1.02$ and this holds for both $s = g$ and $s = b$.

Next, we turn to equity returns. We will ask the equity return to satisfy

$$m(g|s)\frac{2}{3}R(g|s) + m(b|s)\frac{1}{3}R(b|s) = 1,$$

$$\text{with } \frac{2}{3}R(g|g) + \frac{1}{3}R(b|g) = 1.04,$$

$$\text{with } \frac{2}{3}R(g|b) + \frac{1}{3}R(b|b) = 1.10.$$

So set

$$R(g|g) = 1.08 \text{ and } R(b|g) = 0.96$$

and set

$$R(g|b) = 1.17 \text{ and } R(b|b) = 0.96.$$

With these settings, we get the average returns and we get a widening of the variance of returns in bad as opposed to good times. Moreover, getting a bad draw leads to a negative return. All of these are reasonable features given the data.

Now we need to solve for the implied values of the stochastic discount factor. This means solving our system of equations in two blocks—conditional on the current state today. Each block consists of two equations and two unknowns. The solution is

$$m(s'|s) = \begin{bmatrix} 0.735 & 1.47 \\ 0.420 & 2.10 \end{bmatrix},$$

From these values one can see that a high discount rate is applied to return realizations in the good states vs. the bad (column 1 vs. column 2). Also, the gap in the stochastic discount factors for payouts tomorrow is much bigger starting in the bad state (row 2) than starting in the good state (row 1).

Example 4. What is price of a unit delivery in state 1 and state 2?

To solve this, we need to construct the delivery prices, but this is very simple since

$$p(s'|s) = m(s'|s)\Pr(s'|s).$$

So the answer is

$$p(s'|s) = \begin{bmatrix} 0.490 & 0.490 \\ 0.280 & 0.700 \end{bmatrix}.$$

Note that the stochastic discount factor prices the delivery not including the probability, while the delivery price combines the price and the probability.

Example 5. What is the price of risk? And how does it vary with the state?

The price of risk measures the extent to which the state price as captured by m differs across the different states; hence risk (variation in payouts) matters. It is defined as $var(m)/E(m)$, where these are both conditional on the current state. Since we have two possible initial states, we have two conditional market prices of risk. The answer is

$$\frac{var(m|s)}{E(m|s)} = \begin{bmatrix} 0.12 \\ 0.56 \end{bmatrix}.$$

What we see is a lot of variation in the market price of risk. It is much bigger conditional on being in the bad state today than in the good state. So, risk, in the sense of a negative covariation of the payout and m is going to be much more severely priced in bad states than in good.

Example 6. Consider a security whose payout is a function of the realized state s' and an independent risk factor ε. Denote the payoff of the security by

$$Q(s', \varepsilon) = g(s') + f(s')\varepsilon.$$

How are these different forms of risk priced?

To answer that, remember our pricing formula

$$P = E\{m(s'|s)Q(s', \varepsilon)\} = \sum_{s'=\{g,b\}} \sum_{\varepsilon} m(s'|s)\left[g(s') + f(s')\varepsilon\right]\Pr(s'|s)\Pr(\varepsilon)$$

$$= \sum_{s'=\{g,b\}} m(s'|s)g(s')\Pr(s'|s) + \sum_{s'=\{g,b\}} m(s'|s)f(s')\Pr(s'|s)\left\{\sum_{\varepsilon} \varepsilon' \Pr(\varepsilon)\right\}$$

$$= \sum_{s'=\{g,b\}} m(s'|s)\left[g(s') + f(s')\bar{\varepsilon}\right]\Pr(s'|s),$$

where $\bar{\varepsilon}$ is the mean of ε. Note that only the mean shows up here, not the variations of ε around the mean. We would call $f(s')\left[\varepsilon - \bar{\varepsilon}\right]$ idiosyncratic risk, and the rest, $g(s') + f(s')\bar{\varepsilon}$, aggregate risk.

Then, from

$$\sum_{s'=\{g,b\}} m(s'|s)\left[g(s') + f(s')\bar{\varepsilon}\right]\Pr(s'|s) = \sum_{s'=\{g,b\}} m(s'|s)\left[g(s') - \bar{g} + \bar{g} + f(s')\bar{\varepsilon}\right.$$
$$\left. -\bar{f}\bar{\varepsilon} + \bar{f}\bar{\varepsilon}\right]\Pr(s'|s),$$

where $\bar{g}$ is the conditional mean of $g(s')$ and $\bar{f}$ is the conditional mean of $f(s')$. This expression can be rewritten as

$$\sum_{s'=\{g,b\}} m(s'|s) \left[g(s') - \bar{g} + \bar{g} + f(s')\bar{\varepsilon} - \bar{f}\bar{\varepsilon} + \bar{f}\bar{\varepsilon} \right] \Pr(s'|s)$$

$$= \sum_{s'=\{g,b\}} m(s'|s) \left[(g(s') + f(s')\bar{\varepsilon}) - (\bar{g} + \bar{f}\bar{\varepsilon}) \right] \Pr(s'|s)$$

$$+ \sum_{s'=\{g,b\}} m(s'|s) \left[\bar{g} + \bar{f}\bar{\varepsilon} \right] \Pr(s'|s)$$

$$= \sum_{s'=\{g,b\}} m(s'|s) \left[(g(s') + f(s')\bar{\varepsilon}) - (\bar{g} + \bar{f}\bar{\varepsilon}) \right] \Pr(s'|s) + \bar{m} \left[\bar{g} + \bar{f}\bar{\varepsilon} \right]$$

$$= cov\left(m, g + f\tilde{\varepsilon} \right) + E(m)E(g + f\tilde{\varepsilon}).$$

Example 7. How important is the covariance term? And how does it vary with the initial state $s \in \{g, b\}$?

Start from

$$P = cov\left(m, g + f\tilde{\varepsilon} \right) + E(m)E(g + f\tilde{\varepsilon}),$$

and divide by the price to get things in return form, or

$$1 = cov\left(m, \frac{g + f\tilde{\varepsilon}}{P} \right) + E(m)E(\frac{g + f\tilde{\varepsilon}}{P}).$$

Then, define the return as $R = (g + f\tilde{\varepsilon})/P$, and remember that the risk-free rate is $R^f = 1/E(m)$. So we can rewrite this as

$$R^f = R^f cov\left(m, R \right) + E(R),$$

or in terms of the excess return

$$E(R) - R^f = -R^f cov\left(m, R \right).$$

Then, divide and multiply by the right-hand-side (r.h.s.) term by $var(m)$ to get

$$E(R) - R^f = -\frac{cov\left(m, R \right)}{var(m)} var(m)R^f,$$

and finally, replace R^f in the r.h.s. to get

$$-\frac{cov\left(m, R \right)}{var(m)} \frac{var(m)}{E(m)}.$$

The importance of the covariance term can be seen as coming from the product of two factors: (i) $\beta = \frac{cov(m,R)}{var(m)}$, which is our regression term, and (ii) the market price of risk, $\frac{var(m)}{E(m)}$.

If the regression term is independent of the current state, then the importance over time will come from variation in the market price of risk. Hence, it will be more important in bad times than in good.

4. FACTOR MODELS

One concrete example of the sort of pricing model implied by arbitrage pricing is the factor model. In a factor model there are measures of different risks that accumulate to generate the overall price of risk for an asset. A classic example of this is Fama and French's 3-factor model. Their factor pricing model starts from the observation that equity claims on both small firms and high book-to-market-ratio firms have generally earned higher returns than equity claims on the average firm. This leads Fama and French to conjecture that the risks associated with these factors are more highly priced than those for the average firm. From this, they get that the pricing of an individual asset will depend not only on its exposure to the average return on the market, much as in the standard CAPM, but also separately to its exposure to the differential risks.

They posit a linear relationship such as

$$R - R_f = \beta_M R_M + \beta_S R_S + \beta_B R_B,$$

where R_M is the excess return on the market portfolio, R_S is the excess return on a portfolio of small firms, and R_B is the excess return on a portfolio of high book-to-market firms. To get a feel for what this implies, note that Fama and French estimated that the average excess return on the market was around 5%, the excess size return was around 3%, and the excess return on high book-to-market firms was around 5%.

The other terms in this expression capture the exposure of the asset to these forms of risk. This is estimated by taking the time-varying excess returns R_{Mt}, R_{St} and R_{Bt} and regressing the realized excess return of the firm $R_t - R_{ft}$ on these excess returns. Hence, it is the regression coefficient much as in our beta representation above.

Fama and French, and many others, have considered more elaborate versions of this simple structure. To get a sense of how these factors move around and the other sorts of factors one might want to consider, see http://mba.tuck.dartmouth.edu/pages/faculty/ken.french/data_library.html.

5. PROBLEMS

Problem 20. Assume that there are 3 possible states $\{1, 2, 3\}$ both today and tomorrow. Assume that we have a full menu of state-contingent bonds. A state contingent bond pays out 1 tomorrow if the future state is the one agreed to and pays out 0 otherwise. Assume that the prices of these bonds are given by

	State Tomorrow		
State Today	1	2	3
1	.1	.15	.2
2	.05	.1	.15
3	.2	.15	.05

(1) Assume that we had a security that promised to pay out 1 if $s' = 1, 2$ if $s' = 2$ and 3 if $s' = 3$. Try to construct a portfolio of state contingent bonds that will replicate this payoff. Price this portfolio in each of the possible states today. If arbitrage forces the price of the security to be equal to this portfolio, then in which state today will the price be highest and why?

(2) Try to construct the returns for this security for each possible state today. Explain why these returns depend on both the state today and the state tomorrow. Compute the average excess returns and Sharpe ratio both conditional on the state today and as the unconditional values (what we will see in a long time series).

Problem 21. Consider the following example of pricing under uncertainty. Assume that the firm will be around for only three periods including today. Assume that there are only two states of the world in each period, $s = \{$high,low$\}$. Assume that the stochastic discount factors are given by

$m(s'|s)$	Tomorrow's state	
Today's state	$s' =$high	$s' =$low
$s =$high	.75	1.0
$s =$low	.5	.75

Assume that the transition probabilities were always $1/2$; i.e., the probability of going from high to low is the same as going from low to high. Assume that the dividend conditional on the current state was given by

$D(s)$	
Today's state	
$s =$high	2
$s =$low	1

Compute the price of the firm in period 1 for both $s_1 =$high and $s_1 =$ low.

7

Derivatives

Derivatives have become more and more important in financial markets. Here we examine them in greater detail, including how they are priced. Derivatives are contracts whose value is dependent on a collection of underlying assets, which is why we refer to them as "derivatives." Among the modern usages of derivatives, the simplest type of derivative is an agreement to exchange a financial asset at a future date for cash. These are often called *forward contracts* if they are privately negotiated or *futures contracts* if they are traded on an organized exchange.

During the Medieval period, merchants in 12th-century Europe who were traveling from fair to fair made use of a type of forward contract called a *lettre de faire* or letter of the fair. This occurred as part of the economic transformation of Medieval Europe from a largely self-sufficient agrarian economy following the collapse of the Roman Empire and its extensive trading system, to one again based more on trade, especially interregional trade. Medieval fairs, which were gatherings of buyers and sellers and occurred all over Europe, were part of this so-called Commercial Revolution. The letters, which were warehouse receipts, indicated the amount of the good being stored there that was available for future delivery. This allowed the merchants to trade based only on a sample of their goods, rather than undertaking dangerous journeys across Europe carrying them in full.

Another early example of a forward contract comes from feudal Japan. Large landowners would send surplus rice into warehouses in the cities. These warehouses then issued tickets that gave ticket holders the right to come to the warehouse and take delivery of a specified amount of rice at a future date at a specified price. These "rice tickets" came to be traded on the Dojima Exchange during the 1700s. (Interestingly, the Japanese Shogun during this period was generally not receptive to these contracts being traded, and so this market was often somewhat illicit.) The benefit of these tickets was that they allowed the holders to lock in the price at which they would buy their rice in the future. At the same time, tickets also locked in the price for the issuer of the ticket. Thus, future price risk was reduced on both sides.[1]

Agriculture, because of its seasonal production cycle has long been central to futures trading. Chicago became the center for commodity futures in the U.S. starting in the 19th century because of its role in the transportation, storage, and processing of agricultural products. The Chicago Board of Trade was founded in 1848. Around this time, two exchanges were set up in New York: the Cotton Exchange and the Coffee Exchange.

To take a specific example, crude oil futures are traded on a variety of exchanges. One standard benchmark is West Texas Intermediate, or WTI. One of the exchanges on which oil is traded is the NYMEX. These contracts include physical settlement, which means that if you hold the contract when it expires, you are expected to take delivery. The standard length of these contracts is two years. At any given point in time, multiple futures are being traded with different expiration dates. This is all a bit confusing, but a nomenclature has developed to deal with this. For example, "CLH7" means a March 2017 contract, while "CL01" means the closest expiring contract.[2]

Futures, or forward contracts, have a very simple structure relative to other derivatives. In such a contract, once the contract has been entered into, there are no future decisions to be made -other than trading the contract that is, which is not such a simple decision. The components of a futures contract include: (i) the forward price, (ii) the quantity, and (iii) the expiration date. The quantity is normally a multiple of a standardized number, and there are a limited number of expiration dates. For example, many futures contracts have four settlement dates each year, generally the third Friday of every third month in the quarter. So, in 2017, the settlement dates were March 18, June 16, September 15, and December 15. Some futures, like WTI, have monthly settlement dates.

1. David A. Moss and Eugene Kintgen. "The Dojima Rice Market and the Origins of Futures Trading." Harvard Business School Case 709-044, January 2009. (Revised November 2010.) See also http://highered.mheducation.com/sites/dl/free/007337590x/238719/TheOriginsOf Derivatives.pdf

2. https://www.quora.com/What-do-the-abbreviations-in-crude-oil-futures-mean-Eg-CL01-CL02

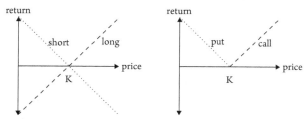

The exercise price in the contracts is *K*. On the left panel are the futures
contracts, on the right panel are the options contracts.

Figure 7.1 Financial Contracts: Future vs. Options. The
exercise price in the contracts is K. On the left panel are the
futures contracts, on the right panel are the options contracts.

An option contract is more sophisticated than a forward or futures contract,
since it involves future decisions with respect to exercising the contract. A European option is either the option to buy a financial asset at a future date at the
agreed price, called the *strike price,* or the option to sell the asset at the agreed
price. The option to sell is called a *put,* since you can "put the asset with the other
party," and the option to buy is referred to as a *call* because you can "call upon the
other party" to sell you the asset at the agreed price.

The left panel of Figure 7.1 shows the payoff for a futures contract in which the
investor has agreed to either buy, (the long position), or sell, (the short position),
an asset at a future date at the exercise price *K*. The return on this contract for the
long position is simply the difference between the price at the time of execution,
here called simply the price, and the exercise price on the contract, or

$$Return = P - K.$$

The return for the short position is simply the reverse of that.

The right panel of Figure 1 shows the payoff from put and call options. Because
investors have the "option" to exercise the option, they will never do so unless
their payoff is non-negative. Hence, the payoff on a call, which is the right to buy,
is given by

$$Return = \max\{P - K, 0\}.$$

while that of a put is similar with $K - P$ replacing $P - K$ in the above expression.

Because the price of the underlying asset in these transactions is taken to be
bounded below by 0, and unbounded above, the potential losses and gains end
up reflecting this asymmetry. In particular, one can see from Figure 7.1 that the
agreement-to-buy side of a forward contract has unbounded gains but bounded

losses of K. This follows because the worst that can occur is that you bought a worthless asset at the price K. Similarly, for an agreement to sell, the best that can occur is that you agreed to sell a worthless asset at the price K, so the maximum gain here is simply K. But the losses are unbounded since you have to get the asset at price P. One way to protect yourself here is to already own the asset when you go short in the futures market. An option means that the gain on a call is bounded below by 0, while the benefit is still unbounded just as in the long future. For a put, the option aspect means that the loss is bounded below by 0. At the same time, it is bounded above by K, just like the short futures. As a result, its return is bounded both above and below.

One natural use of options is to limit or hedge your exposure given your asset position. For example, if you borrowed a stock, and then sold the stock, you are short the stock and will have to buy it and return it in the future. If the price of the stock rises, then you will lose from this transaction and your losses are only bounded by the highest possible rise in the stock relative to the price you sold it at today. To hedge your risks, you might want to enter into a call option. If K is the strike price on the call, then your losses are bounded by $K - P +$ the cost of buying the option. Of course, your risk didn't magically disappear. The risks associated with the spot price of the asset rising above K have simply been transferred to the seller of the call option. This investor, perhaps because she is long in the asset, may feel better able to face this risk, and by selling the call option, she earns a return for this.

An important class of derivatives is swaps. In a swap, the two parties to the derivative agree to exchange some cash flows that arise from the assets they hold. A standard swap contract is an interest rate swap in which, typically, the cash flows from a fixed interest rate asset are exchanged for those from a variable interest rate asset. Financial institutions, like banks or mortgage companies, often borrow under fixed interest rate terms, but can end up lending on variable terms, say, a markup over the fed funds rate or LIBOR (London Interbank Offered Rate). In this case, they are subject to interest rate risk if the base rate falls. To cover this risk, they can enter into a "fixed for floating" swap. Another example of an interest rate swap occurs when an institution has borrowed in, say, dollars and lent in, say, yen. Even if these are both fixed rate contracts, the institution is still subject to exchange rate risk if the value of the yen falls relative to the dollar. In this case, it can agree to a currency swap in which it exchanges yen-denominated interest payments for dollar-denominated interest payments.

In Figure 7.2 I have plotted some data from the Bank for International Settlements on the market values of various types of over-the-counter (OTC) derivative contracts outstanding. The data is bi-annual and is in dollars. In the figure we can see how the total market value of OTC derivatives rose sharply to \$35 trillion, driven largely by the rise in interest rate contracts, which rose to \$20 trillion. One can also see a substantial rise in credit default swaps, which peaked at the same

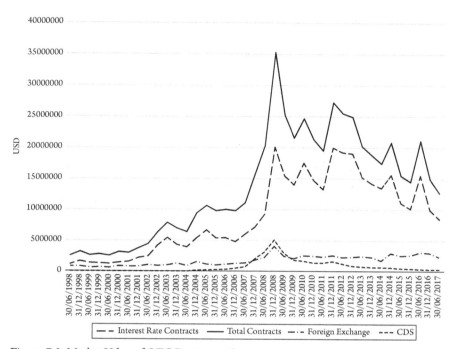

Figure 7.2 Market Value of OTC Derivative Contracts.
SOURCE: BIS Semiannual OTC derivatives statistics.

time at $5 trillion. Since the peak, the market value of OTC derivatives has fallen substantially, beginning with the very steep fall after the second half of 2008. During this period, CDS contracts had fallen to $0.3 trillion by the end of the first half of 2017.

1. DERIVATIVE PRICING

One of the big uses of arbitrage pricing theory is to price different kinds of securities, especially derivatives. One approach to derivative pricing is to use the standard asset pricing formula we have derived. In this case, the price of a European put option contract issued today in state s and which expires tomorrow in state s' and has strike price K can be expressed as

$$P^{put}(K) = \sum_{s'} m(s'|s) \max\{K - P(s'), 0\} \Pr(s'|s),$$

where $P(s')$ is the price of the security on which the put is written. Done in this manner, option pricing is very similar to standard pricing, especially for the European options in which there is no strategic aspect. That is, we do not have to forecast when the option will be exercised.

Another approach is to find a replicating portfolio. Assume that we have N assets and that they span the N possible realizations of the state tommorow. By that we mean that given any payoffs $X(s')$, we can construct a portfolio of our N assets such that

$$\sum_{i=1}^{N} B_i Q_i(s') = X(s') \text{ for each possible } s'.$$

The first method of pricing relied on knowing exactly how the payoff on the derivative, the stochastic discount factor and the conditional probabilities varied with the state at the time the derivative's payoff was realized, which we can think of as the expiration date. The second method required that we know exactly how the payoff to a bunch of assets varied with the realized state at the time of expiration. This can seem like a group of fairly extreme assumptions. There is a third method that makes somewhat less extreme assumptions. This method uses the fact that derivatives derive their value from some underlying asset or assets; this implies that we can use the prices of these underlying assets, perhaps with a bit more information, in order to price the derivative. To sort this out, we start from a simple two-period/two-state example and then generalize slightly.

SIMPLE 2x2 EXAMPLE

Consider the following simple two-state example: We have a stock with price S today that can have two prices tomorrow: $S_h > S_l$. It pays no dividend.

The possible returns must lie between the risk-free rate

$$\frac{S_h}{S} > 1 + r > \frac{S_l}{S}.$$

We have a European call option with strike price K and hence payouts

$$C_i = \max(0, S_i - K) \text{ for } i = h, l.$$

What should be its price (P) today?

The δ of the call option (or relative payoff gap) is

$$\delta = \frac{C_h - C_l}{S_h - S_l},$$

and note that $\delta S_h - C_h = \delta S_l - C_l$. Consider buying δ shares of the stock and borrowing the amount

$$\frac{\delta S_h - C_h}{1 + r} \left(= \frac{\delta S_l - C_l}{1 + r} \right).$$

Then, note that our payoffs are

$$\delta S_i - (\delta S_i - C_i) = C_i \text{ for } i = h, l.$$

So our portfolio replicates the payoff of the option. Hence the price of the option must be

$$P = \delta S - \frac{\delta S_h - C_h}{1 + r}.$$

In constructing this example, note that it is very important that the outcomes of the option and the stock are perfectly correlated above the strike price. This is why one needs to use the underlying security of the option to construct the arbitrage.

This simple example seems very specific, but a two-state type of transition model lies behind the best known stochastic process used in finance: Brownian motion with a drift. That is because a simple step-up/step-down process with i.i.d. transitions is simply a discrete time example of this continuous time process. We don't want to go too far into hardcore math, but for the moment, consider this more general discrete time process.

Remark 3. **Discrete Time Random Walks:** Consider the following discrete time process:

- Time is in Δt units
- The random variable x moves up or down Δh with probability p and q respectively
- It follows that

$$E[\Delta x] = (p - q)\Delta h$$

$$E\left[(\Delta x)^2\right] = (\Delta h)^2$$

and

$$Var[\Delta x] = E\left[(\Delta x)^2\right] - (E[\Delta x])^2$$
$$= \left[1 - (p - q)^2\right](\Delta h)^2 = 4pq\,(\Delta h)^2.$$

If we consider a time interval of length t, it has $n = t/\Delta t$ discrete steps, and the cumulative change $(x_t - x_0)$ is a binomial random variable

$$E[x_t - x_0] = n(p - q)\Delta h = t(p - q)\Delta h/\Delta t$$

and

$$Var[x_t - x_0] = n4pq\,(\Delta h)^2 = t4pq\,(\Delta h)^2/\Delta t.$$

Now assume that the jump size is related to Δt by

$$\Delta h = \sigma\sqrt{\Delta t},$$

and that

$$p = \frac{1}{2}\left[1 + \frac{\mu}{\sigma}\sqrt{\Delta t}\right], \quad q = \frac{1}{2}\left[1 - \frac{\mu}{\sigma}\sqrt{\Delta t}\right].$$

Then

$$E[x_t - x_0] = \mu t$$

and

$$Var[x_t - x_0] = t\left[1 - \left(\frac{\mu}{\sigma}\right)^2 \Delta t\right]\frac{\sigma^2\Delta t}{\Delta t} \rightarrow \sigma^2 t.$$

Hence, we have a stochastic process in which the step size is shrinking to zero with Δt, making it continuous, while at the same time the mean change and the variance is linear in t.

With time naturally comes more states, as Remark 3 illustrates. However, even with a continuous time stochastic process, we can think of the process as the limit of a simple step-up/step-down process with two steps. This leads us to the next example.

Dynamic Trading and Multiple States

With more states, say 4, and only 2 assets, the asset position has to be dynamically adjusted to achieve the arbitrage. Split our time frame into two periods, and assume that there are two possible states in each period $\{s_a, s_b\}$, which leads to 4 possible histories of the form $\{s_1, s_2\}$. This situation is depicted in Figure 7.3. We first need to determine P, the value of the portfolio necessary to achieve the arbitrage conditional states s_a or s_b in the first period. Call this P_a and P_b. Then, construct the portfolio necessary to achieve these two outcomes in the first period:

$$\delta = \frac{P_a - P_b}{S(s_a) - S(s_b)}$$

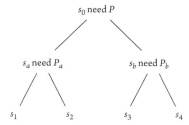

s_0 need P

s_a need P_a s_b need P_b

s_1 s_2 s_3 s_4

Figure 7.3 Derivative Event Tree.

and borrow

$$\frac{\delta S(s_a) - P_a}{1 + r}.$$

We can do this for an arbitrary number of periods using this simple two-outcome transition structure. The key is that we can dynamically adjust our portfolio in order to span the limited set of outcomes over our "period" and then construct a portfolio to just deliver the right amount in each of the two outcomes. Working backward from the end of time, we just need two portfolio values in the first "period" after the initial period in order to price our derivative.

Problem 22. Consider a simple three-period version of our derivative pricing model. Assume that we have an equity security that can increase or decrease in price by one unit each period. We call this the step size. Assume that the security increases in price with probability π and decreases in price by one unit with probability $1 - \pi$ between both periods *1* & *2* and periods *2* & *3*. Assuming that the initial price of the security is 10, then the maximum price after 2 periods is 12 and the price minimum is 8.

(1) For $\pi = .5, 2/3$ and $3/4$ compute the expected price and the variance of this price in period 3 (the last period).
(2) Based on what you've learned, discuss how you could try to calibrate such a model to hit an arbitrary pair of expected return and variance by choosing the step size Δ and the probability π.
(3) Consider the pricing of a European call option on this security, which has a strike price K of 9. Try to use our arbitrage pricing logic to price this option for the case of $\pi = .5$ and $\pi = 2/3$ when the step size is one.

PART THREE

Firm Behavior in Light of Asset Pricing Theory

The asset pricing models we developed suggest that the pricing on payoffs at different points in time and in different states matters. Here we want to reexamine the conventional results on optimal firm behavior. One can anticipate that when the costs and benefits of a potential action are stochastic or separated in time our evaluation of the action will be affected. This in turn can change the predictions about optimal behavior. We will also be interested in examining questions about the optimal capital structure of the firm. The decisions about how much debt and equity to have on the balance sheet are thought to be very important.

8

Investment and Capital Structure of the Firm

Now that we have developed our asset pricing structure, its time to put it to use. We will do this by examining the optimal choices of a firm. We start with a deterministic environment and then add uncertainty later.

1. OPTIMAL DECISIONS UNDER CERTAINTY

How should the firm choose to act? To think this through, let's return to the household's flow budget constraint. We do this in order to ask how the firm can make its net payouts as valuable as possible to the household, and thereby command the highest price for the claims that it sells. To start simply, let's assume that the world is deterministic and hence the household's constraint is given by

$$y_t + D_t + b_t R_t^f - b_{t+1} = P_t c_t,$$

where D_t is the dividend payment of the firm, and b_t is the number of one-period bonds paying the (gross) risk-free rate R_t^f. Then, note that we can rewrite this as

$$b_t = -\frac{1}{R_t^f} \left[y_t + D_t - P_t c_t - b_{t+1} \right]$$

$$= -\frac{1}{R_t^f}\left[\begin{array}{c} y_t + D_t - P_t c_t \\ +\frac{1}{R_{t+1}^f}\left[y_{t+1} + d_{t+1} - P_{t+1}c_{t+1} - b_{t+2}\right] \end{array} \right]$$

$$= -\frac{1}{R_t^f}\left[y_t + D_t - P_t c_t\right]$$

$$- \left(\frac{1}{R_t^f}\frac{1}{R_{t+1}^f}\right)\left[y_{t+1} + d_{t+1} - P_{t+1}c_{t+1} - b_{t+2}\right]$$

$$= -\sum_{j=t}^{T}\left\{\prod_{k=t}^{j}\frac{1}{R_k^f}\right\}\left[y_j + D_j - P_j c_j\right],$$

and we're taking as given that $b_{T+1} = 0$ so you can die neither in debt nor wealth.

If we take the initial period to be $t = 0$, and also assume that the initial bond/debt level is zero, we get the following version of the present-value budget constraint:

$$\left[y_0 + D_0\right] + \left(\frac{1}{R_1^f}\right)\left[y_1 + D_1\right] + \left(\frac{1}{R_1^f}\frac{1}{R_2^f}\right)\left[y_2 + D_2\right]$$

$$+ \dots + \left(\frac{1}{R_1^f}\cdots\frac{1}{R_T^f}\right)\left[y_T + D_T\right]$$

$$= c_0 + \left(\frac{1}{R_1^f}\right)c_1 + \left(\frac{1}{R_1^f}\frac{1}{R_2^f}\right)c_2$$

$$+ \dots + \left(\frac{1}{R_1^f}\cdots\frac{1}{R_T^f}\right)c_T$$

This expression can be rewritten as

$$\left[y_0 + D_0\right] + \sum_{t=1}^{T}\left\{\prod_{k=1}^{t}\frac{1}{R_k^f}\right\}\left[y_t + D_t\right] = c_0 + \sum_{t=1}^{T}\left\{\prod_{k=1}^{t}\frac{1}{R_k^f}\right\}c_j. \qquad (2)$$

This constraint says that the limitation on consumption is the present value of income plus the present value of the firm's dividend stream.

Summary 1. Equation 2, often referred to as the present-value budget constraint, implies that maximizing the present value of dividends will maximize the firm's value to the consumer, and hence its price.

1.1. The Deterministic Investment Problem of the Firm

A firm has a project within which it can utilize its capital and buy labor. The gross output of the project is $F(K_t, L_t)$. Capital evolves according to

$$K_{t+1} = (1 - \delta)K_t + I_t.$$

The dividend of a firm in period t is

$$D_t = F(K_t, L_t) - b_t R_t^f + b_{t+1} - w_t L_t - I_t,$$

where w_t is the wage and L_t is labor hired, K_t is capital, and I_t is investment. The present value of dividends is

$$D_0 + \sum_{t=1}^{T} \left\{ \prod_{k=1}^{t} \frac{1}{R_k^f} \right\} D_t.$$

We can rewrite this present value as

$$F(K_0, L_0) + b_1 - w_0 L_0 - I_0$$
$$+ \sum_{t=1}^{T} \left\{ \prod_{k=1}^{t} \frac{1}{R_k^f} \right\} \left[F(K_t, L_t) - b_t R_t^f + b_{t+1} - w_t L_t - I_t \right].$$

If the firm was behaving in an optimal manner, then we shouldn't be able improve things through simple changes.

1. Consider increasing its labor input in period t and paying out the increase/decrease in profits through the period t dividend

$$\left\{ \prod_{k=1}^{t} \frac{1}{R_k^f} \right\} [F_L(K_t, L_t) - w_t] = 0.$$

So $F_L(K_t, L_t) = w_t$ and we see that static decisions have a simple static optimality condition.

2. Consider increasing the investment level at t, using the extra capital at $t + 1$, and then reducing the investment level at $t + 1$ so that K_{t+2} was unchanged.

$$dD_t = -dI_t,$$

$$dI_{t+1} = -(1-\delta)dK_{t+1} = -(1-\delta)dI_t$$

and so

$$dD_{t+1} = [F_K(K_{t+1}, L_{t+1}) + (1-\delta)]\, dI_t.$$

So it follows that

$$-\left\{\prod_{k=1}^{t} \frac{1}{R_k^f}\right\} + \left\{\prod_{k=1}^{t+1} \frac{1}{R_k^f}\right\} [F_K(K_{t+1}, L_{t+1}) + (1-\delta)] = 0,$$

or

$$\frac{1}{R_{t+1}^f} [F_K(K_{t+1}, L_{t+1}) + (1-\delta)] = 1.$$

Remark 4. Brief aside on investment: If we didn't have offsetting negative investment in period $t + 1$, we would get that

$$dK_{t+1+j} = dK_{t+1}(1-\delta)^j.$$

Then the condition would look like

$$0 = -\left\{\prod_{k=1}^{t} \frac{1}{R_k^f}\right\} + \sum_{j=1}^{T}\left\{\prod_{k=1}^{t+j} \frac{1}{R_k^f}\right\} F_K(K_{t+j}, L_{t+j})(1-\delta)^{j-1}$$
$$+ \left\{\prod_{k=1}^{T} \frac{1}{R_k^f}\right\}(1-\delta)^T$$

where the last term is the value of selling the leftover capital at time T. But note that if $\frac{1}{R_T^f}[F_K(K_T, L_T) + (1-\delta)] = 1$, then the gain of carrying over the capital from $T - 1$ to T is the same as selling it at time $T - 1$. So we could just sell it at time $T - 1$ and get $[F_K(K_{T-1}, L_{T-1}) + (1-\delta)](1-\delta)^{T-2}$. We can continue in this fashion. So in the end, the sum is just the one-period gain.

3. Consider borrowing more at t so you can pay a higher dividend, and then offsetting this at $t + 1$ to keep b_{t+2} unchanged. So it better be that

$$\left\{\prod_{k=1}^{t} \frac{1}{R_k^f}\right\} - \left\{\prod_{k=1}^{t+1} \frac{1}{R_k^f}\right\} R_{t+1}^f = 0.$$

But notice that

$$\left\{\prod_{k=1}^{t+1} \frac{1}{R_k^f}\right\} R_{t+1}^f = \left\{\prod_{k=1}^{t} \frac{1}{R_k^f}\right\},$$

so this is always true. In this simple world debt policy simply doesn't matter.

2. OPTIMAL DECISIONS UNDER UNCERTAINTY

Assume now that the firm is making decisions today in state of the world s, which might impact outcomes in state of the world s' tomorrow. How should the firm behave now?

Under arbitrage pricing with a rich financial structure, we saw that $p = E(mQ)$, where m was the stochastic discount factor and Q was the payout tomorrow. Let's use this to rethink the gains and losses from our three types of deviations. But first we need to price over time.

2.1. Pricing over Time under Uncertainty

Assume that $m(s'|s)$ is the stochastic discount factor if the state today is s and tomorrow it is s'. Let $D(s)$ denote the dividend today if the state today is s. Let $\Pr\{s'|s\}$ denote the conditional probability of going from s to s'.

The value of a firm today in period 1 and state s_1, $P_1(s_1)$ is given by

$$P_1(s_1) = \sum_{s_2} m(s_2|s_1) [D(s_2) + P_2(s_2)] \Pr\{s_2|s_1\}$$

and the value of the firm tomorrow, in period 2 and state s_2, $P_2(s_2)$ is given by

$$P_2(s_2) = \sum_{s_3} m(s_3|s_2) [D(s_3) + P_3(s_3)] \Pr\{s_3|s_2\}.$$

If we put these two expressions together we get that

$$P_1(s_1) = \sum_{s_2} m(s_2|s_1) D(s_2) \Pr\{s_2|s_1\}$$
$$+ \sum_{s_2} \sum_{s_3} m(s_2|s_1) m(s_3|s_2) [D(s_3) + P_3(s_3)] \Pr\{s_2|s_1\} \Pr\{s_3|s_2\}.$$

where $m(s_2|s_1)m(s_3|s_2)$ is the stochastic discount factor applied to income in period 3 and state s_3 conditional on being in state s_1 today and s_2 tomorrow, and $\Pr\{s_2|s_1\}\Pr\{s_3|s_2\}$ is the conditional probability of the history (s_1, s_2, s_3) given that we are in state s_1 today.

2.2. Firm's Objective Under Uncertainty

The firm's objective here is

$$E\left\{\sum_{t=1}^{T} \mathcal{M}(s^t)\left[F(K_t, L_t) - b_t R_t^f + b_{t+1} - w_t L_t - I_t\right]\right\},$$

where $s^t = (s_1, s_2, ..., s_t)$ is the sequence of events that got us to where we are. And the discount factor is the product of the one-step ahead discount factors

$$\mathcal{M}(s^t) = m(s_2|s_1)m(s_3|s_2)\cdots m(s_t|s_{t-1})$$
$$= \mathcal{M}(s^{t-1})m(s_t|s_{t-1}).$$

(Note that we will only need to use the one-period-ahead discount factor m for what follows.)

2.3. Deviations under Uncertainty

1. Consider increasing the firm's labor input in period t and paying out the increase/decrease in profits through the period t dividend. The change in dividends today is
$$F_L(K_t, L_t, s_t) - w_t,$$

   therefore this must once again be 0. (Note that this is still true even though we now allow the state of the world to affect our production.)
2. Consider increasing the investment level at t, using the extra capital at $t + 1$, and then reducing the investment level at $t + 1$ so that K_{t+2} is unchanged.
$$dD_t = -dI_t$$

   and
$$dD_{t+1}(s_{t+1}) = [F_K(K_{t+1}, L_{t+1}, s_{t+1}) + (1 - \delta)]\,dI_t.$$

How do we price this change? Well, we are giving up dD_t for sure and receiving the random payout $dD_{t+1}(s_{t+1})$ tomorrow. The net change in value is going to be

$$dD_t + E\left(mdD_{t+1}\right),$$

so we'd better have that

$$-1 + \sum_{s_{t+1}} m(s_{t+1}|s_t)\Pr\{s_{t+1}|s_t\}\left[F_K(K_{t+1}, L_{t+1}, s_{t+1}) + (1-\delta)\right] = 0.$$

(3)

2.4. Flexible vs. Inflexible Decisions

In our simple example, labor is a very flexible decision, while capital is a somewhat inflexible decision. By this I mean that you can choose the amount of labor at each date and state freely, while capital must be chosen a period in advance, so a given level of capital must hold for each subsequent outcome. This is an important difference.

Looking at Figure 8.1, this means that labor is chosen at each date s_t, s_{t+1}, and so forth, while capital for s_{t+1} is chosen at time s_t. Thus there is only one capital stock level at each successors (of the initial date t) at date $t + 1$. The number of first-order conditions for capital is also smaller and ends up probability-weighted averaging the future discounted marginal product of capital, or MPK. (In the figure, if the world ends after period s_{t+2}, there are 3 capital decisions, but 7 labor decisions, which highlights the difference in flexibility.)

What happens when labor choices become more inflexible? They become more like capital choices. For example, labor unions fight to prevent improper and unfair labor practices. But they also constrain firms, even firms that are behaving correctly, with respect to their hiring and firing decisions. One way to understand the impact of this on hiring/firing choices is to assume that labor, like capital, has to be chosen one period in advance and cannot be freely adjusted in response

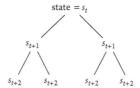

Figure 8.1 Event Tree.

to current conditions. In this case, we will have a labor first-order condition that looks a bit like our capital condition:

$$\sum_{s_{t+1}} m(s_{t+1}|s_t) \Pr\{s_{t+1}|s_t\} [F_L(K_{t+1}, L_{t+1}, s_{t+1}) - w_t] = 0. \qquad (4)$$

Note that in this condition, both labor and capital are fixed, while the shock s_{t+1} is varying and thereby affecting labor's marginal product. This inflexibility may help to protect labor from improper behavior, but it also lowers its effective productivity because it is now more inflexible.

Another impact of this change is that it makes labor now subject to the asset pricing concerns we found with capital. In particular, we can rewrite the first-order condition as

$$\begin{aligned} &E\{m(s_{t+1}|s_t)[F_L(K_{t+1}, L_{t+1}, s_{t+1}) - w_t]\} \\ &= E\{m(s_{t+1}|s_t)\} E\{[F_L(K_{t+1}, L_{t+1}, s_{t+1}) - w_t]\} \\ &+ cov\,(m(s_{t+1}|s_t)[F_L(K_{t+1}, L_{t+1}, s_{t+1}) - w_t]) \\ &= 0 \end{aligned}$$

using our simple covariance result. From this we can see that now the firm's incentive to hire rigid labor will depend on on whether the MPL (marginal product of labor) covaries with the stochastic discount factor, just as it did with capital. If this covariance is negative, as we would normally expect for most industries, then an increase in the market price of risk is likely to lead to a decrease in this covariance and hence depress labor. Since the market price of risk is countercyclical, this factor could depress labor in downturns more than it normally would be.[1]

2.4.1. DISCOUNTING A PROJECT'S RETURN

How do we operationally check our intertemporal investment condition (2)?

One simple way of doing this is to assume all of the projects that a firm undertakes are roughly the same, that is, they have the same risk pricing. Then, if R is the average cost of capital, we evaluate

$$-1 + \frac{1}{R} E\{F_K(K_{t+1}, L_{t+1}, s_{t+1}) + (1 - \delta)\}$$

and check if this is equal to 0.

---

1. While the role of discount rate fluctuations in investment decisions has long been recognized, its role in other less long-lived decisions has not received much attention. An exception to this is a recent paper by J. Borovicka and K. Borovickova ("Discount Rates and Employment Fluctuations"), Research Memo 2017, which argues that discount rate fluctuations play an important role in employment dynamics.

How do we compute the cost of capital for a firm? Suppose the firm's balance sheet looks like

Balance Sheet of Our Firm

Assets		Liabilities	
Asset Value	100	Debt (D) Value	40
		Equity value (E)	60
Asset Value	100	Firm Value	100

Then the company cost of capital = the return on its assets = return on its implicit portfolio which is given by

$$R = \frac{D}{D+E} r_{debt} + \frac{E}{D+E} r_{equity}$$

However, a firm's projects will typically have very different risk characteristics. So this may be a very bad approximation.

So we need a better method of estimating the appropriate discount rate. Two methods suggest themselves.

The first method is to use our arbitrage pricing model to estimate the appropriate discount rate. To do this, let the project beta be given by

$$\beta = \frac{cov(m, [F_K(K_{t+1}, L_{t+1}, s_{t+1}) + (1 - \delta)])}{var(m)}.$$

Then the expected project return should be

$$E(R) = R^f + \left(\frac{cov(m, R)}{var(m)} \right) \left(-\frac{var(m)}{E(m)} \right).$$

However, estimating β can be hard, particularly if the project is new or novel.

The second, and alternative, method is to find a traded security whose payout tomorrow looks like $Q(s') \propto F_K(K_{t+1}, L_{t+1}, s_{t+1}) + (1 - \delta)$. Then, if R is its implicit rate of return,

$$P = \frac{1}{R} E\{Q(s')\}$$

we form

$$-1 + \frac{1}{R} E\{F_K(K_{t+1}, L_{t+1}, s_{t+1}) + (1 - \delta)\}$$

and check if this is equal to 0. However, finding the right security with the right risk profile to get the right risk-adjusted discount rate $1/R$ is the key to making this check work.

3. Consider borrowing more at t so you can pay a higher dividend, and then offsetting this at $t + 1$ to keep b_{t+2} unchanged.

Then we're getting 1 more unit today and giving up R^f_{t+1} units tomorrow. So the impact on the value at t is

$$-1 + E\left(mR^f_{t+1}\right) = -1 + E(m)R^f_{t+1}.$$

But $E(m) = 1/R_{t+1}$ because of arbitrage, and hence this always nets to 0. Once again, debt policy does not matter.

3. CAPITAL STRUCTURE

To try to understand why so much time and energy is spent on capital structure decisions, we need to understand how they can matter. To do that, we're going to consider a very simple model of the firm in which its output tomorrow is given by $Y(s')$. Assume the firm is initially all equity-owned and ask what happens if it issues debt claims B'? Then

$$D(s') = Y(s') - R^f_{t+1}B'.$$

And

$$E\{mD(s')\} + E\left\{mR^f_{t+1}B'\right\} = E\{mY(s')\}.$$

This is the same result we found before. It says that the value of the firm, which is the value of the claims to dividends (i.e., equity), and the claims to debt are equal to the net value of the firm.

3.1. Bankruptcy

But what happens if $Y(s')$ is very low? Then the firm may not be able to pay $R^f_{t+1}B'$. Assume now that the interest rate is R, and that the firm pays $\min[Y(s'), RB']$. Then

$$D(s') = \max[Y(s') - RB', 0],$$

and

$$E\{m\max[Y(s') - RB', 0]\} + E\{m\min[Y(s'), RB']\} = E\{mY(s')\}.$$

Assume that the company's cost of capital is R, where

$$R = \frac{D}{D+E}r_{debt} + \frac{E}{D+E}r_{equity}.$$

Then, if the firm changes its capital structure, the returns on its debt and its equity will be adjusting to maintain this relationship. If D goes up so that bankruptcy becomes more likely, then r_{debt} will fall and r_{equity} might rise due to more leverage. But this won't affect R. So bankruptcy per se doesn't change our original answer that the capital structure doesn't matter.

3.1.1. COSTLY BANKRUPTCY

What happens if bankruptcy involves a loss in output? Assume that the debt holders get

$$Q(s') = \begin{cases} RB' & \text{if } Y(s') \geq RB' \\ \gamma Y(s') & \text{if } Y(s') < RB' \end{cases}$$

while

$$D(s') = \max\left[Y(s') - RB', 0\right].$$

Then

$$E\{Q(s')m\} + E\{D(s')m\} = E\{Y(s')m\}$$

$$-(1-\gamma) \sum_{\{s' : Y(s') < RB'(s')\}} Y(s')m(s')\Pr(s'|s)$$

$$= E\{Y(s')m\} - (1-\gamma)E\{Y(s')m|Y(s') < RB'\}\Pr\{Y(s') < RB'\}.$$

Now the capital structure of the firm matters.

The total value of the firm is

$$E\{Y(s')m\} - (1-\gamma)E\{Y(s')m|Y(s') < RB'\}\Pr\{Y(s') < RB'\}.$$

Bankruptcy costs imply that issuing debt is expensive, since it increases the likelihood of bankruptcy and having those costs realized. But then no firm should issue debt.

3.2. Taxes

Let's go back to our baseline model and allow for taxes. This isn't by chance. It will turn out that the tax system has one important feature that impacts the

capital structure. The corporate tax rate is applied to profits net of interest costs.
Therefore

$$D(s') = (1 - \tau)\left[Y(s') - R^f_{t+1}B'\right],$$

where τ is the corporate tax rate.

Now the value of the firm is given by

$$E\{mD(s')\} + E\left\{mR^f_{t+1}B'\right\} = (1 - \tau)E\{mY(s')\} + \tau B'.$$

3.3. Optimal Capital Structure Involves a Trade-Off

This gives us a nice trade-off story:

(1) Having a lot of debt raises the likelihood of bankruptcy and therefore
    its expected costs.
(2) Having debt raises the value of the firm because payouts via debt are
    shielded from corporate taxes, while those via dividends are not.

The optimal capital structure emerges from trading off these two factors.

3.4. Modigliani-Miller and Irrelevance

The Modigliani-Miller (MM) theorem is one of the best known results in corporate finance. It argues that the capital structure of the firm is irrelevant to the total
value of the outstanding claims on the firm. This theorem is really composed of
three propositions:

(1) The firm's market value is independent of its capital structure, i.e., the
    debt-equity ratio.
(2) The firm's market value is independent of its dividend policy.
(3) The firm's cost of capital is independent of its capital structure.

Under this theorem, firms don't care about how they finance themselves: issuing equity, issuing bonds, or borrowing from a bank are all the same. Moreover,
financial intermediaries do not have any significant role given MM.

Their results rely on the following assumptions:

(1) no bankruptcy costs,
(2) no differential taxation of dividends vs. interest payments,

(3) no moral hazard: managers seek to maximize the value of the firm, and

(4) no adverse selection: information is symmetric.

We have already discussed how breaking the first two assumptions leads to a trade off theory of the capital structure. Breaking the second two assumptions are important components in the theory of financial intermediation. However, in the meantime, we will think about empirically determining the role of capital structure in terms of the cost of capital for the firm.

3.5. Capital Structure in the Data

What does the balance sheet of firms look like? A standard source here is the Flow of Funds of the Federal Reserve. It can show us the balance sheet of various sectors. Here we look at the non-financial non-farm corporate sector.

Non-financial Non-farm Corporate Sector

Year	2006	2007	2008	2009
Debt/Equity Ratio	41.5	43.8	72.1	56.1

You can really see here the impact of the stock market boom through 2007 and the bust in 2008. By the way, leverage varies by sector and is much higher in the financial sector.

3.6. Reservations about Our Theory

All theories have limitations, and it's always wise to think over what these are before wrapping up a topic. So, here goes on our theory of capital structure.

1. We have taken as given that the owner of the firm can freely trade in asset markets to offset his risks and allocate his consumption optimally. If he cannot do this, then his own risk aversion will factor in. This could be very important in cases where the owner/manager has to retain a large stake in the firm.

2. We've also implicitly assumed that any uncertainty was symmetric; that is, everyone has common information and common beliefs about future probabilities. This means that you are not trying to infer things from the rm's actions about its information.

3. We have not worried about how the capital structure might affect the firm's future incentives. For example, if a firm's stockholders are highly

leveraged, they will generally prefer high-return/high-risk projects to low-return/low-risk projects. This may affect the investment choices they make.

4. PROBLEMS

Problem 23. Consider our model of capital structure in which the future output of the firm is given by $Y(s')$. Assume that if the firm goes bankrupt the output of the firm is reduced by the factor γ, because $(1-\gamma)Y(s')$ is consumed in bankruptcy costs. Assume also that any dividends are subject to the tax on corporate profits, but that interest payments are deductible and hence are not. The payouts to debt and equity holders are

$$Q(s') = \begin{cases} RB' \text{ if } Y(s') \geq RB' \\ \gamma Y(s') \text{ if } Y(s') < RB' \end{cases}$$

and

$$D(s') = \max\left[(1-\tau)\{Y(s') - RB'\}, 0\right].$$

Assume that the output of the firm, $Y(s')$, is uniformly distributed on the interval $[0, 10]$. Then, the value of the firm is given by

$$V = \int_{RB}^{10} \{(Y - RB)(1-\tau) + RB\}\frac{1}{10}dY$$
$$+ \int_{0}^{RB} \gamma Y \frac{1}{10}dY.$$

And the derivative of the value is

$$\frac{dV}{d(RB)} = \int_{RB}^{10} \tau\frac{1}{10}dY + (\gamma - 1)RB\frac{1}{10}.$$

Note that at $RB = 10$, this derivative is negative, while at $RB = 0$ it is positive. This implies that the value is optimized for an interior level of RB. Assume that $\tau = .35$ and that $\gamma = .9$ (which are roughly reasonable values) and try to determine the optimal capital structure of the firm. To do this, compute the value at a grid of points for values of RB between 0 and 10.

Problem 24. Consider an entrepreneur who can finance the one-unit cost of an investment project by issuing either equity or debt claims on that project.

Assume that the project has 3 output possibilities next period given by $y_h > y_m > y_l$. Assume that the (gross) riskfree rate is R^f, that bankruptcy costs are zero, and that lenders are risk-free. So, if RB is the value of the debt claim coming due, bondholders will get min $[y_i, RB]$ while the equity holder will get max $[y_i - RB, 0]$.

A. Compute the expected return to the entrepreneur from financing the one unit cost of the project using debt or equity when the three states are equally likely. For debt it must be the case that

$$R^f = \sum_i \min [y_i, RB] \frac{1}{3} \text{ when } B = 1.$$

For equity finance, if he sells off the project, the price of the equity claim is

$$P = \frac{\sum_i y_i}{3R^f},$$

so to finance the project he needs to sell off $\alpha\%$ of the total shares where $\alpha P = 1$. Assume that $y_l = 1, y_m = 2$, and $y_h = 3$. Also assume that the gross risk-free rate is $R^f = 1.1$. Try to explain your result and whether it holds generally.

B. Now, imagine that the entrepreneur finds out the probabilities of the three states are

	Case 1	Case 2
y_h	.5	0
y_m	.5	.5
y_l	0	.5

Assume that the entrepreneur alone knows this information. Compute the returns to debt finance and equity finance for the entrepreneur for each of these two cases. Why do your results differ from A?

C. Given what you found out about the payoff to the entrepreneur and the incentive to issue debt vs. equity to finance his project based on his private information, discuss how the lenders should react to seeing the choice he makes.

PART FOUR

Money, Exchange Rates, and Payments

We turn now to the payments system and money in its various forms. Money is one of the great inventions. A medium of exchange is fundamental to exchange and the specialization of production. We start by discussing money and some standard monetary models. We turn next to different monies and the exchange rate. This leads us to think about the impact of different currency denominations on bond interest rates and risk. Finally, we turn to more modern payment methods; this leads us into the cryptocurrencies. These modern payment methods are horning in on the medium of exchange role of money and thereby reducing its importance.

9

Money

The ability to exchange goods and services underlies everything we see in the modern world. Money and finance play a fundamental role in allowing this to take place. As such, money is one of the key inventions of man. It allows specialization by fostering exchange. This in turn has played a crucial role in economic development. Marx and Engels saw money as an instrument of capitalist exploitation. However, even communist societies have not been able to do without it.

Early money came in a variety of forms, including minted coins of rare metal, salt blocks, and commodity receipts. The earliest minted coins come from around 600 BCE in Turkey. The Roman system of coinage utilized three different coins: one of gold, one of silver, and one of bronze. Their coins long outlasted the Roman empire. Prices were still being quoted in silver denarii in the early AD 800s. Interestingly, one of the early issues was that the relative price of the different coins was not stable. The relative price depended on the relative price of the metals and the relative scarcity of the different coin denominations. Fiat money (often referred to as unbacked money), which consists of pieces of paper, is a fairly recent invention. However, since the government has agreed to accept it as a means of payment for things like taxes, there is a sense in which all of the moneys we see in widespread use have some backing.

Money has three key features: (i) It is a store of value: one can use money to transfer wealth or purchasing power through time. (ii) It is a unit of account: one prices various goods in terms of money. (iii) It is a medium of exchange: one sells goods or services to acquire money, not because we desire money per se, but in order to hold it and use it to acquire the desired final good at a later moment in time.

This last function is really the distinguishing feature of money. But in order to understand why it arises, we need to allow for exchange frictions. The reason for this is that we need to rule out simple barter as an efficient means of exchange. To see this, think about how you interact within your family. You generally do not use money to get dinner on the table, the clothes washed, or the house cleaned if it is being done within the family. Instead, you divide up tasks, with some tasks being done now and some later. In essence, you are exchanging tasks through time. In this same way, one could imagine exchanging goods and services. However, in the family we all know each other and interact again and again. This makes it possible to undertake simple barter. To explain money we need to add impediments. These include only seeing people occasionally or once. It also includes not being sure that they will be around to complete the exchange we agreed to.

Understanding why people want money and how much they want it turns out to be important for understanding macroeconomic variables like the price level, which is a measure of the cost of a basket of goods in terms of money. This is because the price level also measures how valuable money is relative to this basket. Thus, the demand and supply of money ends up being a key determinant of the price level. It also determines how the price level changes over time, in other words, it drives inflation. Inflation in turn plays an important role in determining the nominal interest rate.

We are going to develop three increasingly sophisticated models to understand money. The first is the velocity model, which is really an accounting identity coupled with a behavioral assumption. The second is an inventory model, which we can use to think about money demand. This model really focuses on money's store-of-value role. The third is a search model of money, which focuses on money's most important role as a medium of exchange.

1. VELOCITY MODEL

The velocity model of money starts with an accounting identity. If M is the money supply and P is the price level, then M/P describes real money balances. If Y is nominal income, then in order for this nominal income to arise, money is needed to facilitate a certain number of transactions. If we think that these transactions are proportionate to the level of income, then it makes sense to focus on the speed with which money must turn over. Define the income velocity of money, typically simply called the *velocity of money*, as

$$V = PY/M.$$

If velocity is constant, then we have a nice relationship that links three key variables since $MV = PY$. This implies that an increase in the nominal money supply will lead to a proportionate increase in the nominal value of output,

$$\% \triangle M = \% \triangle p + \% \triangle Y.$$

Generally, this is thought to occur over the long run through a proportionate increase in the price level. However, if money has real effects, this could lead to short-run changes in output too.

Technological innovation has affected how money circulates. Inventions like ATMs, credit cards, and money market accounts have changed velocity over time. These innovations have led to a secular rise in velocity $V = PY/M$. At the same time, the nominal interest rate tends to have a systematic impact on velocity, with increases in the interest rate raising V.

2. INVENTORY (BAUMOL-TOBIN) MODEL OF MONEY

The inventory model of money is one of the first models of money demand. In this model we consider the problem of an individual who wants to finance a constant stream of consumption, $P * c$, where P is the price level and c is the real quantity. Time in this model is continuous, so over the interval of time $\triangle t$, the individual consumes c at each point in time and therefore spends $Pc \triangle t$. The individual gets his cash by withdrawing money from his bank account. We assume that going to the bank is costly and that it costs γ in real units per trip. Money, or wealth, left in the bank has the nice feature that it earns interest. We assume that money in the bank earns net interest r. The unfortunate feature of money that one holds directly is that the money in your pocket earns 0 net interest.

The problem of the individual is to minimize his costs, which consist of lost interest and costly trips to the bank, while funding his consumption. We represent these costs as follows. If he goes to the bank T times per period, then his *nominal* costs are

$$\gamma PT + M(T) * r,$$

where γPT is the cost of his trips; here we use the price P to convert his real trip costs to nominal trip costs. And $M(T) * r$ is the forgone interest earnings from holding money. Here, $M(T)$ is his average money holdings.

To see how we get this formulation, consider the following. Assume that he withdraws M units of money at time 0 :

- Then at time t' : $M - t' * P * c = 0$, or $t' = \frac{M}{Pc}$, he has to go back to the bank.
- If he always withdraws M units of money, the number of times he goes to the bank per period is $T = 1/t'$.

His forgone interest on his money between time 0 and t' is $\int_0^{t'} M(t)r\,dt$, and per period it is simply $1/t'$ times this number, or r times his average per period money holdings. His average money holdings are

$$\frac{1}{t'} \int_0^{t'} [M - Pct]\,dt = \frac{1}{t'} \left[Mt - \frac{1}{2}Pct^2 \right]\Big|_{t=0}^{t'}$$

$$= M - \frac{1}{2}Pct' = \frac{M}{2}.$$

So, if he goes to the bank T times per period, then $M = Pc/T$ and his forgone interest is $r\frac{Pc}{2T}$.

Given that he goes to the bank every $1/T$ units of time, he must withdraw $(1/T)Pc$ units of money, which implies that his average money holdings are $(1/T)Pc/2$. Hence, his total costs as a function of T are given by

$$\gamma PT + \frac{Pc}{2T}r.$$

This is the formulation we were seeking and it gives his overall costs in terms of T, the number of times he goes to the bank.

Minimizing these costs implies that

$$\gamma P - \frac{Pc}{2T^2}r = 0$$

or

$$T = \left(\frac{cr}{2\gamma} \right)^{1/2},$$

and hence

$$\frac{M}{P} = \frac{1}{2T}c = \frac{c}{2\left(\frac{cr}{2\gamma}\right)^{1/2}} = \frac{(c)^{1/2}\gamma^{1/2}}{2^{1/2}r^{1/2}}.$$

This gives us an analytic form for real money demand. However, the real insight we get from this expression is thinking about how changes in things like r and γ, or in c will affect money demand. To understand this, we first take logs of the above expression and then differentiate. This leads to

$$d \log \left(\frac{M}{P} \right) = \frac{1}{2} d \log(c) - \frac{1}{2} d \log(r) + \frac{1}{2} d \log(\gamma).$$

This expression shows how real money demand responds to interest rates and real consumption. What we see is that a 1% rise in consumption will raise real money demand by 1/2%. At the same time, a 1% increase in the net nominal interest rate will lower real money demand by 1/2%.

A key assumption in this model is that the cost of going to the bank is independent of income. This is unlikely to be true in practice since time costs may rise with income. In addition, one can often reduce these costs by setting up certain arrangements. Setting up these arrangements acts as if you are paying a fixed cost to reduce the flow cost of going to the bank.

3. SEARCH MODEL OF MONEY

In this section we set out a more complete and elaborate model of money. The model has three frictions that are going to lead to money being used as the medium of exchange. First, we will have a large number of agents in the model who have different goods and want different goods in exchange. The fact that they do not want what they can produce means that exchange is vital to consumption. In addition, we will use the large number of goods to make finding someone for which there is a double-coincidence of wants—being able to find someone who wants what I have and has what I want—rare. This means that direct barter will be inefficient. Second, we will assume that no intertemporal agreements can be enforced. This will rule out using intertemporal barter, or borrowing and lending. Finally, we will assume that agents are anonymous (in other words, the history of their actions is not public information). This last assumption means that we cannot try to enforce some sort of community arrangement where you are supposed to produce a good for anyone you meet who wants your good, and you do so anticipating the same treatment so long as everyone continues to cooperate. All these frictions will open the door to money being used. The version of the model we will consider is loosely based on Kiyotaki and Wright's classic articles.[1]

1. For a more detailed discussion of the basic search money model see P. Rupert, M. Shindler, A. Shevchenko, and R. Wright, "The Search-Theoretic Approach to Monetary Economics: A Primer," *Federal Reserve Bank of Cleveland, Economic Review,* vol. 36, no. 4, pp. 10–28, 12.01.2000. Kiyotaki, Nobuhiro, and Randall Wright. "A Search-theoretic Approach to Monetary Economics." *The American Economic Review* (1993): 63–77. Also, Kiyotaki, Nobuhiro, and Randall Wright. "On Money as a Medium of Exchange." *Journal of Political Economy* 97.4 (1989): 927–954.

Let us lay out the formal aspects of the model. We will assume that there are a continuum of anonymous agents. Each agent's private name is given by a number on the unit interval $[0, 1]$. These agents live forever and discount the future at a constant rate β. Agent i produces good i. These goods are non-storable, so they cannot be used as some sort of commodity money. There is a utility cost c for agent i to produce a unit of good i, and they can only produce one unit per period. Unfortunately for these agents, they do not produce the good they like to consume. Instead, agent i would like to consume some bundle of goods J and j will denote a generic element in this bundle. When agents consume a unit of a good they desire, they get utility u, where $u - c >> 0$ (read $>>$ as "much larger than"). So exchange is a good thing.

We will assume that these agents randomly bump into each other over time. When they do so, they run into one and only one other agent at a time. At the point in time at which they meet, they can produce and exchange goods. The likelihood that an agent runs into someone else over the time interval $\triangle\, t$ is $\gamma \triangle\, t$. We will assume that the time interval is sufficiently short that the likelihood of running into two people is effectively 0 so we can ignore it. This means that over this time interval one of two outcomes occurs: (i) you run into no one, and (ii) you run into one other person.

When you meet someone, he will want a particular good and will be able to produce a particular good. Conditional on meeting someone, the likelihood that agent i runs into someone who produces the same good as he does is zero. Conditional on meeting someone, the likelihood that agent i runs into someone who produces the good he likes is $x > 0$. The final meeting outcome we are concerned with is the very fortunate event that agent i meets agent j and there is a double coincidence of wants. The conditional likelihood of a double coincidence is given by y, where $x >> y$.

We will assume that money in the model comes in the form of identical coins. These coins cannot be duplicated or counterfeited. We will assume that a fraction M of the agents start off with a coin. No agent has more than one coin. We will assume that when you have a coin you cannot produce (perhaps because you need to eat something first). This means that people with coins can look for people without coins who can produce what they want. They would then exchange the coin for the good and consume the good. Alternatively, everyone with a coin could discard it and then people would just search for someone with whom there is a double coincidence of wants.

Start by conjecturing that a barter equilibrium exists in which everyone throws away his money and searches for a double coincidence of wants. Denote their payoff in this case by V_B for barter. This payoff will satisfy the following simple formula,

$$V_B = \gamma \triangle ty (u - c) + \beta^\tau V_B.$$

Here, $\triangle t$ units of time pass, and the probability of meeting someone who wants your good and whose good you want is $\gamma \triangle ty$. When this happens, you produce your good, which costs you c, and you get his good which benefits you u. So, $u - c$ is the net. In any case the future always looks the same; hence, your continuation payoff is $\beta^\tau V_B$ where β^τ is the discount factor. Note that this implies that

$$(1 - \beta^\tau) V_B = \gamma \triangle ty (u - c).$$

This is the payoff from a barter equilibrium. As $y \to 0$, this payoff goes to 0.

Conjecture that there exists an equilibrium in which an individual with money can exchange the money for the good he/she likes if he/she meets someone who does not have money and can produce the good that he/she likes. The probability of meeting someone is $\gamma \triangle t$, the probability that the person does not have money is $1 - M$, and the probability that this person can produce the good you like is x. Hence, the likelihood of an exchange is $\gamma \triangle t(1 - M)x$, and the likelihood of no exchange is $1 - \gamma \triangle t(1 - M)x$. If we denote the payoff to someone with a unit of money by V_1, then if that person does not have an exchange after $\triangle t$ units of time, his future payoff is still V_1. But, as of today, we discount this by β^τ. In a similar fashion, denote the payoff function for someone who has no money by V_0. This gives us two simple formulas that their payoff functions must satisfy. For V_1, it is

$$V_1 = \gamma \triangle t(1 - M)x (u + \beta^\tau V_0) + \left[1 - \gamma \triangle t(1 - M)x\right] \beta^\tau V_1.$$

The first term is the event that the individual meets someone who wants his/her money and can produce the good he/she wants. The second is the payoff if this does not occur, in which time passes but the individual remains in the same condition. For V_0 the expression is a bit more complicated since three different things can happen: the individual could run into a double coincidence where the person he meets does not have money, he could meet someone with money who wanted his good, or he could meet no one. Thus,

$$V_0 = \gamma \triangle t(1 - M)y (u - c + \beta^\tau V_0) + \gamma \triangle tMx (-c + \beta^\tau V_1)$$
$$+ \left[1 - \gamma \triangle t(1 - M)y - \gamma \triangle tMx\right] \beta^\tau V_0.$$

The first term captures the event that the individual meets someone for whom there is a double coincidence of wants—hence, the conditional probability y. Note that this can only occur if the other agent also does not have money, hence,

$1 - M$. In this case, both agents produce a unit of the good, which costs them c, and they get a unit of the good they desire, which gains them u. The second term captures the case in which the individual meets someone with money who wants his good, hence, the conditional probabilities x and M. In this case the individual produces the good, which costs c, and changes his state from not having money to having it, hence his continuation payoff changes by $V_1 - V_0$. Finally, the third term captures the case in which the individual either meets no one or no one who can make an exchange for his good.

The expected payoff to someone in the monetary equilibrium is

$$MV_1 + (1 - M)V_0.$$

If we make y smaller or make x large relative to y, while setting M close to 0.5, then it is easy to construct examples in which people are much happier in the monetary equilibrium than under barter. The rate at which money will turn over here, called the velocity of money, will depend positively on γ, the meeting rate. In general, a higher meeting frequency benefits both the barter and the monetary equilibrium. Thus, we can use the model to explain why barter may be preferred in situations in which the meeting rate is very high.

We can extend the model in a crude fashion to think about the impact of inflation. To do this, assume that there is a cost per period of holding money. This cost is meant to capture the utility loss from inflation. One can imagine it as the amount of work that must be done to restore the coin to its original value. To keep things simple we will model this cost as a utility cost and denote it by ω. With this change, the payoff equation for holding money becomes

$$V_1 = \gamma \triangle t(1 - M)x\,(u + \beta^\tau V_0) + \left[1 - \gamma \triangle t(1 - M)x\right]\beta^\tau\,(V_1 - \omega)\,.$$

The utility cost is paid in the next period if the money is unspent, and this reduces the continuation benefit from holding money by the cost term ω. In a similar fashion, the payoff from not holding money becomes

$$V_0 = \gamma \triangle t(1 - M)y\,(u - c + \beta^\tau V_0) + \gamma \triangle tMx\,(-c + \beta^\tau\,[V_1 - \omega]) $$
$$ + \left[1 - \gamma \triangle t(1 - M)y - \gamma \triangle tMx\right]\beta^\tau V_0.$$

This expression now reflects the fact that if one receives money today and carries it over, then the utility cost must be paid tomorrow.

Now if we compare the benefits of barter exchange to exchange intermediated by money, the benefits of barter exchanges are not affected by ω, while those of money-based exchanged are reduced. From this, one can see how a high rate of inflation, which here is a high value of ω, can potentially drive out money as a medium of exchange. This will force the economy back into barter. This is why it is common for people to switch to barter exchange during hyperinflations.

We can also extend our model to think about the impact of theft. A natural way to model this would be to have a probability, say z, that a person switches from having money or getting payoff function V_1, to getting payoff function V_0. I won't bother to trace out all the steps for this. I just want to note that it will lower the payoffs to money exchange and not affect the payoff to barter exchange. In this way, a high probability of theft can also lead to a switch from money exchange to barter exchange.

Finally, I want to think about the role that confidence in the value of money can play. Here, people are only acquiring money in order to exchange it for goods down the road. We can think of confidence as the probability that people assign to the fact that money will retain its current value when they go to exchange it. Denote this probability by $\triangle t\Pi$. What happens if money loses its value? Then we can think of the economy switching back to barter and everyone discarding his/her money. Under this scenario, our payoff functions become

$$V_1 = \gamma \triangle t(1 - M)x\,(u + \beta^\tau \Pi V_0) + \left[1 - \gamma \triangle t(1 - M)x\right]\beta^\tau \Pi V_1$$
$$+ \triangle t(1 - \Pi)V_B$$

and

$$V_0 = \gamma \triangle t(1 - M)y\,(u - c + \beta^\tau \Pi V_0) + \gamma \triangle tMx\,(-c + \beta^\tau \Pi V_1)$$
$$+ \left[1 - \gamma \triangle t(1 - M)y - \gamma \triangle tMx\right]\beta^\tau \Pi V_0 + \triangle t(1 - \Pi)V_B.$$

Note here that after $\triangle t$ units of time, confidence may not have collapsed, in which case we continue with money exchange, or it may have collapsed, in which case everything reverts to barter exchange ever after.

A couple of things to note here. First, if $\Pi = 0$, it will never be optimal to produce a good today in exchange for money. This is because you pay a cost c today and get no future benefit tomorrow. But if no one will give up a good for money today, then its value has already collapsed. To understand this better, note that money is, in a fundamental sense, a bubble asset here. It only has value because people think it will have value in the future. Because of this belief money can intermediate exchange, even if only temporarily. But the collapse of the bubble can never be certain, or even too likely or it will collapse today.

This model has been kept very simple. It can be enriched in a wide variety of ways. It nicely captures using a friction to rationalize why money is being used. However, it relies on the search friction. Historically, when people traveled around, this friction and our environment seemed very natural. However, in the modern context, it seems somewhat less so. For example, almost all transactions that can be done with money can increasingly also be done via the credit or debit card systems. The real reason we use money is largely to avoid the fees on small transactions associated with these systems. Additionally, many monetary transactions seem to involve very little search activity and the transactions that do involve a lot of search, like home buying, are typically not intermediated with cash. Still, this model seems to capture something fundamental about exchange via money, which is why it is considered the premier model of money.

4. STANDARD MONEY DEMAND FUNCTIONS

We close out the chapter on money by discussing a couple of standard money demand functions that are often used in empirical analysis. The first is

$$\ln (M_t/P_t) = \alpha \ln(Y_t) - \gamma r_t,$$

where α is the elasticity of money demand with respect to income and γ is the semi-elasticity of money demand with respect to the interest rate. Lucas (2000) estimated $\gamma = 7$ based on long-run evidence. The second function is similar to what we found in the inventory model of money and is given by

$$\ln (M_t/P_t) = \alpha \ln(Y_t) - \chi \ln(r_t),$$

where χ is the elasticity of money demand with respect to the interest rate. Lucas (2000) estimated $\chi = 0.5$, which is exactly the inventory coefficient. The income elasticity α is thought to be somewhat below 1.[2]

5. PROBLEMS

Problem 25. Use the inventory model of money and compute the level of average money holdings for an individual for the following cases, taking as given that $c = 100$ and $P = 1$:

γ	R
.1	1.05
.1	1.10
.5	1.05
.5	1.10.

---

2. Robert Lucas, Jr., "Inflation and Welfare," *Econometrica*, vol. 68, no. 2 (March 2000).

Then compute the level for the first case when c goes from 100 to 200. Use these results to discuss the comparative static result of this model.

Problem 26. The interest elasticity in the inventory model is $1/2$. Discuss how this will be affected if we assume that along with an interest cost to holding money r, there is also a theft/loss cost of d, so the flow cost is $r + d$.

10

Exchange Rates and Nominal Interest Rates

In this chapter we want to understand exchange rates, which are the relative price of two currencies. We also want to understand how exchange rates interact with nominal interest rates when these interest rates are denominated in different currencies. The determination of exchange rates and their interaction with interest rates turns out to be a surprisingly complex, yet important, topic.

The foreign exchange market (Forex) is an over-the-counter market between large financial institutions. This means that it is a decentralized market with major centers in the financial capitals of the world: New York, London, Tokyo, and somewhat surprisingly, Singapore. A typical exchange involves the swap of some quantity of one currency for some quantity of another. The market is extremely large, with as much as $5 trillion being exchanged in a single day. It is in this market that foreign exchange rates are determined.[1]

The multi-currency debt market is a product of the fact that one can choose which currency to borrow in. Originally, this was done by choosing where to borrow. So, to borrow in dollars, one had to issue one's bond in the U.S. and to borrow in pounds, in the U.K. But this is no longer the case, and hasn't been since the 1960s. One can issue a bond in, say, New York, that promises a future payment in yen. A bond that is being issued in a currency that is not the currency of the country where it is being issued is called a "eurobond." A eurobond can come in many different denominations, such as euroyen, eurodollar, and so forth, where

---

1. See Wikipedia's entry under "Foreign Exchange Market" for more.

the name reflects the currency in which the bond is issued. London is the major center for the eurobond market.[2]

The dollar plays a special role in international markets. It is the most commonly used currency in trade invoicing. It is also commonly used as the reference currency against which other currencies are valued. The dollar inherited this role from the pound after WWII.[3]

1. EXCHANGE RATES

Let's start with a definition: the *exchange rate* is the price of domestic currency in terms of a particular foreign currency. For Americans, the pound-dollar exchange rate is $/£, or the number of dollars you must give up to get a British pound. Because exchange rates can be quoted as $/£ from the American perspective and as £/$ from the British perspective, a standard terminology has arisen to avoid confusion. A rise in the $/£ exchange rate or a fall in the £/$ exchange rate means that the dollar has become less valuable relative to the pound. We refer to this as a *depreciation* of the dollar and an *appreciation* of the pound.

Exchange rates are determined in part (sometimes in large part) by government actions. Governments have chosen to exercise this power to varying degrees over time. There are three basic types of exchange rate regimes, depending upon the degree to which a government seeks to exercise control over its exchange rate. The loosest regime is called a *floating exchange rate*, and this occurs when the government has simply allowed the market to determine its exchange rates vis-a-vis other countries' currencies. The tightest regime is called a *fixed exchange rate*, and this occurs when a country has sought to fix the value of its currency vis-a-vis that of another country. In between is something called a *pegged float* or a *controlled float*; this is when the government allows the value to fluctuate within some band relative to another currency.

To fix an exchange rate, a country (or pair of countries) pledges to stand ready to buy and sell the two currencies at the specified price, in much the same way the Federal Reserve stands ready to exchange 5 one-dollar bills for 1 five-dollar bill. The most famous examples of this sort of arrangement include the various gold standard intervals during which countries pegged their currency to gold and, through this, to each other. The fixed exchange rate regime is in many respects an

---

2. See Wikipedia's entry under "Eurobond" for more.

3. Gita Gopinath, "The International Price System," Working Paper No. w21646. National Bureau of Economic Research, 2015. See also H. Rey (2001), "International Trade and Currency Exchange." *The Review of Economic Studies*, 68(2): 443–464.

ancient regime. Governments typically minted their coins in gold or silver. This led to a coin that had 1 oz of gold being worth 1/4 as much as one containing 4 oz of gold. During the Roman Empire, silver minted coins called *denarii* were the standard. During the Middle Ages these were superseded by the gold minted *solidi* of the Byzantine Empire. Things became more complicated when both gold and silver coins were in wide circulation, since their relative value depended to a substantial degree on the relative price of gold versus silver. This is an early example of a floating regime.[4] The certainty of fixed exchange rates has often been held out as promoting economic activity and international trade in particular. For this reason, countries have attempted to reconstruct this sort of arrangement.

The gold standard system, in which countries pegged their exchange rate in terms of gold, had been in place prior to WWI. As usual the system was suspended during the war when many countries used inflation as a way to finance their wartime spending. The gold standard was resumed after the war. For the U.K. returning to the old parity required a substantial deflation, and this deflation was blamed in part for the economic stagnation the U.K. experienced during the 1920s. The gold standard then broke down during the Great Depression as various banking panics, including that in the U.S., led to a collapse in the currency-to-gold ratio and, as a result, in a substantial deflation. In the U.S. prices fell by 25% between 1929 and 1933. Many countries, including the U.S., suspended convertibility to gold in order to expand their currencies and generate a recovery in prices.

After WWII there was a strong desire to return to the stability of the old gold standard but without some of its shortcomings. This led to the Bretton Woods agreement, which was made in 1944 and was in force until 1971. Under this agreement, the U.S. pegged its currency to gold, but only backed it to a partial degree, while all of the other parties to the agreement pegged their currencies to the dollar. The dollar was chosen because the U.S. economy was clearly the strongest at that time, having superseded England, and because there was a concern that trying to resurrect the gold standard would be problematic given a shortage of gold and the need to sharply deflate prices to restore the old parities. The U.S.'s subsequent currency expansion, especially during the Vietnam War era, made maintaining its peg to gold problematic, and in 1971, President Nixon ended convertibility to gold, thereby ending the Bretton Woods arrangement.

After the end of Bretton Woods, many developed countries went into a period of floating or controlled floating exchange rates. Figure 10.1 plots the U.S./U.K. exchange rate between the dollar and the pound for the entire post-Bretton

---

4. For more on this, see Thomas J. Sargent and Franois R. Velde. *The Big Problem of Small Change.* Princeton University Press, 2014. Also see the Wikipedia entry "Gold standard."

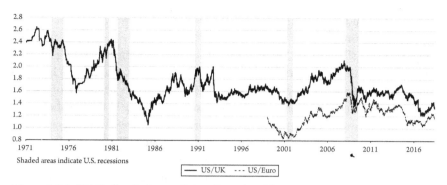

Figure 10.1 U.S. Dollar Exchange Rates: Pound and Euro.
SOURCE: FRED. Data Source: Board of Governors of the Federal Reserve System (U.S.).

Woods period. One can see immediately that the exchange rate is much more volatile than a standard price index like the Consumer Price Index (CPI) or the GDP deflator.

This came as a surprise to most economists, since the exchange rate is a factor in determining the relative price of any good that is being sold in any two countries. For example, if the price of tapas in country i at time t is given by $p_t^{i,tapa}$, and the exchange rate between currency i and currency j is given by $e_t^{i/j}$, then the relative price of tapas is given by

$$\text{Relative price of tapas} = \frac{p_t^{i,tapa}}{e_t^{i/j} p_t^{j,tapa}}. \tag{5}$$

To understand this expression, note that the price in country j is in terms of the number of units of j's currency per tapa, and the exchange rate is in terms of the number of units of i's currency per unit of j's currency. So, multiplying by the exchange rate converts the cost of this good into the number of units of i's currency one needs to exchange into j's currency in order to buy the good.[5]

What surprised economists is that price indices tend to move fairly smoothly, much more smoothly generally than exchange rates. Moreover, this smooth movement is largely independent of the exchange rate regime. This means that the high volatility in floating exchange rates, relative to zero volatility in fixed exchange rates, will lead to much more volatile relative prices across countries. The volatility of exchange rates and the role this plays in distorting relative prices seems even more surprising when one focuses on traded goods. This is because,

---

5. *Tapas* is the Spanish word for bar snacks, something at which Spain excels.

modulo trade and shipping costs, one can always simply move the good to the highest price country.[6]

Figure 10.1 shows that there have been large systematic swings in the U.S./U.K. exchange rate since the end of Bretton Woods. Starting in 1971 the exchange rate is initially roughly equal to its Bretton Woods fixed rate of 2.4, but then falls to 1.7 in 1977, before recovering to 2.4 in late 1980. After that, it fell again, and has since fluctuated fairly wildly around 1.5. The fall in the exchange rate was an appreciation in the U.S. dollar relative to the U.K. pound. Figure 10.1 also shows what has happened to the euro after its initial introduction as part of the European Monetary Union in January 1991. The euro started at its targeted value of 1.18, but then quickly fell, and was below 1 during the early 2000s. It then recovered fairly sharply, and has since fluctuated between 1.1 and 1.5.[7]

1.1. Real Exchange Rate

When we use the exchange rate in combination with price indices, we derive something called the *real exchange rate*. For example, if the CPI in country i at time t is given by p_t^i, and the exchange rate between currency i and currency j is given by $e_t^{i/j}$, then the relative price of the basket used in the CPI is given by

$$\text{Relative price of basket} = \frac{p_t^i}{e_t^{i/j} p_t^j}. \tag{6}$$

Movements in the real exchange rate can have important implications for a country since they represent a change in the overall cost of goods in the country relative to that in another country. A rise in the relative cost of goods and services, especially labor services, can indicate that a country is becoming less competitive in terms of its production costs relative to its trading partners.

There is a general presumption that over some sufficiently long interval, trade and economic pressure will force real exchange rates into an appropriate alignment. This is often referred to as purchasing power parity (PPP). The evidence in favor of PPP is pretty weak however, and it is natural to think that economic development can have a substantial impact on the local cost of living. So perhaps

6. See Charles Engel and John H. Rogers (1996), "How Wide Is the Border?" *American Economic Review* 86: 1112–1125.

7. Source: Board of Governors of the Federal Reserve System (US), U.S. / U.K. Foreign Exchange Rate [EXUSUK], and Board of Governors of the Federal Reserve System (US), U.S. / Euro Foreign Exchange Rate [EXUSEU], retrieved from FRED, Federal Reserve Bank of St. Louis

we should not be too surprised. After all, it is much cheaper to live in Omaha, Nebraska than in New York City.

1.2. Boom-Bust Cycles and the Real Exchange Rate

A commonly observed phenomenon is for a reduction in restrictions on foreign investment and foreign borrowing to lead to an increase in capital inflows for so-called middle-income countries. This in turn leads to a lending/investment boom for these countries and rapid growth. Sometimes these booms have ended badly. When that occurs, the real exchange rate normally rises during the boom as non-traded goods in particular rise in price. Eventually this leads to a deterioration in export performance and a reversal of the capital inflows, with money now flowing out of the country. This reversal is often called "a sudden stop" because the reversal can be quite abrupt. Normally at this point, both the real exchange rate deteriorates and the country experiences a banking crisis as many of the loans and investments that were made during the boom become insolvent.[8]

To illustrate one example of this occurrence, we examine what happened in Mexico during the 1990s. In Figure 10.2, one can see the initial rise in the real exchange rate during the first half of the 1990s. This was driven by a rise in prices and wages within Mexico generated by the boom in economic activity and large capital inflows. Starting in 1994, there is a reversal as economic conditions

Figure 10.2 Mexico's Real and Nominal Exchange Rates During the 1990s. SOURCE: FRED. Data Source: Organization for Economic Co-operation and Development.

8. See Aaron Tornell, and Frank Westermann (2002), "Boom-Bust Cycles in Middle Income Countries: Facts and Explanation." *IMF Staff Papers* 49.1: 111–155. See also Guillermo A. Calvo, Leonardo Leiderman, and Carmen M. Reinhart (1996), "Inflows of Capital to Developing Countries in the 1990s." *Journal of Economic Perspectives* 10.2: 123–139.

deteriorate. This eventually leads to a sharp depreciation in the U.S./Mexico exchange rate (measured in terms of unit labor costs), and this, combined with a fall in domestic prices and wages, leads to a sharp fall in the Mexican real exchange rate.[9] The Mexican crisis of 1995 leads to a sovereign debt crisis, something we will return to when we discuss sovereign debt later.

2. INTEREST RATE PARITY

Exchange rate fluctuations over time also play an important role in evaluating the relative returns from saving in bonds denominated in different currencies. This is because one uses the exchange rate to convert money holdings in one currency into another currency in order to purchase a foreign bond, and then converts the proceeds back using the then prevailing exchange rate.

2.1. Exchange Rates and Interest Rates in the Risk-Neutral Model

To begin to see the connection between interest rates and exchange rates, consider the problem of acquiring some euros to spend in the next period. There are several ways to do this:

A. Exchange dollars for euros today at exchange rate e_t, and save at the nominal interest rate on euro accounts $1 + i_t^*$.
B. Save dollars today at interest rate $1 + i_t$ and exchange dollars for euros tomorrow at rate e_{t+1}.
C. Agree to a forward contract that exchanges dollars for euros tomorrow at rate f_t and save dollars today at interest rate $1 + i_t$.

To understand what our risk-neutral model implies about these transactions and their prices, consider the following two-period version of our risk-neutral pricing model:

$$\max_{a_1} c_1 + E_1\beta \left\{ \max_{a_2} c_2 \right\},$$

where the flow budget constraint is given by

$$p_1 y_1 - b_1 - b_1^*/e_1 = p_1 c_1,$$

9. Source for figure is Organization for Economic Co-operation and Development, Real Effective Exchange Rates Based on Manufacturing Unit Labor Cost for Mexico [CCRETT02MXA661N], and National Currency to US Dollar Exchange Rate: Average of Daily Rates for Mexico [CCUSMA02MXM618N], retrieved from FRED, Federal Reserve Bank of St. Louis

where p_1 is the period 1 price level, b_1 is domestic nominal bond purchases, e_1 is the euro/dollar exchange rate, and b_1^* is eurobond purchases. This budget constraint allows the individual to exchange b_1^*/e_1 units of nominal dollar income for b_1^* units of eurobonds of price 1 euro. To keep things simple, we will assume that the individual only buys euro-denominated consumption goods, spending $p_2^* c_2$ in euros. We will also assume that he converts the fraction λ of his savings in dollar-denominated bonds to euros using the current exchange rate, and the rest using a foreign exchange contract that he had agreed to, in which the contracted exchange rate was f_1. With these assumptions, the second period budget constraint is given by

$$(1 + i_1)\, b_1 \left[\lambda e_2 + (1 - \lambda) f_1\right] + \left(1 + i_1^*\right) b_1^* = p_2^* c_2.$$

To derive our optimality conditions, take λ to 0 and note that the change in the payoff from increasing b_1 is given by

$$-1/p_1 + \beta E\left\{(1 + i_1) f_1/p_2^*\right\} = -1/p_1 + \beta(1 + i_1) f_1 E\left\{1/p_2^*\right\}$$

since all period 1 prices, including f_1, are known. At the same time, the gain from changing b_1^* is given by

$$-1/e_1 p_1 + \beta E\left\{\left(1 + i_1^*\right)/p_2^*\right\} = -1/e_1 p_1 + \beta \left(1 + i_1^*\right) E\left\{1/p_2^*\right\}$$

Thus, if we compare methods (A) and (C) using our two expressions, we get that

$$\left(1 + i_t^*\right) e_t = f_t(1 + i_t),$$

or there is an arbitrage opportunity. This is called *covered interest rate parity* and it holds very strongly in the data. This is unsurprising because there is no risk in this comparison beyond p_2^*; which washes out because it is completely common.

Now consider doing a similar comparison when we take $\lambda = 1$. In this case the gain from changing b_1^* has changed and it is now

$$-1/p_1 + \beta E\left\{(1 + i_1) e_2/p_2^*\right\}.$$

These gains will both need to be zero in equilibrium; hence, we can rearrange them to get that

$$1/p_1 = \beta E\left\{\left(1 + i_1^*\right) e_1/p_2^*\right\},$$
$$1/p_1 = \beta E\left\{(1 + i_1) e_2/p_2^*\right\}.$$

From these two conditions we get that

$$(1 + i_1)E\{e_2/p_2^*\} = (1 + i_1^*)E\{e_1/p_2^*\}.$$

This condition is a bit tricky, since we actually have two random variables on the l.h.s. expression. However, price level uncertainty is often taken to be small enough to be ignored, in which case we get

$$(1 + i_t^*)\, e_t = E\{e_{t+1}\}(1 + i_t). \tag{7}$$

Condition 7 is called *uncovered interest rate parity*.

In a risk-neutral model we would expect uncovered interest rate parity to hold. But our prior asset pricing discussion already illustrated that the world does not act like the risk-neutral model, at least with respect to aggregate risk. Since exchange rate fluctuations affect things in aggregate, it should come as no surprise that this condition does not hold in the data.

Finally, consider the optimal choice of λ. In this case we end up comparing taking the risk of exchanging currency using e_2 or the certainty of f_1. In this case, we are comparing

$$-1/p_1 + \beta(1 + i_1)f_1E\{1/p_2^*\} \text{ vs.} -1/p_1 + \beta E\{(1 + i_1)e_2/p_2^*\}.$$

If we again take price-level uncertainty to be small enough to ignore, we get that

$$f_1 = E\{e_2\}.$$

This condition says that the forward rate should be a good predictor of the future spot rate.

Note that the future exchange rate is a random variable, so we would not expect f_1 to equal e_2. However, in a risk-neutral world we would expect the forward rate to get the future spot rate right on average. To test this, one would need to get a time series of forward and future spot rates for different countries and examine whether

$$f_t - e_{t+1}$$

was on average equal to zero. If it was not, then shifting f_t by the average error would improve the forecast. If one wanted to be even more severe, one would expect that no information available at time t could improve our forecast of the future spot rate. Sadly, even our simple average test is systematically violated in the data.

The failure of uncovered interest parity to hold, and the failure of the forward rate to efficiently predict the future spot exchange rate, illustrate the fact that the data deviates from our simple risk-neutral pricing model in a quantitatively important manner.

2.2. Interest Rates, Exchange Rates, and Risk Premia

The failure of uncovered interest parity gives a nice starting point to organize our thinking about interest rates and exchange rates. The relative deviation from interest parity is given by

$$\frac{\left(1 + i_t^*\right) e_t}{(1 + i_t)E_t\{e_{t+1}\}}.$$

If we take logs and note that the $\log(1 + x) \approx 1$, then we get that the relative deviation in interest rate parity, γ_t, is given by

$$\gamma_t \equiv i_t^* - i_t + \log(e_t) - \log(E_t\{e_{t+1}\}). \tag{8}$$

The term γ_t is often referred to as a risk premium. Holding this premium fixed, we can see that a rise in the foreign interest rate should imply an offsetting depreciation in the foreign currency, which here means that e_{t+1} is expected to rise relative to e_t. Alternatively an increase in the foreign interest rate with expected depreciation in the foreign exchange rate implies that the risk premium must have risen.

A major surprise in the data is that an interest rate premium, which theory says should generally be associated with a currency depreciation to offset the interest rate surplus, is often associated with a currency appreciation instead. This means that on average, someone who takes advantage of interest rate premium stands to gain. This observation has led a number of major banks and other large financial institutions to invest in the *currency carry trade*. Under this investment strategy, investors seek to borrow in the currency of countries with low interest rates and invest in bonds denominated in the currency of countries with high interest rates. A lot of this borrowing has been done in yen because of Japan's long history of low interest rates.

One possible explanation of the seeming existence of a profitable arbitrage opportunity coming via the currency carry trade is that a large depreciation of the currency is a low probability event and we do not often see it. This explanation would argue that over a sufficiently long history, this investment strategy will eventually run into some large losses that will offset the frequent small gains. Sorting this out in the data is difficult. But large losses do sometimes occur.

11

Moving away from Money

Money in the physical form of bills and coins and transactions involving its physical exchange are being gradually supplanted by electronic exchanges and digital currencies. To understand why this is occurring, it is useful to focus clearly on what money is actually doing. If we stand back and look at the system of monetary exchange from afar, basically money is serving as a decentralized recordkeeping system for a large collection of exchanges that are taking place at different locations and points in time.[1] Thought of in this way, it seems very natural that we might move away from using a physical record and requiring a physical exchange in the electronic and digital age. In fact, the ability to transfer funds without any physical exchange is quite old. In addition, some sort of digital money is not new. The Federal Reserve System has two forms of the monetary base: currency and reserves. But reserves are really bookkeeping entries maintained by the Fed with respect to the different member banks. The Fed fixes the relative value of these two forms of money by pledging to exchange one dollar for one unit of reserves, which is why we use the dollar as the unit for reserves too.

1. ELECTRONIC PAYMENT METHODS

Electronic payment methods have a long history. The first electronic payment system was developed by the telegraph company Western Union, when, in the

---

1. This point was first made by N. Kocherlakota in "Money Is Memory," *Journal of Economic Theory* (August 1998).

1870s, the company set up the Electronic Funds Transfer system. To transfer money the sender goes to a telegraph office, provides some basic information about the sender and the receiver, hands over the funds, and gets a special code number. The sender then informs the receiver of the code number and the receiver goes to an office of the telegraph company, presents the code number and some identification, and receives the funds. The first credit card was introduced in the 1950s. Initially, information about these transactions was transferred using reasonably secure means, such as the phone system or the Federal Reserve's wire transfer system. But, with the advent of e-commerce, more and more information on these transactions is being transferred wirelessly and over the internet.

Any electronic payment system requires that a record be kept of the current balance an individual has, and of shifts in funds from one individual's account to another. If there is a trusted central record keeper, this can be done by that agent. At the same time, the system must prevent individual account holders from spending their funds multiple times—the electronic analog of check kiting. These accounts work very much like standard checking accounts and are easy to set up even within a decentralized environment with multiple record keepers when there is trust. Examples of such a system include Fedwire, which is a settlements or payment system run by the Federal Reserve that allows a very wide range of financial intermediaries to hold balances with the Fed and make payments to each other. The system allowed financial intermediaries to move away from having to physically deliver cash to other intermediaries in order to settle claims with each other. The amount of funds transferred on Fedwire is huge: $766 trillion in 2016 with almost 600 thousand transfers on average being made on a daily basis.[2]

The Federal Reserve conducts an annual payments study that reports on how transactions are being made. In the 2017 study, the Fed reported that total credit card payments continued to grow sharply and had a total value of almost $6 trillion in 2016. It also reported that "remote general-purpose" card payments are growing roughly twice as fast as the standard old-fashioned "in-person" card payment. While the value of credit card payments is still less than 1/5 of check payments, they are used around 5 times as much.[3] This implies that, more and more, credit card payments are taking over everyday transactions. In fact, one might anticipate that electronic payment methods will eventually drive conventional money out of the transactions business.

The prospect of electronic payments taking over seems most salient in Sweden, where according to *Bloomberg News*:

2. See the Board of Governors of the Federal Reserve System data on this system at https://www.federalreserve.gov/paymentsystems/fedfunds_ann.htm.

3. "The Federal Reserve Payments Study: 2017 Annual Supplement."

Sweden is widely regarded as the most cashless society on the planet. Most of the country's bank branches have stopped handling cash; many shops, museums and restaurants now only accept plastic or mobile payments.[4]

The extent to which cash usage is shrinking has even got the Riksbank, the central bank of Sweden, to begin studying this phenomenon and to consider forcing banks to provide customers with cash.

2. CREDIT CARD TRANSACTIONS AND THE INTERNET

Using our credit cards to purchase things on the internet has become ubiquitous. However, for something that we now take for granted, making it happen was not so easy. In fact, the first major attempt to do so failed because participants were forced to jump through many procedural hoops. This is because the system had to overcome the problem of transmitting information over an insecure network. These kinds of insecure transfers of information only became possible with the development of modern encryption systems—a development which has ushered in the creation of cryptocurrencies.

   To allow for widespread use of credit cards over the internet, a consortium of companies came together to develop a common protocol that could be widely used. This protocol was called the Secure Electronic Transaction (SET) protocol and was developed in the mid-1990s by a group of companies including Visa, Mastercard, IBM, and Microsoft. To maintain security, the buyer's credit card information is not actually shared with the seller. Instead, the buyer, having decided to purchase something through the seller's website, transmits both her purchase order and her encrypted credit card information to the seller, who then passes on both pieces of information to their bank. The bank then confirms the legitimacy of the transaction with the credit card issuer. The issuer authorizes the transaction and this is passed along by the bank to the seller. The seller then processes the order and sends a confirmation to the buyer. The issuer then passes on the payment to the seller's bank, while also charging the buyer. The key innovation was both to encrypt the buyer's credit card information in such a way that only the issuer could decrypt it, and, at the same time to come up with a way to link the buyer's purchase order and credit card information. This system ultimately failed because of the need for every buyer to have a secure encryption key known only to the issuer. This requirement was so onerous that the system never gained widespread acceptance.

---

4. "'No Cash' Signs Everywhere Has Sweden Worried It Has Gone too Far," Bloomberg.com 2018-02-18.

The second attempt to develop a payment system, 3-D Secure, had the buyer actually temporarily switch his internet connection from the seller's web page to the issuer's web page. The buyer then logs into his account at the issuer's web page and thereby authorizes the transaction. This login is not trivial, since the login information must itself be encrypted. The SSL (secure sockets layer, which has now been superseded by the Transport Layer Security standard) relies on the two parties establishing a shared private cryptographic key when they first interact. How they are able to do this is a bit of a miracle of modern cryptography, a miracle that allows internet credit card transactions to take place, with some further advancement, this led to the development of cryptocurrencies.

3. CRYPTOCURRENCIES AND BITCOIN

There is a variety of cryptocurrencies, including, most notably, Bitcoin, as well as Ethereum, Litecoin, Zcash, Dash and Ripple. The other cryptocurrencies were created in response to the success of Bitcoin and they incorporate many of its features.[5] Besides speculation, the main benefit these currencies provide is the ability to transact in an untraceable manner; this is one reason why they have been quite popular with criminals and criminal enterprises. However, the public ledger aspect of Bitcoin (more on this later) has led to the development and popularity of more anonymous alternative cryptocurrencies.[6] Vladimir Putin has even recently suggested creating cryptorouble to get around various sanctions being levied against the Russian state.[7]

So, what is Bitcoin? First, it's a set of rules written in the form of computer programs that seek to create and manage a supply of digital currency (called Bitcoins). These programs also seek to maintain an elaborate system of ledgers for each participant and to process payments between the users of this system by crediting and debiting their accounts. It tries to do all this anonymously and also in manner so that it cannot easily be hacked or disrupted. The inventor of this system is unknown, but goes by the alias Satoshi Nakamoto. The program is open source and there is a group of people who seek to maintain it. Bitcoins themselves are just credits on these accounts. Both Ethereum and Litecoin are essentially

---

5. Go to https://coinmarketcap.com/ to see a list of these currencies and their current prices and market capitalizations.

6. See Jason Bloomberg, "Using Bitcoin or Other Cryptocurrency to Commit Crimes? Law Enforcement Is Onto You," *Forbes Magazine* Dec. 28, 2017.

7. Ben Chapman, "Bitcoin latest: Vladimir Putin 'Considers Launching cryptocurrency to Help Russia Evade Sanctions'," *Independent,* January 2, 2018.

more recent spawns of the original Bitcoin protocol with some minor differences. Because Bitcoin is open source, this kind of spawning and competition between various cryptocurrencies is to be expected.

When Bitcoin started, a unit of the currency was worth very little—only 6 cents in July 2010. By December 2013 the value had risen to almost a thousand dollars. However, the value has been highly volatile. For example, on December 2, 2013 the closing value was $979.45, while on December 23 it had fallen to $716.53. Starting in mid-2017, the value of a Bitcoin started rocketing upward in much the way we would expect from a bubble. On March 20, 2017 a Bitcoin was worth $1012.81, but by December 11, 2017 it was worth $17,549.67, then declined to $7964.42 on February 5 2018. Since then it has rebounded. When I last checked (in March 2018) a coin was worth more than $10 thousand and the total market capitalization was $166 billion dollars with almost 17,000 coins in existence. A unit of Ethereum was worth around $750 and a Litecoin $185. Both of these alternatives have smaller market capitalizations; for example Ethereum's is only $73 billion.[8]

Any person can participate in the Bitcoin system. To do so, one downloads a digital wallet that can be stored on your computer or USB drive. This wallet is an encrypted computer file where your bitcoins can be stored and comes with a public Bitcoin address and a private key. The encrypted file is labeled wallet.dat and it is important that you do not lose your copy. An individual can have more than one such wallet to make tracking the wallets more difficult. While the identity of the owner of a wallet is not known, the contents of every wallet are public knowledge. To prevent loss, a wallet can be stored with an intermediary, such as the Coinbase. For a service fee, Coinbase will store your wallet, thereby trying to prevent loss or theft.[9] If someone can access your wallet, they can steal the Bitcoins in it and spend them. This appears to have happened to one of the biggest Bitcoin exchanges, Mt. Gox, which was located in Japan. Mt. Gox originated in 2010, and suspended operations in 2014 when it announced that 850,000 bitcoins had been stolen.

Unlike other old-fashioned digital currencies, such as the Fed's reserves, Bitcoin has a decentralized ledger system. In this ledger system, the record of transactions is kept at a wide range of locations simultaneously. These locations are called *miners* and one becomes (or constructs) a miner by setting up a computer server at a given location that stores and shares data with other locations in the network. Miners are compensated to give them an incentive to maintain and update these records. Someone who wants to make a transaction in the Bitcoin network system

---

8. https://www.coindesk.com/price/.

9. They also store Ethereum and Litecoin.

sends a message out to all of the miners in the Bitcoin network stating her account name, the amount to be transferred, and the receiving account name. Her name here is not the person's real name, just the public address associated with her Bitcoin wallet. It also includes a digital signature that is constructed from her private key and is special in that decrypting and verifying it includes checking the decrypted information against the information in the transaction message. This decryption is done with a public key that everyone in the system knows. Sending a false transaction message means forging someone's digital signature, and by design, this is computationally infeasible.

Transactions data are stored in blocks. Each block includes a record of a set of recent transactions, a reference number and the hash number of the block before it, and the solution to a computational problem that serves as proof-of-work. Both the hash number and the solution to the computational problem involve something called a *hash function*. The hash number of the prior block involves computing something that depends upon the prior block in a nearly unique manner. The proof-of-work is done by trying to find a number that, when added to the hash of the prior message block, will lead the hash value of the transaction block to have a certain number of 0s at the start of the number. All of this is called a *block* because the information transmitted must fit into a 1M block of data. The block is then transmitted to the network of miners and this block is added in a linear chain to the overall record if over 50% of the miners accept it as valid. This overall chain constitutes a record of all the past transactions going back in time to the beginning; hence it's called a *block chain*. The energy being burned in this process, which primarily involves all the guessing to solve the proof-of-work, is currently estimated to be about the energy consumption of Israel.[10]

A transaction is not considered valid until it has been included in the block chain. Since a block may be judged to be invalid, it is customary to wait until the transaction is several blocks deep in the chain. This process of validation is designed to prevent double-spending. If a bitcoin transaction is rejected, then the transfer never takes place, and the wallet balance returns to its prior level. (Note that this does not lead to a credit for an attempt at double-spending.)

A miner who is attempting to augment the block chain first verifies the chain it is working on. By design, this is fairly easy to do, since computing the hash of a given message or number once is easy, as is verifying digital signatures. As part of his reward for successfully updating the block chain, a miner enters an initial transaction that credits his wallet. The amount being credited started at 50 Bitcoins and falls in 1/2 at regular intervals. This means that the maximum level of the total Bitcoin currency is capped at 21 million. Someone seeking to

10. See "Bitcoin Energy Consumption Index" at Digiconomist, https://digiconomist.net/

have her transaction processed by a miner can include a payment to the miner in her transaction message. It is anticipated that these payments will more and more become the main source of revenue for a miner.

Solving the proof-of-work puzzle is too complicated to simply invert the hash function, and the only computationally feasible way to do it is simply to guess and try out various numbers. Computational power is very important here, since it takes an extremely large number of guesses to arrive at a successful result. The difficulty of the proof-of-work is reset every couple of weeks so that the efforts of the last two weeks would have yielded one block every 10 minutes, given the pool of miners (which includes both their number and their computing power). This amount of time was set to allow the miners to examine the new block before accepting it. Other cryptocurrencies feature faster processing times. The fact that it takes an increasingly difficult "lucky" guess to generate a solution to the proof-of-work hash function has made mining a pretty risky business. The miners have responded by organizing themselves into pools. The pools break the overall problem down into smaller and easier components that they distribute among the pool. This can readily be done by partitioning the set of guess numbers to try.

Attempting to introduce fraudulent transactions into the block chain means introducing a fraudulent transaction block. This could lead to there being more than one possible block chain in existence. The rule on deciding which of several possible block chains to treat as valid is to always accept the longest chain, which also has had the most computational work done on it. This is supposed to prevent anyone from successfully generating and maintaining a false chain, since he would be competing against all of the other miners in order to update it.

Anyone can examine the block chain and see the transactions in it. To do so, simply go to Bitcoin Block Explorer. All of the early blocks have no transactions besides the 50 BTC credit to the miner. But more recent blocks have many transactions. For example, Block #513221, which has a time stamp of March 12, 2018 2:25:10 PM is the 513221 block in the chain, with 599 transactions. The proof-of-work value of the nonce is 1475494586.[11] The miner's direct reward was 12.5 BTC.

To make this kind of system function, it must be the case that a miner can readily verify a digital signature and that this signature cannot be forged. The miner must also be able to verify the transactions log which is in the form of a block chain and detect when fraudulent changes to the chain have been attempted. At the same time, the actual identity of the message sender is being kept secret, as is the true identity of the transfer recipient. Moreover, all

11. A nonce is a word or expression coined for one use or circumstance. In information theory, it is taken to be a "number used once." Typically this is done for authentication or time-stamp purposes.

communication is being done over an open network. This is a pretty tall order, and it is only fairly recently that it all became possible. Because having some notion of how successful encryption works is so central to understanding the modern and future transactions systems, the next section lays out some of the basics. (See https://www.stlouisfed.org/dialogue-with-the-fed/the-possibilities-and-the-pitfalls-of-virtual-currencies/; A. Narayanan, J. Bonneau, E. Felten, A. Miller and S. Goldfeder, "Bitcoin and Cryptocurrency Technologies," Draft Feb. 9, 2016; the "bitcoinwiki" entry on Wikipedia;

4. EVERYTHING STARTS WITH KEEPING SECRETS

All of the modern transaction methods seem to start from solving the following very old problem. How can two parties secretly communicate information across a public line? To understand why this is so important, note that everything communicated through the phone system, especially wirelessly or through the internet, has a public aspect, since many others could find a way to listen as the message is passed between our two parties. The solution to this problem is also very old: Encrypt the message using a secret key that only the two parties know.

A standard method of doing this sort of encryption is the following. Let $\mathcal{P}$ be a set of symbols. A natural set for our purposes would include the letters from A to Z and the integers from 0 to 9. However, other symbols could be included, for example, "$". Assume that the symbols are ordered in a particular fashion indexed by $i = \{1, ..., I\}$, where I is the number of elements in $\mathcal{P}$. An encryption takes each index i and maps it to another index j in our set of indexes $\{1, ..., I\}$. The key here is that the mapping $\epsilon(i) = j$ is one-to-one (which means that it maps to a unique element j). Because of this and the fact that we have a finite set mapping back into itself, it must be onto (i.e., for each j there is some i that maps to it). Also, more important, because it is one-to-one we can invert this mapping $\epsilon^{-1}(j) = i$. This gives us our encryption system. We use the mapping ϵ to encrypt the message and ϵ^{-1} to unencrypt the message.[12]

A very old example of such a system was used by Julius Caesar, who simply shifted each letter by 3. So A becomes D, ..., X becomes A, Y becomes B. This sort of cypher was used for a long time. Unfortunately, this sort of simple cypher has a fundamental flaw that was first discovered by an Arab mathematician some 800 years ago: The frequency with which we use certain letters is not uniform. For

---

12. Here we are assuming that the original set of characters $\mathcal{P}$ and the encrypted set are the same. This need not be the case but is very commonly done. Doing so means that any encryption must be a permutation of the original set of characters.

example, the letter E is the most common; all of the other vowels are also quite common, while certain letters are very uncommon. Also, to make matters worse, military or financial transactions tend to use the same words with high frequency. So if one sees a lot of messages, then one can use the lack of uniformity and the repetitiveness of certain words to quickly infer the encryption.

A way around this problem is to vary the encryption in a systematic fashion. For example, we could shift the first letter in the message by 3, the second by 6 and the third by 9, before returning to 3. So our cycle is {3, 6, 9}, which is repeated over and over again. The number 369 is called our *key*. Using a key like this increases difficulty of figuring out our code, since a simple examination of the letters will not reveal the standard nonuniform pattern. However, if the person seeing our messages has enough of them and realizes that we are going to repeat ourselves, she can try different repeating groups: (i) start with all the letters, (ii) group them into odd and even letters, (iii) group them in a 3-cycle where the first letter is in group 1, the second in group 2, the third in group 3, then the fourth is back in group 1, and so forth. When this person hits the 3-cycle, she will detect the familiar pattern and be able to read our message and find out our secrets.

The solution to this problem is to come up with a long series of shifts. These shifts are referred to as the key, and a good key has the property that it flattens out the distribution of the letters (or symbols) that we end up using in our encrypted message so that they look close to uniform. But not all keys, which we can just think of as numbers, are good. For example 123123 is bad. Even though it is 6 elements long, it repeats after 3, so really it's just a 3-cycle. So we want to stick with non-repeating numbers. However, we cannot go too far, since any non-terminating non-repeating number is an irrational number and does not have a finite representation, so we would need to have a key of infinite length. That is infeasible; sooner or later, we will need to repeat ourselves. So in the end there must be a cycle.

The latest encryption methods for generating a good cycle do so by using the residuals from simple division. This works especially well when augmented by powers. For example, consider the residuals from dividing 2^n by 13 for $n = 0, 1, 2, \dots$. This leads to the sequence

$$\frac{2^n}{13} = 1, 2, 4, 8, 3, 6, 12, 11, 9, 5, 10, 7, 1, 2\dots\text{for } n = 0, 1, \dots$$

Notice how this leads to a nice random spreading over the numbers $0, \dots, 12$. The cycle starts repeating when $n = 12$ as 2^{12} divided by 13 has a remainder of 1.

Math Fact: Consider a rational number of the form a/b, then the residual r of dividing a into b once must be less than b. But there are only $b - 1$ possible numbers here, so within at most b times we are going to get a repeat. But once we get a repeat, we start the cycle again. Thus, all rational numbers must terminate or repeat within at most b steps. This problem gets much worse if a and b share a common factor, say c, because of course

$$\frac{a}{b} = \frac{a/c}{b/c} \tag{9}$$

and now we know that our number must repeat within b/c units. So, it would be best *not* to pick a base number b that is going to have a common factor with any number we might pick for the numerator. This leads us naturally to prime numbers to be sure that this won't happen.

But this all relied on our two parties getting together and privately exchanging their keys. For many forms of communication, this initial private exchange is not possible. So, the critical problem to be solved here is how to determine the two parties' keys without a private exchange of information; that is, with only a public exchange of information. The answer relies on each of the two parties coming up with a number and passing on some condensed information about that number to the other party. Each party then combines the condensed information they have received along with their private number to construct a second private number. The cleverness in this construction is that the set of possible numbers which are consistent with the condensed information must be (computationally) infinite so no one can guess the number through repeated trials, and yet the condensed information plus a party's actual number must lead both parties to the exact same resulting numerical value when they construct their second private number. It may seem quite surprising that this is even possible, and figuring all this out leads us into a fairly abstract corner of number theory.

4.1. Residuals and Modular Math

We start with modular arithmetic. If we do division the old-fashioned way with a remainder, we can define

$$\frac{N}{D} = Q \operatorname{rem} R, \tag{10}$$

where N is our numerator, D is our denominator, Q is the quotient, and R is the remainder. This representation is unique (i.e. there is a unique value of N and R given D) and every integer number can be represented in this manner. This means that this operation divides up all of the integer numbers into mutually exclusive groups based on the value of their remainder. Of course all of these groups have an infinite number of members because Q can run from minus infinity to plus infinity.

Moreover, addition in terms of the remainder works in the following simple fashion. The remainder from the sum of two numbers, $N + M$,

$$\frac{N + M}{D} = Q \operatorname{rem} R \tag{11}$$

is just the result from running the remainders through the quotient operation or

$$\frac{R_N + R_M}{D} = Q' \operatorname{rem} R. \tag{12}$$

Moreover, multiplication works the same way since in any operation of the form

$$\frac{(Q_N * D + R_N) \times (Q_M * D + R_M)}{D}, \tag{13}$$

any product being multiplied by D or by D^2 will end up in the quotient. So, the remainder is again simply the result of applying our quotient operation to the product of the remainders.

The fact that things work out so neatly led to a whole branch of mathematics developing around this with its own formalism. The quotient operation expression is also expressed as

$$N \bmod D = R,$$

where D is referred to as the modulus. The following two examples will help us understand how this is applied to positive and negative integers.

$$17 \bmod 5 = 2 \tag{14}$$

$$-17 \bmod 5 = 3 \tag{15}$$

The first is fairly obvious, but the second is more tricky. Remember, we are seeking the closest lower number in $Q \times D$, and in the second case, this lowest number is -20, and that gives us a remainder of 3.

The next result is neat and a bit surprising

$$
\begin{array}{lll}
-3 \bmod 3 = 0 & -2 \bmod 3 = 1 & -1 \bmod 3 = 2 \\
0 \bmod 3 = 0 & 1 \bmod 3 = 1 & 2 \bmod 3 = 2 \\
3 \bmod 3 = 0 & 4 \bmod 3 = 1 & 5 \bmod 3 = 2
\end{array} \tag{16}
$$

So, modular arithmetic comes in the form of a cycle, which starts at 0 when $N = 0$ and climbs by $+ 1$ up to $D - 1$ before starting over at 0. If we subtract 1 from $N = 0$, then it counts down in the same fashion. So everything forms a cycle. This leads to the following key result.

Proposition 1. *We start with two fairly straightforward results that follow from the cyclical aspect of modular arithmetic*

$$N \bmod D = (N + I \times D) \bmod D$$

for any integer I. Also,

$$(N + A) \bmod D = (N \bmod D + A \bmod D) \bmod D.$$

And finally,

$$(N \times A) \bmod D = (N \bmod D \times A \bmod D) \bmod D.$$

Now for one more key fact about modulus math.

Proposition 2. *The cyclical nature of modular arithmetic also implies that*

$$N^A \bmod D = ((N \bmod D)^A) \bmod D.$$

This last result, obscure as it seems, turns out to be the *key*. This is because you might think I would need to know N^A and D to compute $N^A \bmod D$, but in fact, all I need to know is $(N \bmod D)^A$ and D. This is actually much less information, since there are many different values of N that will lead to the same remainder, since $N \bmod D = (N + I \times D) \bmod D$. But, despite this, we will arrive at the same result.

And now for the trick.

(1) Party 1 picks a prime modulus D and a prime generator N and sends this information to Party 2 over the *public* line.

(2) Party 2 selects her private prime number A and calculates $N^A \bmod D = X$ and sends this result to Party 1.

(3) Party 1 then selects his private random number B and calculates $N^B \bmod D = Y$ and sends this result to Party 2.

(4) Party 1 calculates $X^B \bmod D = N^{A^B} \bmod D$ to get his side of the shared private key.

(5) Party 2 similarly calculates $Y^A \bmod D = N^{B^A} \bmod D$ to get her side. This common number is the encryption key they will use.

These private numbers are the same, since the order of exponentiation does not matter. Notice here that the calculation performed by each party, Y^A, for example, is pretty easy. But to start from Y and N and try to infer A, we need to solve for all of the integer solutions to $N^c = Y$. This turns out to be much harder, especially when the numbers N, D, A, and B all get big. This problem even has a special name: the discrete logarithm problem. Modern encryption relies on the notion that doing this reverse calculation can be made to take so much time, it will never be done.

Table 11.1 provides a numerical example of just such an exchange. The exchange leads to the agreed private number 4. If we changed Party 1's private number from 7 to 5, this would lead X to change to 9, and the private number to change to 8. It was hard for me to go much beyond these simple examples because my math software automatically rounds numbers and so it did not work with bigger numbers.[13]

Table 11.1. Example of Private Key Exchange

Public generator	Public modulus
$N = 2$	$D = 23$
Private number 1	Private number 2
$A = 7$	$B = 5$
Public Communication	
$X = N^A \bmod D = 13$	$Y = N^B \bmod D = 9$
Common Key 4	

Note that if we wanted to add another party, Party 3 to this exchange and Party 3 also wanted to send secret messages to Party 1, we simply have Party 3 pick her private number C, calculate $N^C \bmod D = Z$, and send Z to Party 1. Party 1 then picks a new B' and sends $Y' = N^{B'} \bmod D$ to Party 3 and calculates $Z^{B'} \bmod D$, while Party 3 calculates $Y'^C \bmod D$. The results are a new private key that is shared between Party 1 and Party 3, but is not even known to Party 2. So, this encryption system expands very nicely. This is important if we want to think of Party 1 as a bank or some other major financial institution. In a similar manner, we can make our keys harder to discover by having our two parties redo the above algorithm to generate fresh keys each time they start to communicate.

To summarize, a system of encryption has been developed that enables two parties to communicate secretly over a public system without ever having to meet first and decide on the common encryption key they will be using to encrypt and decrypt their messages.

---

13. Computers are generally set up to do floating point calculations and this means that they naturally round off numbers. A better modular calculator can be found at http://ptrow.com/perl/calculator.pl, where there is a link to an even better one which gets around the floating point problem.

To go a bit further, it would be nice to provide the encryption and decryption keys rather than just the common key for encryption. To do this, we need another bit of number theory that is related to Fermat's last theorem. Consider any integer raised to a prime modulo that prime, and note that

$$A^N \bmod N = A \text{ if } A < N.$$

To see how this works, first note that it must hold for $N = 2$, since the only candidate is 1, and $1^2 \bmod 2 = 1$. So, let's try $N = 3$ or 5. The following table lays out some examples.

$$
\begin{array}{lll}
1^3 \bmod 3 = 1 & 2^3 \bmod 3 = 2 & \dots \\
1^5 \bmod 5 = 1 & 2^5 \bmod 5 = 2 & 3^5 \bmod 5 = 3
\end{array}
\tag{17}
$$

In particular, $2^5 = 32$, which once divided by 5 and computing the remainder gives us 2. This would be wonderful *if we could factor a prime*, since then we would just raise the message to factor one to encrypt and factor two to decrypt. But, of course, that is impossible by construction. However, it turns out that this is not the only case in which we can get this result. If p and q are primes where $p * q = N$, then

$$M^{[(p-1)*(q-1)+1]} \bmod (p * q) = M \text{ if } M < N.$$

Moreover, the number $[(p - 1) * (q - 1) + 1]$ will generally not be prime and hence it can be factored into two parts

$$a * b = [(p - 1) * (q - 1) + 1].$$

This encryption and decryption system which we have just outlined was first proposed in a paper by Rivest, Shamir and Adleman in 1977, and is named the RSA Cryptosystem. It is widely used now, for example, in creating the digital signatures which underpin all of our internet transactions along with many others. A *digital signature* is a pair of encryption and decryption keys. They are used in conjunction with a message and typically contain additional information, such as the date and time, and information about the associated transaction, that ties the signature to the message or transaction.

Example 8. Here is an example of a pair of RSA encryption and decryption keys that I generated using the online webpage of Professor J. Popyack of Drexel University. I choose $p = 71$ and $q = 29$, which leads to $N = p \times q = 2059$. Then we want a number which has a remainder of 1, when we divide it by $r = (p-1)(q-1)$. Some candidates were

$\{1961, 3921, 5881, 7841, 9801, 11761, 13721, 15681, 17641, 19601\}$.

I choose 1961, because it can be factored into $37 * 53 = 1961$. Then, I checked that these numbers are relatively prime relative to r, which they are. So these are my encryption and decryption keys given the modulus 2059. To verify that this works, I went to an RSA express encryption/decryption web page and encrypted the following quote:

I have not failed. I've just found 10,000 ways that won't work. Thomas A. Edison

The quote must first be put in (ASCII) numeric form, since computers only really understand numbers

073032104097118101032110111116032102097105108101100046
032073039118101032106117115116032102111117110100032049
048044048048048032119097121115032116104097116032119111
110039116032119111111141070460100841041111090971150320 65
046032069100105115111110

I then encrypted it using ($e = 37, N = 2059$) to yield

070845614671057731194569642026110245617371051187304119
197719314561708181677311945620412002118811024561 7372026
200296419774563421026196910261026102645612391051 2221188
456110214671051102456123920269641816110245612392 026358
115419314561748146720267341051188456745193145617711977
118711882026964

Last, I verified that I got back my quote when I supplied the decryption key ($d = 53, N = 2059$).[14]

One final piece of the system remains. How can we verify that a block of data, such as a transactions log, has not been tampered with? The RSA system we

14. https://www.cs.drexel.edu/~introcs/Fall/notes/10.1_Cryptography/Rsa:Express_Encrypt Decrypt.html and https://www.cs.drexel.edu/~jpopyack/IntroCS/HW/RSAWorksheet.html

have just described is aimed at verifying a small block of data, since the message must be smaller than the modulus. We could simply apply it over and over, but this becomes cumbersome and slow. Also, the message might be manipulated by rearranging the encrypted blocks. This leads us to hash functions.

A *hash function* is a special function that takes in an input string of arbitrary length and maps it into a numerical value with a fixed upper bound on its size. It is important for cryptography that the value be easy to compute, but that it be hard nearly to the point of impossible to reverse this computation. To make this work, the hash function must compress the information in the original input when that is very long and extend the input length when it is too short. At the same time it must have a rich enough set of possible outputs so that verification has bite. By this I mean that it is hard to construct input blocks that will lead to the same output. One way that hash functions can be used is to verify that a message block has not been tampered with. To do this, one simply computes the hash value of the message block and sends it separately. The receiver can then compute the hash value of the message received and compare it to the separate hash value to verify the message. The hash of a message block can be encrypted as part of the digital signature to provide an unforgeable link between the signature and the message block. A final use of hash functions is the so-called proof-of-work computations which are designed to create a computational cost to sending a message block.

Modular arithmetic gives us a natural method for restricting the length of the output value since it cannot be greater than the modulus. Hence, it again plays a key role. At the same time, some way of converting any message to a numerical string must be used for message verification. With long messages this often also involves using compression software. The proof-of-work asks the computer to construct an input whose hash value begins with a certain specified number of zeros. One version of a hash function that has seen wide use is the MD4 hash function first proposed by Rivest in 1990. The current standard hash function that is being commonly used is called the SHA256. For example, the SHA256 hash of the following message:

> *What all the wise men promised has not happened, and what all the damned fools said would happen has come to pass.* William Lamb 2nd Viscount Melbourne.

is the following

03AC2107A857621ECAD66B9010C46088ED84142D7EE41CFC79761744B5
9B696D

To test it out, go to https://passwordsgenerator.net/sha256-hash-generator/ and try for yourself.

To learn more about this go to the "modular arithmetic" and "cryptography" sections of the Khan Academy web page (https://www.khanacademy.org/computing/computer-science/cryptography). Even more detail can be found in D. Stinson, *Cryptography: Theory and Practice,* CRC Press Series, 1995.

PART FIVE

Financial Intermediation

We turn now to financial intermediation. We start with an analysis of simple lending and some of the frictions that impede credit markets along with some history of early intermediation. We discuss the roles played by banks and bankers. This leads us into a history of banking in the United States. One key role of U.S. banks has been financing home purchases. We discuss how financial intermediaries have evolved and how this evolutiion, along with changes in mortgage finance, contributed to the financial meltdown that occurred during the Great Recession of the 2000s.

12

Lending and the Development of Banks

One of the earliest forms of financial intermediation seems to have been debt. The use of debt finance led to the development of banks. Here we lay out some of this early history and talk through several models to help us sort out some of the issues facing these early financial investors and intermediaries.

1. A BIT OF FINANCIAL HISTORY

Early merchants needed a means of financing their operations. One of the earliest mechanisms was the *bill of exchange*. The bill of exchange was a promise in writing by the payer, which promised to pay a certain amount either at a future date or on demand. The person issuing the bill need not be the payer (though it often was), but it could be someone empowered to issue such notes. Also, the bill could be transferable, in which case, the payment was to be made to whoever had the bill. When a bill was transferred, the person receiving the bill might not give the full amount of the promised payment to the person presenting the bill. This was called *discounting*.

The bill of exchange was an early example of a *bearer bond*. Bearer bonds are different from standard bonds in that no records are kept as to the identity of the owner of the bond. The holder of the bond is treated as the owner and can redeem the bond. This is great for anonymity, but it makes the bond very vulnerable to theft or loss. In recent times, bearer bonds have largely been supplanted by book entry bonds, which are registered to a specific person/institution. However, the

U.S. Treasury only stopped issuing bearer bonds in the 1980s, and there are still a substantial number waiting to be redeemed.

Some time after the emergence of bond lending, primitive forms of bank lending began to emerge as early merchants gradually started broadening their financial activities, taking on partners, and establishing offices in the major trading centers. In Europe these centers consisted of places like London, Paris, and Rome. These merchants began to take in interest-bearing deposits and started issuing commercial paper—short-term promissory notes. Eventually, they started selling longer-term bonds and stocks to take on longer-term capital financing. Famous examples of these early investment bankers include the Medici of Florence and the Barings and the Rothschilds of London.

The emergence of the modern investment bank, which undertook activities like underwriting and assisting in the placement of securities, started on a major scale early in the 19th century. However, its role in placing corporate securities came into play as the modern corporation began to arrise. This began late in the 19th century and these early corporations were known as *limited liability companies* or LLC. One early driver of this development was the need to finance wars. In the United States, this surge in the government's need to borrow came to the fore during the Civil War.

Especially when funding longer-term loans and investments, these banks faced the possibility of a serious liquidity problem. This meant that these banks often used a large equity or long-term debt component in their financing. In England, this led to the development of two types of banks: investment banks which specialized in long term financing and commercial banks, which took in short term deposits and specialized in shorter term financing.[1]

While the term *stock market* is very old, referring to the early forms as a "stock market" is a bit of a misnomer, since the trading of stocks would have to wait until the creation of the first publicly traded companies. The first of these was the East India Company in 1600. However, the legal basis for the modern corporation would not come for some time.

Instead, these markets generally sold both private and government debt claims, commodities and other such claims. A number of them grew out of coffee houses. These early coffee houses were very different from coffee houses today. In those early days, residential houses did not have numbers, so it was not uncommon to receive one's mail at a nearby coffee house. Moreover, they were places where people of different classes interacted. This is why many financial institutions grew out of these early coffee houses.

1. C. Fohlin, "A Brief History of Investment Banking from Medival Times to the Present," Johns Hopkins Department of Economics Working Paper, 2014.

One famous example is Lloyd's Coffee House in London. This coffee house catered to merchants and sailors, and as a result many shipping industry deals were done there. As this continued, the coffee house grew into Lloyd's of London, a major insurance company that historically has been quite important. Another famous coffee house was Jonathan's Coffee House, which was frequented by many business people. After Jonathan's burnt down, it was rebuilt and took on the name *The Stocks of Exchange*.[2]

To sum up our history, early financial intermediation or investing (outside of partnerships) seems to have primarily taken place through debt finance. Equity finance comes much later. This leads to several natural questions: (i) What were the hurdles these early investors had to clear? (ii) Why was debt such a popular means of doing so? In the sections 2 and 3 of this chapter we will explore some models to help us answer these two questions.

2. A SIMPLE MODEL OF LENDING

We start with a very simple model of lending to illustrate the roles of limited liability and information frictions We want to show how these factors can affect loan markets.

Assume that we have two projects. The first project pays off a relatively small amount r with high probability Π. We call this the *safe project*. The second project pays off a large amount R with low probability π. We call that the *risky project*. All projects require one unit of investment today, which the owners of the projects, whom we call the borrowers, must borrow from the owners of the funds, whom we call the lenders. Each project pays off tomorrow. The opportunity cost of funds to our lenders, by which we mean the return on their funds in the best alternative use, is taken to be 1 for simplicity. Let S be the total supply of funds available for lending by the lenders. Let D be the number of borrowers. We will assume that there are enough lenders and borrowers so that everyone behaves competitively. We will assume that the lenders are offering simple loan contracts with an interest rate I. Finally, we will assume that both the borrowers and lenders are risk neutral.

Case 1: Assume that there is unlimited liability and that $S > D$. In this case, the lenders will compete among themselves and bid the interest rate on loans to $I = 1$. Because there is unlimited liability, the lenders do not have to worry about being repaid. The safe borrower will borrow one unit if

$$\Pi * r > 1$$

2. See Wikipedia "English Coffee Houses in the 17th and 18th centuries."

and the risky project will also borrow one unit if

$$\pi * R > 1.$$

Note that loanable funds are the long side of the market here. If instead loanable funds were in short supply, then the borrowers would bid up the interest rate to its highest feasible level, or

$$I = max[\Pi * r, \pi * R]$$

and only the best project in terms of its expected payoff would be funded. Moreover, this best project would just break even.

Case 2: Assume now that there is limited liability, and that the safe project has a positive NPV (net present value), while the unsafe project does not, or

$$\Pi * r > 1 > \pi * R.$$

With limited liability, the payoffs to the borrowers and lenders are now quite different and both depend on the project type:

$$\text{Safe Borrower} = \Pi max\{r - I, 0\} \quad \text{Lender} = \Pi min\{r, I\}$$
$$\text{Risky Borrower} = \pi max\{R - I, 0\} \quad \text{Lender} = \pi min\{R, I\}$$

Note that both the borrower and lender payoffs are random and we have put down their expected payoffs since we are assuming that they are risk neutral. From our assumptions, the lender must lose when it lends to the unsafe project. At the same time, because of limited liability, and the fact that $R > r$, the risky lender is willing to borrow at a higher interest rate I than the safe borrower. However, since we are assuming that the lenders can tell the two types of projects apart, this really is not a problem. The lenders simply refuse to lend to risky borrower who have a negative NPV project and only lend to the safe borrowers, who have a positive NPV project. The interest rate is determined by which is the long or the short side of the market. So, $I = 1$ if there are more lenders than safe projects, and $I = r$ if the reverse is true.

Case 3: Now, assume that the lenders cannot distinguish between the two types of projects. This means that they will randomly end up making a loan to one or the other type of project. In this case, it seems natural to assume that the probability of making a loan to, say, the safe project depends on its share of the borrowing population. Let's denote this share by $Pr\{safe\}$. The payoff to the borrowers are unchanged relative to case 2, but now the expected payoff to the lender is given by

$$Pr\{safe\}\Pi \min \{r, I\} + Pr\{unsafe\}\pi \min \{R, I\},$$

assuming that $I \leq r$ so safe borrowers will still show up. If the reverse was true, then the safe borrowers would drop out and only unsafe borrowers would show. This means that their payoff would become $\pi \min \{R, I\}$ with probability 1. Since in this case, the lenders must lose, there are now two possibilities. Either the interest rate does not exceed r and the lenders can profitably lend at this rate or the lending market collapses. For the lenders to profitably lend, it must be the case that the share of safe borrowers is sufficiently high.

When there are more lenders than borrowers, the lenders will competitively bid down the interest rate I until they just break even, which means that their payoff is equal to the opportunity cost of their funds (which here is taken to be 1), so

$$Pr\{safe\}\Pi \min \{r, I\} + Pr\{unsafe\}\pi \min \{R, I\} = 1.$$

This is only possible if the share of safe borrowers is sufficiently high. If it is too low, then such an interest rate for $I \leq r$ will not exist and the lending market will collapse. (Remember, the interest rate cannot go above r or the borrowers with safe projects will drop out and all who will be left trying to borrow are those with unsafe projects—and the lenders lose money on unsafe borrowers.)

With the cap on the feasible interest rate of r, when the number of borrowers is greater than the number of lenders, there will be excess demand for loans at $I = r$. But the rate cannot go higher to clear the market. This means that borrowers will be rationed in the sense that some fraction of them will get loans and some, who want to borrow, will not. This is called *credit rationing* and is commonly thought to be an important feature of credit markets under certain conditions.

The fact that the composition of lenders changes in a manner that is adverse to the interests of the lenders as the interest rate on loans increases is called *adverse selection*. Many markets with incomplete information are thought to have this feature.

Remark 5. Normally, market clearing would have the demand for funds, $D(I)$, be decreasing in I and the supply of funds, $S(I)$, be increasing. The market clearing interest rate would have $D(I) = S(I)$. But now the composition of borrowers is declining in quality as I increases. This can mean that having a high I and getting only unsafe projects will *lower* the supply $S(I)$. So market clearing cannot be done in the normal way. Instead, if $D(r) > S(r)$, borrowers will be rationed: some borrowers will be rejected so that the lenders don't loan out more than $S(r)$.

Example 5. To help us see concretely how this all works, consider the following numerical example. The parameters of the example we are working with are given in Table 1. From the table, one can see that the probability of the safe project paying off is 0.8, and when it does so, the output realized is 1.4, while for the risky project the numbers are 0.4 and 2, respectively. This means that the overall expected return on investing in the safe project is 1.12 and in the risky project is 0.8. Since the lender's opportunity cost is taken to be 1, only the safe project is a positive NPV project.

Table 12.1. LENDING MARKET
EXAMPLE

Project	Probability	Output
Safe	0.8	1.4
Risky	0.4	2

In Figure 12.1 I have plotted the lender's expected payoff for different shares of the safe project under a variety of interest rates, which range from a gross interest rate of 1.1 to 1.4. When we look at the lender's expected payoff under

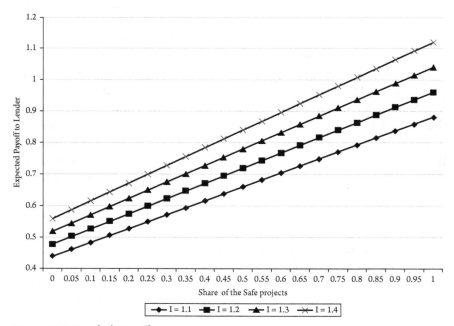

Figure 12.1 Lender's Payoffs.

the different interest rates, we see that the interest rate has to be above 1.2 for there to be a possible share of safe projects such that the lender's expected payoff is equal to the lender's opportunity cost of funds, which is 1. From the figure, one can see that the lender can just break even at an interest rate of 1.3 if the share of safe projects is 0.93, and at an interest rate of 1.4 if the share of safe projects is 0.78. One can see that if the share of safe projects is below 0.78, then the market for lending will collapse due to the impact of adverse selection.

2.1. Collateralized Lending

A lot of lending involves borrowers posting collateral that can be seized and sold to repay debts when the borrower fails to do so. Classic examples include mortgages for which the house or building being purchased is used to collateralize the loan. To see how collateral works, we want to extend the analysis in case 3 to include collateral. Assume that the borrowers have a unit of capital that they will be using in the project along with the loaned funds. Assume that the value of this collateral next period is C. In this case, they can pledge the collateral to back up their loan. This means that in the event the borrower cannot pay off the loan, the lender can seize and sell the collateral, thereby recovering $min\{C, I\}$. With this change, the payoff to the lender becomes:

$$Pr\{safe\}\left[\Pi min\{r, I\} + (1 - \Pi)min\{C, I\}\right] +$$
$$Pr\{unsafe\}\left[\pi min\{R, I\} + (1 - \pi)min\{C, I\}\right].$$

For any given interest rate, the presence of collateral increases the return to the lender. Hence, collateral can make lending possible in circumstances in which it would not otherwise be possible. Note that the presence of collateral also changes the payoff to the borrowers since now they must factor in that they will be giving up their collateral if they default on the loan. This can help to induce the risky borrower to drop out of the loanable funds market if C is big enough.

Assume now that the collateral has positive value only when the project is successful. In this case the lender's payoff collapses back to what it was without collateral. This is because when the collateral is valuable, the loan can be fully repaid from the proceeds of the project, and when it is not, the collateral is worthless. This extreme example illustrates why collateralized lending is not as simple a business as it might seem.

Changes in the perceived risk and payoff correlation of collateral can lead lenders to demand more and better collateral from borrowers when things become more suspect. This aspect played an important role in the collapse of several of the major investment banks at the height of the Great Recession. These investment banks were borrowing short-term from a variety of lenders, which meant that as soon as the lenders saw things going downhill they demanded higher rates on their loans and more collateral. This in turn helped to usher in the collapse of these banks. For example, J.P. Morgan, which was doing a lot of business with Lehman Bros. and acting as a middleman in many of Lehman's transactions, became nervous about the risks to which this was exposing Morgan. In September 2008, Morgan demanded $5 billion of additional collateral. This collateral call, along with a major outflow of hedge fund money led Lehman Bros. to finally declare bankruptcy on September 15.

3. AUDITING AND DEBT: TOWNSEND'S COSTLY STATE VERIFICATION MODEL

So why was debt finance one of the earliest and most common methods of arms-length finance? The need to monitor in order to induce repayment can explain why lenders use debt contracts. To illustrate this, we use Townsend's classic model of efficient monitoring and optimal financial contracting when it is costly to determine the true condition of the borrower's project.

3.1. Model

This is a two period model. In the first period contracting and investment are carried out, and in the second period, output is realized. Outcomes are random, and to capture this, we have the state of the world, s, which contains all of the relevant information about exogenous random events. There is an entrepreneur who has a project that costs 1 unit to set up in the first period and produces $Y(s)$ units of output next period when the state is s. Let $\Pr(s)$ denote the probability of state s for each s in the set of possible states S. We assume that the entrepreneur has no funds of his own. We also assume that the output of the project is *private information* to the entrepreneur (which means that only he can directly see it). However, the intermediary can find out the outcome of the project by monitoring at cost C. Otherwise, he must go with what the entrepreneur reports. We assume that the entrepreneur and the intermediary are risk neutral.

In the first period, the lender and the entrepreneur agree to a contract that specifies everything that is supposed to happen. The contract will say how much will be invested, when monitoring will occur, and how much is to be paid to the lender. In particular, the contract will say

- Invest 1 in period 1.
- In period 2, when state s is realized, the entrepreneur is supposed to report state s. We will call his report $\hat{s}$. (We could also have had him report $Y(s)$ and called his report $\hat{Y}$.)
- Given the report $\hat{s}$, the intermediary monitors or not according to the contract. We will capture this using the function m. Let $m(\hat{s}) = 1$ if the project is monitored and $= 0$ if not. Note that this is a function of the report because until monitoring occurs, that's all the intermediary knows.
- The contract will specify an amount X to be paid to the intermediary in state s of period 2. Since the only resources the entrepreneur has are the output of the project, we will require that $X(s) \leq Y(s)$ (i.e., no blood from a stone).
  - If the intermediary doesn't monitor, then he only knows $\hat{s}$, and so the payment has to be made according to the report only; i.e., $X(\hat{s})$. If he monitors then the payment can depend on both s and $\hat{s}$.
  - If the intermediary does monitor, then he can demand a payment that in principal depends upon both the report and the true state. However, to discourage lying, the intermediary will want to always take everything if $\hat{s} \neq s$. But given that the entrepreneur knows this, he will never want to lie when his report will lead to monitoring.

If the contract induces the entrepreneur to tell the truth, it is straightforward to specify expected profits and payoffs. The intermediary's expected profits are

$$\sum_{s} [X(s) - m(s)C] \Pr(s)$$

and the entrepreneur's expected profits are

$$\sum_{s} [Y(s) - X(s)] \Pr(s).$$

Since both are risk neutral, these are also their expected payoffs.

3.2. Incentive to Misreport Output Leads to Debt

With complete information, the payments of the entrepreneur to the intermediary can be conditioned on the state, that is, $X(s)$, subject only to the no blood from a stone upper bound. However, with private information, things are more complicated. To see this, let's take as given the monitoring schedule $m(s)$ and the payment schedule $X(s)$ as given and think about the reporting incentives of the entrepreneur.

- Consider the set of states in which monitoring does not occur: $S' \subseteq S$ where $m(s) = 0$ for all $s \in S'$. Next, consider the state s' in which $X(s)$ is smallest given that $m(s') = 0$; i.e., $s' : X(s') = \min_{s \in S'} X(s)$.
- Then, note that the entrepreneur should always report state s' if $X(s) > X(s')$ to reduce his payments. Since there is no monitoring for a report of s', his lie can never be detected. But this means that $X(s')$ puts a ceiling on the maximum recovery in any state because the entrepreneur can always safely report this state.
- The efficient contract should seek to make s' large enough for the lender to recover enough to break even on his investment while also seeking to make monitoring costs as low as possible. This leads to the following set of observations about the efficient contract:
  (1) The intermediary should recover his costs most efficiently by taking everything when he monitors. Hence, if $m(s) = 1$, then $X(s) = Y(s)$.
  (2) There is no point in monitoring at s_1 and s_3 but not at s_2 where $Y(s_1) < Y(s_2) < Y(s_3)$. The reason is that the most that can be asked of the entrepreneur in states s_1 and s_3 is $Y(s_1)$ irrespective of whether monitoring takes place in s_3. So monitoring at s_3 is purely a waste. This implies that monitoring will follow a cut-off rule: monitor for all $Y(s) \leq \bar{Y}$, and don't monitor for all $Y(s) > \bar{Y}$.
  (3) To make this monitoring cut-off as low as possible, the efficient contract should also take as much output from the project as possible when the monitor doesn't monitor. This implies that $X(s) = \bar{Y}$ for all $s : Y(s) > \bar{Y}$ and hence $m(s) = 0$.

Proposition 3. *The efficient contract looks like debt with*

$$X(s) = Y(s) \text{ and } m(s) = 1 \text{ for all } s : Y(s) < \bar{Y}$$
$$X(s) = \bar{Y} \text{ and } m(s) = 0 \text{ otherwise.}$$

This simple model implies that a debt-like contract is an efficient means of reducing costs while inducing the appropriate payments.

4. THE RISE OF FINANCIAL INTERMEDIARIES

Finance could have stayed very decentralized, with individual investors buying up debt or IOU claims, but even fairly early on, larger more organized entities arose. Why? Here we provide a simple model that gives us one answer to this question.

Monitoring is a key feature commonly associated with financial intermediaries. This monitoring occurs for a variety of reasons:

(1) auditing borrowers who fail to repay,
(2) screening projects to relax adverse selection, or
(3) preventing opportunistic behavior to relax moral hazard.

Intermediaries audit borrowers who fail to repay both to find out how much repayment they can extract from them, and to make sure that they're not simply trying to avoid repayment. They also screen potential borrowers to try to determine who is and is not a good risk. They want to make loans to or invest in those individuals or projects which have a high enough return to the intermediary. Finally, they want to monitor individuals and projects in which they have invested to make sure that they are behaving in a proper manner as required under the contract both parties agreed to.

Why are financial intermediaries commonly used for this monitoring role? There are a couple of natural reasons:

(1) scale economies in monitoring and
(2) sole investor and free riding

The first reason is scale economies: Intermediaries can monitor at low cost because they have invested in people and equipment that specialize in this function. They do this because they are monitoring on a mass scale. So, for example, intermediaries may find it useful to have full-time accountants who specialize in looking for fraud and abuse in the projects they are monitoring. They may also have fancy computer systems that allow them to go through the projects' books quickly and easily. The second reason is that intermediaries can have sufficient funds to set themselves up as the sole investor in a project and thereby avoid having other people free ride on their monitoring. We talk about this and a number of other things in what follows.

4.1. Project Evaluation, Scale Economies, and Free Riding

Assume again, as in the first model, that there are a large number of potential investors who each have 1 unit to invest. Assume that there are a lot of entrepreneurs who have one of two kinds of projects:

- safe projects, which return r with probability Π where $\Pi r > 1$
- unsafe projects, which return $R > r$ with probability $\pi < \Pi$ where $\pi R < 1$

All of these projects require an investment of X, where $X > 3$. An investor can determine if a project is safe or unsafe by paying a cost C. Let I denote the gross interest rate being charged to the entrepreneurs.

With direct investing, the payoff to investing at interest rate I is

$$\Pi \min (I, r) [1 - C] \text{ if cost is paid and project is safe,}$$

and

$$\Pi \min (I, r) \Pr \{\text{safe}\} + \pi \min (I, R) \Pr \{\text{unsafe}\} \text{ if the cost is not paid.}$$

So either I pay the screening cost or take on the risk of an unsafe project where I lose money.

Even if the project is profitable

$$X\Pi \min (I, r) - C > 0,$$

having each investor pay the screening cost may lead it not to be

$$\Pi \min (I, r) [1 - C] < 0.$$

Free riding may stop investment even when direct investing is profitable. Note that even if

$$\Pi \min (I, r) [1 - C] > 0,$$

if I see you invest with Harry and know that you would only do so if you paid C and found his project to be safe, then I can get return

$$\Pi \min (I, r)$$

by lending to Harry. But then everyone should seek to avoid this cost.

Intermediaries can fix this free riding problem. To do so, they collect enough funds from investors to fully fund the project while paying the monitoring cost. Of course, one may need to monitor the bank, but nothing comes for free.

Financial intermediaries produce information by evaluating different potential projects and entrepreneurs and selecting the better ones to finance. One of the key problems here is that once information has been produced, transferring it incurs a very low cost.

13

More on Banks and Banking

1. BANKING IN THE U.S.

Originally, a bank in the U.S. was chartered or created by an act of a state legislature. This changed in 1837, when states began to change the rules to allow freer entry. This change ushered in the "Free Banking Era," which ran from 1837 until 1863. During this period, all banking was done by state-chartered banks. These banks operated with somewhat mixed success, with many of them proving to be unstable.

In response, there was an attempt to more tightly control banking. In 1863, the National Banking Act allowed banks to be chartered at the national level. The act restricted banks from purchasing ownership claims (i.e., stocks) on non-financial firms. The Federal Reserve Act of 1913 created the modern Federal Reserve System with its system of regional federal reserve banks. All nationally chartered banks were required to join the Federal Reserve System.

The Great Depression led to another big transformation in the banking sector. Prior to the Great Depression, banks were small and almost always had only one branch. They generally specialized in local mortgage and commercial lending. Mortgages were short term, say 5 years, and households were typically required to make large down payments. Moreover, a given bank's mortgage contracts could be quite different from those of other banks. Finally, both banks and securities markets in general were much less tightly regulated than they are today.

Table 13.1. NUMBER OF BANK SUSPENSIONS PER YEAR

1921	1922	1923	1924	1925	1926	1927	1928
505	366	646	775	618	976	663	498
1929	1930	1931	1932	1933	1934	1935	1936
659	1,350	2,293	1453	4,000	57	34	44

Bank suspensions—when a bank closed its doors in order to try to satisfy its creditors in an orderly manner—had been a regular event. However, many of these banks were quite small. The stock market crash, which started in October 1929, led to a slew of deposit withdrawals, and the rate of suspensions jumped dramatically, as one can see in Table 13.1. During the early years of the Depression, suspensions rose to an unprecedented level, peaking in the first 3 months of 1933 when 4000 banks went into suspension.[1]

At the height of the Great Depression, President Roosevelt and Congress passed the Emergency Banking Relief Act on March 9, 1933. The act imposed a bank holiday during which time the Treasury was to audit every bank and certify it sound before it could reopen. Three-quarters of the nationally chartered banks were able to reopen within three days. In June, the Banking Act of 1933 set up the Federal Deposit Insurance Corporation (FDIC) to insure ordinary deposits and, at the same time gave the FDIC regulatory power over the state-chartered banks, while the Fed was to regulate the nationally chartered banks.

In 1938, the Federal National Mortgage Association (FNMA), or Fannie Mae, was created to make a secondary market in mortgages and to securitize them. To do this, it bought up mortgages issued by banks and then sold them in the secondary market with a guarantee, often back to the same banks. Since it was known that banks would like to dump their bad mortgages, Fannie Mae would only accept prime mortgages. "Prime" has come to mean a high credit (FICO) score and a good loan-to-value ratio. In 1970, Fannie Mae was split in two, with a new entity, the Federal Home Loan Mortgage Company, or Freddie Mac, being created so as to promote competition and efficiency in the securitization of mortgages.

The Roosevelt administration also passed the Glass-Steagall Act, which separated commercial banks from investment banks. The administration did this because investment banks were thought to involve a more risky aspect of financial activities. In 1999, the main provision of the Glass-Steagall Act was repealed by the Gramm-Leach-Bliley Act, which removed the separation between investment and commercial banks.

---

1. The suspension data are from the Federal Reserve Bulletin.

2. DIAMOND AND DYBVIG'S MODEL

Diamond-Dybvig is a three-period model. There is a technology that converts the final good today at $t = 0$ into

- 1 unit of the final good tomorrow at $t = 1$,
- $R > 1$ units of the final good in two periods at $t = 2$.

This project is illiquid in that early termination involves a loss, since output does not grow at a constant rate.

We assume that there are a lot of investors, and π of these investors will end up wanting to consume only in $t = 1$ and the remainder will only want to consume in either period. Each investor has one unit of the final good in period $t = 0$. The $t = 1$ consumers are hit with a liquidity shock and need cash.

2.1. Direct Investing

Each investor will invest his one unit in the project. He will liquidate the project if he is hit with the liquidity shock. If not, he will run it to completion. His payoff is

$$\pi u(1) + (1 - \pi)u(R),$$

which is suboptimal (as we will see next). The reason is that he has to fully absorb the consequences of a liquidity shock directly.

2.2. First Best

The ex-ante payoff is given by

$$\pi u(c_1) + (1 - \pi)u(c_2)$$

subject to

$$\pi c_1 + (1 - \pi)c_2/R = 1.$$

So, we want to choose c_1 and c_2 to maximize this payoff.

The optimal consumption program has

$$u'(c_1) = \lambda,$$
$$u'(c_2) = \lambda/R.$$

So long as

$$u'(1) > u'(R)R,$$

this program involves providing insurance to the liquidity shock investors (true if risk aversion is greater than 1).

2.3. Financial Intermediation

Now assume that there is a financial intermediary who promises

- a return of $c_1 > 1$ if the investor withdraws his funds in the first period
- and $c_2 < R$ in the second period.

So long as the intermediary breaks even, or $\pi c_1 + (1 - \pi)c_2/R = 1$, then we can implement this under symmetric information. The intermediary gets to see whether the investor has been hit by the shock.

2.4. Private Information

Assume that only the investor gets to see whether he is being hit by the liquidity shock. Now the intermediary has to go by the investor's report. The investor needs to have the right incentives to withdraw his funds only if he is hit by a liquidity shock, or $c_2 > c_1$. In the optimal program $u'(c_1) = u'(c_2)R$, which implies that $c_2 > c_1$. So this condition can be satisfied.

2.4.1. EXCESS WITHDRAWALS AND INSOLVENCY

Because $c_1 > 1$, if everyone asked to have their funds, promises could not be kept. We can deal with this by asking all investors if they want to withdraw, and then give them the smaller of c_1 and an amount that ensures that c_2' was bigger than c_2. This is given by

$$\min\left[c_1, \frac{R}{[1 - \pi' + R\pi']}\right],$$

where π' is the fraction who ask for their money. Now late withdrawers are protected since

$$[1 - \pi'x]R = x(1 - \pi') \Rightarrow x = \frac{R}{[1 - \pi' + R\pi']}.$$

Everyone who withdraws in the first period gets the same amount. Everyone who withdraws in the second period gets weakly more than first period withdrawers.

2.4.2. SEQUENTIAL SERVICE AND SUSPENSIONS

If the intermediary must deal with its withdrawers sequentially, then our proposal to deal with excess withdrawals is not feasible. Investors at the front of the line get c_1 and later investors may get less. Now, $t = 2$ withdrawers could get nothing unless $t = 1$ payments are decreased for some or even suspended, in which case they are forced to get their money in period $t = 2$. Suspensions may be efficient if $t = 1$ withdrawers can trade claims to $t = 2$ withdrawals among themselves. And suspensions occur at π. But if the lack of $t = 1$ output means that c_1 is worth more than the remaining claims, then those people who managed to withdraw are better off (even if claims are tradable).

2.4.3. GAME THEORY

The decision problem of an investor is now *strategic*—the investors must forecast the decisions of others in deciding what to do. If he thinks that the fraction π' of people are going to choose to withdraw in the first period, then

if $c_1 > [(1 - \pi' c_1)R]/(1 - \pi')$ he is better off withdrawing, and

if $c_1 < [(1 - \pi' c_1)R]/(1 - \pi')$ he is better off not withdrawing.

So, the investor's optimal action depends crucially on his forecast of the actions of others. Moreover, the higher his forecast of the fraction of people who withdraw, the bigger are his gains from withdrawing. This is sometimes referred to as a *strategic complementarity* and is what leads to two possible equilibrium outcomes: Either the fraction of people who only want to consume in period 1, π, withdraws, or everyone tries to withdraw. The second outcome is called the *run equilibrium* because it is thought to resemble a bank run.

2.5. Insolvency Shocks, Illiquidity Shocks, and Pure Runs

If both R and π are stochastic two sorts of fundamentals-based bank-run outcomes are possible, as well as non-fundamentals based runs. This stems from the fact that both c_1 and c_2 have to be chosen before R and π, so it is not possible to choose things as nicely as before. Now it is possible to run out of funds (without having a run) in period 1 if R is low or π is high. We can apply the following labels to these crises:

1. Insolvency Runs: If in period $t = 1$ investors find out that $(1 - \pi c_1) \times R < c_1$ then investors will want to withdraw their funds in $t = 1$.
2. Liquidity Runs: If π turns out to be large, then lots of people will want to withdraw their funds. If the bank plans on suspending at some cut-off $\bar{\pi} < \pi$, then those at the end of the line will be stuck with less valuable claims to funds at $t = 2$.
3. Sunspot Runs: If suspensions only occur once $(1 - \pi)R < 1$, then everyone will want to run if they think everyone else will.

As a result of this greater uncertainty, the costs of attempting to give investors certainty with respect to their returns (conditional on period 1 or 2 withdrawals) and at the same time insuring them against a liquidity shock have gotten higher.

2.6. Good and Bad

We have a nice model of a financial intermediary:

- It features security mismatch—the bank's assets are illiquid and its liabilities are liquid.
- It rationalizes various types of runs, deposit insurance and lender of last resort functions.

Unfortunately, there is an arbitrage possibility that can undo everything. Here's how it works. I should invest directly in the project:

- If I turn out to have a liquidity shock:
  - Find someone who didn't and who deposited their funds.
  - Have them withdraw their funds. Now we have c_1 at $t = 1$ and R at $t = 2$ to split between us. Give them R and I get c_1
- If I don't have a shock, then I just consume R at $t = 2$.

My expected payoff is $\pi c_1 + (1 - \pi)R$, which is higher than $\pi c_1 + (1 - \pi)c_2$ since $c_2 < R$. However, note that the other individual didn't do better. We can fix that with a bit more work.

This arbitrage can also be effective for a group. Get a large group of people together. Then the fraction π of them will have a liquidity shock and $1 - \pi$ will not. So, randomly choose a fraction π of them to invest with the intermediary and withdraw their funds at $t = 1$, while the rest invest directly in the project and get R in period $t = 2$. The group then gives the π individuals who had a liquidity shock c_1 in period $t = 1$ and the rest consume R in period $t = 2$. Now everyone earns expected payoff $\pi c_1 + (1 - \pi)R$.

How is it possible to make everyone better off? It happens because the inter-mediary suffers losses on this deal. With probability 1 everyone in the group who invested with the intermediary withdrew c_1 in period $t = 1$. But there was only 1 unit of output available for each person, so the intermediary lost $c_1 - 1$ on each member of this group.

2.7. Bank Runs with Maturity Transformation

There are two key aspects of the Diamond-Dybvig model. First, there is the bank's balance sheet. On one side, the bank had some long-run assets that were hard to liquidate in the short run, and on the liability side, it had short-run deposits that could be called in at any time. This contrast in maturity is one of the essential features we see in commercial banks, and it goes to the heart of their fragility.

The second key aspect is the deposit contract, which promises to pay off its customers as they show up, rather than accumulating their claims and paying everyone off as best it can at the end of the period. Here we discuss how to construct a model of banking with these two aspects and how these two aspects generate the possibility of a bank run in our model.

Assume that we have people who live for three periods. In each period t a new group is born. These people like consumption in periods 2 and 3 of their lives. They have preferences given by

$$\theta u(c_2) + u(c_3).$$

where θ is a preference shock. In normal times it takes on a value of 1, but in abnormal times it takes on a higher value, say, 2. These consumers are going to want to choose their consumptions so that

$$\theta u'(c_2) = u'(c_3).$$

This means that they will want to consume the same amount in the second and third periods of their lives if $\theta = 1$, and more in the second period than in the third if $\theta = 2$. The household's budget constraint is given by

$$(I - c_2)I = c_3$$

where I is the return per period that households earn on their bank deposits, and households are assumed to have one unit to invest.

The bank has two types of investments. The first is a short-run investment that will return 1 unit the next period for every unit invested. The other is a less liquid investment. It will return $R > 1$ units in two periods, or $r < 1$ after one period.

If withdrawals were constant each period, then the bank could adopt a policy of just investing in the high-return illiquid asset. Each period it would receive a constant inflow of deposits from young households in the first period of their lives, and each period it would invest that amount in the illiquid asset. At the same time, the bank could cover withdrawals from investments that it made two periods ago. The bank's net flow earnings would be given by

$$R - c_2 - c_3$$

which reflects the fact that each period the bank has 1 unit of investment maturing that pays R, while the period 2 households withdraw c_2 and the period 3 households withdraw c_3. At the same time, the bank is taking in 1 unit of deposits from the period 1 new households, but this increases the bank's liabilities by 1, so that nets to zero.

So long as I is not too large, the bank will have a positive net flow each period. Even if the bank gets a surprise increase in the amount of withdrawals because more households received a high θ than expected, the bank would still be able to meet this demand either by having a small net worth reserve that it invested in the liquid asset, or by selling some of its illiquid investments to another bank that had lower than expected withdrawals.

This will work fine unless there is an aggregate shock in which many households at many banks received high θ levels. This could lead to a crisis in which banks did not have enough liquid assets to cover the higher withdrawals and together they ended up flooding the market with the illiquid asset, driving its price down so far that the banks could no longer honor their outstanding claims.

Even without a real shock coming through θ, we could generate a bank-run type crisis here if every period 2 household suddenly thought that its next period claims would not be honored. In this case, all the period 2 households should withdraw everything in now, not just those that had the high θ realization.

Thus the logic of Diamond and Dybvig's bank-run type of outcome seems to carry over quite generally to any institution in which there was a maturity mismatch and in which a sudden need to pay off all claimants could not be honored within the system as a whole.

2.8. Maturity Transformation and Interest Rates

One other aspect of maturity transformation is that long-run claims are very sensitive to interest rate changes. This is because payments t periods away are being valued at Q_t/R^t, where R is the discount rate and Q is the payment. Small increases in R lead to big decreases in the valuation of this payment. At the same time, short-run liabilities are due next period, so their value looks like L/R today, and hence they are not as sensitive.

Mortgages are one major example of a standard bank asset with this sensitivity. They often run for 30 years and have a fixed stream of payments associated with them. Adjustable-rate mortgages (ARMs) are mortgages that have a payment that is adjusted in response to prevailing interest rates. These types of mortgages effectively transfer interest rate risk back onto the household.

Consider the following scenario, which lays out how an increase in interest rates can affect a bank's balance sheet in a negative way:

(1) A bank borrows 100 for one period at 4% and uses it to buy mortgages issued at 6%. So roughly speaking

$$\frac{X}{.06} = 100.$$

It is counting on being able to roll over its loan. Assume that immediately after that, interest rates rise, with the borrowing rate going to 6%.

(2) In the second period, it receives $X = .06 * 100$, and pays out $1.04 * 100$. So, it needs to borrow 98. Assume that when it goes to do so, interest rates on that loan are 8%.

(3) So, this period it owes $1.08 * 98 = 105.8$. The mortgages again pay off $.06 * 100$. So it needs to borrow 99.2.

(4) In this period, it owes $99.2 * 1.08 = 107.1$, which means that once it receives the mortgage payment means it has to borrow 101.1. Assume that the borrowing rate has come back down to 6% and is expected to stay there.

(5) Now it owes $101.1 * 1.06 = 107.6$, which means that, once it receives the mortgage payment, it has to borrow 101.6. From now on the problem will continue to get worse. The bank is insolvent if the bank's capital was small relative to this loan.

Of course, lenders will anticipate the eventual collapse of this scheme and refuse to lend at some point. This cessation will take the form of a bank run if there is some sort of sequential service aspect to the loan contract, as in demand deposits. If instead it is borrowing using bonds, a rollover crisis will occur.

2.9. Bank Runs in History: The Great Depression

The Great Depression began in the U.S. with the downturn in industrial production starting in July 1929, followed by the stock market crash beginning in

October. Both real activity and the nominal price level declined sharply, reaching their trough in 1933. By 1930, the banking system as a whole was under great stress, and the first wave of banking failures hit. The failing banks were primarily small banks in agricultural areas due in large part to the steep decline in farm prices.

> Mobs of shouting depositors shouldered up to tellers' windows to withdraw their savings. The banks, in turn, scrambled to preserve their liquidity in the face of these accelerating withdrawals by calling in loans and selling assets. As the beleaguered banks desperately sought cash by throwing their bond and real estate portfolios onto the market—a market already depressed by the Crash of 1929—they further drove down the value of assets in otherwise sound institutions, putting the entire banking system at peril.[2]

There was a second, much bigger wave of banking panics in 1933. This led Roosevelt to institute a bank holiday between March 9 and March 12. After this, only banks approved by the Federal Reserve could reopen and they did so with deposit insurance. After this, the waves of bank closings ceased.

2.10. Lender of Last Resort

Both our model and the brief history of banking during the Great Depression lead naturally to a question: What can the government do to prevent these crises? Several actions are commonly suggested: deposit insurance and lender of last resort. How might this work in our simple model?

If the government pledges to step in and buy up the $t = 1$ claims at a price of c_1, then no one will want to run since they are insured. What's nice about this policy is that it can remove the sunspot run equilibrium as an outcome. However, in the case of insolvency (R low) or liquidity (π high), the value of the claims the government ends up buying may be worth less than c_1. So there can be losses. As a result, the government needs to have deep pockets. It's also the case that we are simply moving these losses from the private sector to the government, and ultimately the taxpayers will have to pay for them.

2.11. Incentive Effects of Deposit Insurance

Deposit insurance is frequently cited as one way to prevent runs. However, it reduces and in many cases eliminates depositors' need to care about how much

2. David M. Kennedy, *The American People in the Great Depression: Freedom from Fear, Part One.* Oxford University Press, 2003, p. 66.

risk their bank is taking on. As a result, banks will not face standard risk pricing, and this can lead to stronger incentives to engage in risky activity.

Example 6. The gross interest rate is taken to be 1, and the bank can invest in projects that pay out after one period. Each project requires a loan of $100 today.

- Loan 1 yields $105 for sure tomorrow so its net return is $5.
- Loan 2 yields 200 with probability 1/4 and 0 with probability 3/4. So, its expected return is .25 * 200 − 100 = −50.

If the bank has deposit insurance, then it will be charged 1 on its deposits. And the expected payoff to the bank from Loan 2 is .25 * (200 − 100) = 25. The difference is coming from the expected payment from deposit insurance of .75 * 100 = 75.

The bank likes Loan 2 and society likes Loan 1. Note that the problem isn't that stockholders face no losses; they get wiped out 3/4 of the time. The problem is that the bondholders—here, the depositors—face no losses and so the price of risk is wrong.

The incentive problem coming from deposit insurance has been well understood for a long time. One way to try to get around this problem is to impose capital requirements on banks. This reduces the bank's incentive to engage in risk-taking. To understand how this works, we return to our example.

Example 7. Assume that everything is as before, except that now the bank has to fund $30 of the loan from its (or rather the stockholders') money. Now, Loan 2 yields .25 * (200 − 100) − .75 * 30 = 2.5. Now Loan 1 is preferred to Loan 2.

This solution to the incentive problem is limited in the sense that banks can still get around capital requirements by engaging in even more risky activity. The increasing proliferation of sophisticated financial instruments means that it is fairly easy to come up with a way to take on as much risk as you want. To see this, we return once again to our example.

Example 8. Now, augment our example by adding an even more risky loan.

- Loan 3 yields 325 with probability 0.15 and 0 with probability 0.85.

Even with our capital requirement, the bank nets $0.15 * (325 - 100) - 0.85 * 30 = 8.25$. Note that this is occurring despite the fact that Loan 3 has a lower overall expected return than does Loan 2.

3. SAVINGS AND LOAN ASSOCIATIONS AND THE CRISIS OF THE 1980S

Savings and loan associations (sometimes called *thrifts*) are sort of junior banks. They take in deposits and use them to finance mortgage lending. The first S&Ls arose in the 1800s. Because they concentrate on short-term borrowing and long-term lending, S&Ls are very sensitive to interest rate fluctuations. Even a small increase in the interest rate that they have to pay on their deposits can make them insolvent because the loans on the asset side of their balance sheet were typically fixed-rate 30-year mortgages. As a result, the value of their mortgage assets would fall with a rise in the interest rate due to high discounting of the future receipts promised in these contracts. At the same time, the interest costs on their deposits would rise.

This unpleasant potential for disaster came into its own during the late 1970s, when the sharp rise in inflation and interest rates sent many S&Ls' balance sheets into the red. These problems were made even worse by the development of NOW (negotiable order of withdrawal) accounts, which circumvented the law that prohibited paying interest on demand deposits, and brokered deposits which moved large deposits from bank to bank seeking the highest rate of return.[3]

When inflation and interest rates declined in the early 1980s, many S&Ls started to recover, but many were also still insolvent. Since the deposits in S&Ls were insured, this insolvency was a problem for the government as well. In 1983, the cost of paying off the insured depositors at insolvent S&Ls was estimated at $25 billion. However, the FSLIC (Federal Savings and Loan Insurance Corporation), which was the insurance fund that was suppose to handle this, had only $6 billion in assets.

The decision was made to allow these insolvent thrifts to continue operating. Congress sought to aid things by passing legislation that allowed them to seek higher yields. In 1980, thrifts were allowed to make consumer and commercial loans and to issue transaction (read credit card) accounts. In 1981, thrifts were

---

3. Regulation Q, which was part of the Banking Act of 1933, essentially barred paying interest on deposit accounts. This was done to make the banking system more robust since it limited competition for deposits.

allowed to sell their mortgages and use the cash to generate better returns. However, the slowing of the "housing boom" in the early 1980s sent them back into serious trouble. In the end, the S&Ls had to be bailed out by the U.S. government at a cost that is estimated to be about $160.1 billion, much more than the initial estimate before the problem had been allowed to fester.

To understand why the regulators showed such forbearance and how the problems of the S&Ls were allowed to get so bad, it is helpful to review the history of the Lincoln Savings and Loan Association and the so-called Keating Five. The "Five" consisted of 5 U.S. senators who would be accused of improperly interfering in the Federal Home Loan Bank Board's (FHLBB) oversight and regulation of Lincoln, which was run by Charles Keating. The FHLB backed off on taking major action against Lincoln in response to pressure from the 5 senators. The S&L collapsed after its very speculative investments went bad, which cost the taxpayers over $3 billion. Among the Keating 5 were some very well-known senators, both Democrats and Republicans, including Alan Cranston (D), John Glenn (D), and John McCain (R).

The story of the Keating Five makes clear why financial sector regulation and oversight is such a tricky business. There is a tremendous concentration of liquid or fairly liquid funds in these institutions. These funds can be used conservatively or speculatively. The people controlling these funds do not want to be interfered with and they have a lot of money to offer people in power who can help them get what they want.

4. MORE RECENT TRENDS IN BANKING

In 1975, there were over 14,000 banks in the U.S.. By 2009 there were fewer than 7,000. This period saw a tremendous consolidation of the banking sector. Consistent with this, the size of the largest banks has grown dramatically. As a result, the top 10 banks accounted for 45% of all deposits in 2009 (Table 13.2).

We can also use the Federal Reserve's Flow of Funds accounts to see what the overall balance sheet of the banking sector looked like at this point in time.

Table 13.2. SHARE OF DEPOSITS IN TOP BANKS 2009

Bank of America	12.4%
JP Morgan Chase	9.3%
Wachovia Bank	6.0%
Wells Fargo Bank	4.9%
Citibank	4.0%

The striking aspect of the asset side of their balance sheet is how big agency and GSE-backed (government-sponsored enterprise) assets are. These assets are primarily MBS (mortgage-backed securities) issued by Fannie Mae and Freddie Mac. Overall the banks' exposure to mortgages is large.

On the liability side of banks' balance sheets the big surprise is how small checkable deposits are. Another is how little long-term claims (i.e., corporate bonds) there are.

The data is from table 11 of the Flow of Funds Accounts from the Federal Reserve. This data is available at https://www.federalreserve.gov/releases/z1/current/default.htm.

In addition to these balance sheet items, there are now also a lot more off-balance sheet items that reflect fee-generating activities. By their nature, they affect banks' bottom line, but not their balance sheets. These items include:

(1) Standby letters of credit, which are promises to lend issuers of commercial paper enough to cover a bond when it comes due. The bank absorbs the issuers' credit risk for a fee, even though it did not actually issue the loan.

(2) Loan commitments, which are promises to lend up to a certain amount over a specified time period. This earns the bank an upfront fee and a non-usage fee on the unused portion of the loan.

(3) Loan sales, which are typically sold with recourse so that the risks are transferred to the buyer..

(4) Trading activities, which include fees earned from trading in futures, options, and interest-swap markets. Returns from the bank's own investment activities also show up here.

Many of these off-balance-sheet items have large risks, and therefore they can have a big impact on the profits or losses the banks end up realizing.

Table 13.3. U.S. Chartered Commercial Banks Balance Sheet in 2005 ($ billions)

Assets		Liabilities	
Financial Assets	6903.9	Checkable Deposits	588.0
Vault Cash and Reserves	65.5	Small Time and Savings Dep.	3494.3
Treasury Securities	64.2	Large Time Dep.	837.7
Agency and GSE-backed Sec.	992.7	Fed. Funds and Security Repos.	898.7
Mortgage Sec.	731.3	Corporate Bonds	121.7
Municipal Sec.	157.2		
Corp and For. Bonds	411.6		
Mortgages	2902.1		
Consumer Credit	707.0		

Investment banks have also changed a lot over this period. These banks are primarily engaged in the following activities:

(1) providing advice on new security issues
(2) underwriting new security issues, guaranteeing a minimum price for a fee, 6-8% for an IPO and 2-4% for secondary offerings (sales by a firm that has sold securities before)
(3) advising on mergers and acquisitions
(4) financial engineering and risk management - developing new securities and investment strategies
(5) research
(6) proprietary trading

Prior to the 1990s, most investment banks were partnerships that concentrated on traditional banking activities and did little proprietary trading. The banks largely financed themselves from partner equity. During the 1990s and 2000s, most of these banks converted to public corporations. They became much more involved in proprietary trading financed by extensive short-term borrowing, which led to large increases in their leverage ratios. Leverage ratios were over 30 at Morgan Stanley and Bear Stearns in 2007, and over 25 at Merrill Lynch and Lehman Brothers. In contrast, Citibank had a 20 leverage ratio and the other big banks were around 10-12.

The investment banks financed these high leverage ratios using commercial paper and repurchase agreements. Some of this commercial paper was explicitly backed by financial assets.[4]

Repurchase agreements are collateralized loans where the borrower hands over a security to the lender and agrees to a repurchase price as part of the loan. If the lender on a repo thinks the borrower will default, then the lender worries that they will be left with just the security and hence are exposed the risk that the security will lose value and the costs of selling it. Repos are typically overnight or short term. The investment banks were borrowing short in order to purchase things like mortgage-backed securities (MBS), which were long-term assets that traded in illiquid markets.

The change in the ownership structure of investment banks may have changed their incentives. Before the 1990s investment banks were primarily self-financed partnerships that would be exposed to any risk they took on. After restructuring,

---

4. In January 2007, there was $2 trillion in commercial paper outstanding. Of this, more than $700 billion was issued by financial corporations, with more than $500 billion coming from domestic financial corporations (Board of Governors of the Federal Reserve System (US), Commercial Paper Outstanding).

they were transformed into heavily debt financed corporations whose owners bore only a small part of the risk. With this change, it seems like moral hazard may have become much more of a problem, especially for poorly controlled traders.

5. THE DEMAND FOR SAFE ASSETS AND SECURITIZATION

Much of the growth in financial transactions has come in the form of collateralized activities. In addition, many institutions, such as insurance companies, pension funds, banks, and so forth, are either legally restricted or choose to limit their risk exposure. This wish to limit risk creates a large demand for low-risk securities and a limited demand for high-risk securities. This in turn lead to the explosion in the issuance of asset-securities, the most well known of which were MBS. In addition, it has generated a huge growth in the demand for safe assets that can be used as collateral.

Figure 13.1 shows how these securities first began to be issued in significant quantities during the latter half of the 1980s. It also shows how their issuance exploded in the 2000s, before collapsing during the financial crisis associated with the Great Recession.

The means by which a pool of moderately risky mortgages were transformed into low risk securities was through some clever financial alchemy called *tranching*: Multiple securities are issued on the same underlying pool of assets, where each security is differentiated in terms of its seniority. The most senior security is paid first, and the most junior security is paid last. The senior tranches are safer, while the junior tranches are more risky. In this way a given pool of mortgages can generate different securities with different levels of risk. Often, the senior tranche was AAA or AA rated, which meant that it was rated above investment grade and could be held by highly regulated institutions. However, the junior tranches would often be rated below investment grade and would be held by those seeking higher expected returns.

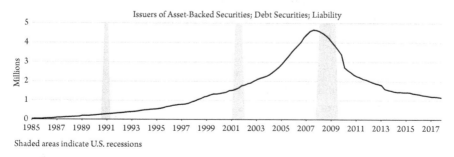

Figure 13.1 Asset-Backed Securities

SOURCE: FData Source: Board of Governors of the Federal Reserve System (U.S.).

To understand how this works, assume that we have a pool of mortgages. We want to take the payments coming from this pool and create two assets: a safe asset and an unsafe asset. At the same time, we would like to make the value of the safe asset as large as possible by assigning it the bulk of the value of the mortgage payments. To do this, we assign the first $W\%$ of the payments to the safe security and the remainder to the unsafe one. Note that if less than the amount assigned to the safe security is realized, then the unsafe security pays out nothing. In this way, we are trying to assign almost all of the risk in the underlying pool of mortgages to the unsafe security. In designing this security, we are first trying to take advantage of the diversification gains from having a pool of mortgages. This allows us to predict the fraction of the mortgages that will go bankrupt with a high degree of accuracy. We then use the tranching of the payments for to the two securities to do the rest of the job.

Consider the following simple example to see how this is supposed to work and what can potentially go wrong. Assume that we have a pool of 30-year fixed-rate mortgages with an interest rate of 5%. Assume that there is a 0.5% chance of any single mortgage going bankrupt in any given year. Then, the probability that an individual mortgage has not gone bankrupt over the 30-year span is given by $(1-\pi)^{30}$.

If the default realizations of the households are independent of each other, then the number of households that will not be in default is distributed according to a binomial distribution. We can exploit this to get a handle on the frequency distribution of defaults. In particular, if the outcomes are 0 and 1, and the probability of a one is Π, then the probability that out of N draws the number of 1's is less than Z is given by the cumulative distribution of the binomial.

Assume that our pool of mortgages has 10,000 mortgages. A simple way to think about the lack of independence is to assume that some of these outcomes are perfectly correlated: if mortgage a defaults then mortgage b does as well because, say, it is in the same location. This reduces the number of independent draws and hence the gains from risk diversification. We can visualize the impact of the reduction in the number of independent draws by looking at Figure 13.2. Using the information in this figure, we can say with 95% confidence that the share of defaults will be less than

- 14% with 10,000 independent draws,
- 16% with 1000 independent draws, and
- 20% with 100 independent draws,

Given these cutoffs, the likelihood of a loss of more than 1% or 2% for a safe security is quite small, and the vast majority of the payments are going to it. So

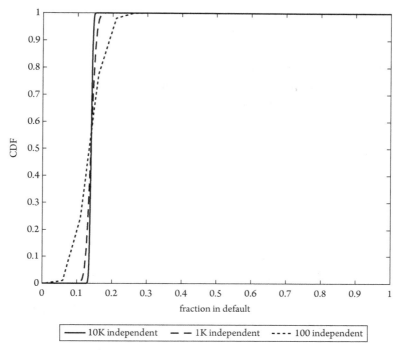

Figure 13.2 Tranching Experiments.

its share of the value will be quite large. But we can also see that for this to work, the independence assumption is critical.

An alternative to the lack of independence model is the extreme events model. In this statistical model, the 10,000 mortgages are drawn from the independent binomial model with probability ρ, and from a very different model—say, one with a very high degree of correlation with probability $1 - \rho$. If ρ is close to 1, then the draws from the second distribution are very rare events, and hence even fairly long time-series tell us very little about them. This kind of outcome is often called a "black swan" event: something rare, but possible.

The MBS had a slightly higher yield than similarly rated corporate bonds, suggesting that the investors realized that the MBS were more risky than their rating might suggest. At the same time, the higher yields made them attractive to institutions that faced ratings-based constraints on how much risk they could take on.

A second aspect of the financial alchemy that created very low-risk MBS was credit default swaps. A *swap* is an agreement between several parties to exchange cash flows over some future period. It is similar to a futures contract, but it is more flexible, since it is a private agreement between parties. In the mid-1990s, several investment banks, including Bankers Trust and JP Morgan, developed credit default swaps. These swaps were supposed to be triggered in the event of a default by the issuer of the bond that underlay one side of the swap. Swaps are a form of insurance in which, in exchange for a fee, the insurer agrees to make the borrower's payments on the underlying bond if the borrower defaults. American International Group (AIG), the largest insurance company in the world, issued a great many of these credit default swaps on MBS.

6. PROBLEMS

Problem 31. Consider an augmented version of the Diamond-Dybvig model described above. In this version there are 4 investors, 2 of whom will have a liquidity crisis and need funds in period $t = 1$, and 2 of whom will not and hence can use funds in either $t = 1$ or $t = 2$. Each depositor has 1000 units to invest. The bank has two possible means of investing its money: a long-term investment and a short-term investment. The long-term investment pays $R = 2$ times the amount invested at $t = 2$. Early liquidation of the investment at $t = 1$ pays $L = 0.5$ times the original amount invested. The short-term investment pays the original amount if it is withdrawn at $t = 1$ or $t = 2$.

(1) Try to come up with a resource constraint that indicates the available combinations of consumption in period $t = 1$ and consumption in period $t = 2$ that the bank can offer its customers.
(2) Given this resource constraint, and the fact that the customers are all ex ante identical and would like to be insured against having a liquidity crisis, construct the social planning problem and use it to characterize the optimal contract the bank should offer its customers, given that it knows ex post which of its investors has had a liquidity shock.
(3) Assume that the bank cannot tell who had the liquidity shock, and that preferences over consumption are given by

$$u(c) = \frac{c^{1-\gamma}}{1 - \gamma},$$

with $\gamma \geq 2$. Try to argue that your contract is incentive compatible. By that, I mean that if the other investor who did not have a liquidity shock is not withdrawing his funds at $t = 1$, then the first investor without a liquidity shock shouldn't either. Can there be an equilibrium in which the efficient contract is realized?

(4) Explain why, if the other investor without a liquidity shock is going to withdraw his funds early, then the first investor without a liquidity shock should as well. Can there be a run equilibrium as well?

(5) Discuss why the threat of a run here is more severe than in the model in discussed above because of the assumptions about the investment technology. Try and relate this to concerns about fire sales.

Problem 32. Consider again the simple example about using capital requirements to reduce the perverse risk-taking incentives of banks' caused by capital controls. What level of required capital would cause banks to not take loan 3? What does this say about the size of capital requirements as we increase the riskiness of the available menu of projects?

14

The Financial Meltdown and the
Great Recession

The so-called Great Recession in the latter half of the 2000s was a major economic event in both U.S. and world history. For the U.S. it was the second largest decline in economic activity in the last 100 years, exceeded only by the Great Depression. However, unlike in the Great Depression, when industrial production turned downward several months before the stock market collapsed, in the Great Recession financial events preceded the downturn in economic activity, and in a relative sense were probably more important than in the Great Depression. The catalyst within the financial sector came from housing, and the lengths that financial institutions went to finance it. We start first with housing and financial events; then we examine some standard macro aspects.

1. HOUSING AND FINANCE

The main driver of the financial meltdown in the U.S. was the interconnected market that financed home mortgages. Figure 14.1 shows how the long boom in housing came to an end in 2006.[1] This boom in house prices and demand for housing in general was financed by a large run-up in household debt, and mortgage debt in particular. Historically, much of this mortgage debt had been

1. SP Dow Jones Indices LLC, S&P/Case-Shiller U.S. National Home Price Index [CSUSHPINSA], retrieved from FRED, Federal Reserve Bank of St. Louis; https://fred. stlouisfed.org/series/ CSUSHPINSA, April 14, 2018.

Figure 14.1 Housing.
SOURCE: FRED. Data Source: S&P Dow Jones Indices LLC.

bought up by the two government-sponsored enterprises (GSEs), Fannie Mae and Freddie Mac, which used them to form mortgage-backed securities (MBS). These MBS were then sold to a variety of financial institutions, including many banks. The MBS issued by the GSEs came with a guarantee. During the 2000s, privately securitized MBS also became a large part of the securitization market, and in 2005-6 they accounted for over half of the MBS that were originated. These privately issued MBS, were often created using senior and junior tranches, such as those described previously. They also often came with some insurance through credit default swaps, which promised to swap the payments of the MBS for some (even less risky) securities in the event of a default.

The overall creditworthiness of mortgage borrowers appears to have deteriorated during the 1990s and early 2000s. Mortgages are rated by the FICO score of the borrower, and the highest rated of these are called prime mortgages; those slightly below prime are referred to as alt-prime, and the next group down is referred to as subprime. The U.S. government had pressured the GSEs to help extend housing finance to lower-income areas, and the privately issued MBS often included large shares of altprime and subprime mortgages. Figure 14.2 shows the boom in both subprime lending and securitization right before the crisis.[2]

At first, there was a great deal of confusion about what these events meant for the U.S. economy because many of the crucial securities that were to play an important role in the meltdown were traded in over-the-counter (OTC) markets, which are primarily used to trade bonds, currencies, and so-called structured products, such as derivatives. An OTC market is a loose collection of dealers who make up the market. These dealers trade with the public and also with each other. Since the trades made in this market are not reported, an outsider will not know

2. Final Report of the National Commission on the Causes of the Financial and Economic Crisis in the United States, p.70, figure 5.2.

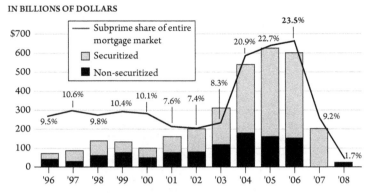

Figure 14.2 Subprime Mortgages Subprime Mortgage Originations: In 2006, $600 billion of subprime loans were originated, most of which were securitized. That year, subprime lending accounted for 23.5% of all mortgage originations. Percent securitized is defined as subprime securities issues divided by originations in a given year. In 2007, securities issued exceeded originations.

SOURCE: Inside Mortgage Finance (IMF).

what a particular security is being traded for, either between dealers or between the dealers and their other customers. They will also not know the volume of trading. Aside from being quite opaque, OTC markets can freeze up if dealers withdraw from the market.

In August 2007, investors such as money market mutual funds became increasingly nervous about the underlying value of asset-backed commercial paper and began to withdraw from these markets. This led to a sharp rise in the spreads on these securities. This in turn meant that the holders of asset-backed securities who were counting on being able to issue commercial paper backed by these securities could no longer finance their balance-sheet positions. To help the holders of these securities, the Federal Reserve pumped "money" into these markets through repurchase agreements in which the Fed bought the securities for short periods from the dealers. The European Central Bank undertook similar measures at this time.

However, events continued to unfold in a negative fashion. The investment bank Bear Stearns pioneered the securitization and asset-backed securities markets. As investor losses mounted in those markets in 2006 and 2007, the company actually increased its exposure, especially to the mortgage-backed assets that were central to the subprime mortgage crisis. In March 2008, the Federal Reserve Bank of New York provided an emergency loan to try to avert Bear Stearn's sudden collapse. The company could not be saved, however, and was sold to JPMorgan Chase for as little as $10 per share, a price far below the 52-week high of $133.20

per share at which it traded before the crisis, although not as low as the $2 per share originally agreed upon by Bear Stearns and JP Morgan Chase.

The mortgage crisis also meant that the loan guarantees issued by Fannie Mae and Freddie Mac, the two government-sponsored enterprises, were now proving very costly. In September 2008, the Treasury placed Fannie and Freddie in conservatorship, effectively nationalizing them and taking on their obligations.

The next shoe to fall concerned another investment bank, Lehman Bros. In 2008, Lehman faced an unprecedented loss due to the continuing subprime mortgage crisis. Huge losses accrued in lower-rated mortgage-backed securities throughout 2008. In the second fiscal quarter, Lehman reported losses of $2.8 billion and was forced to sell off $6 billion in assets. In the first half of 2008 alone, Lehman stock lost 73% of its value as the credit market continued to tighten. In August 2008, Lehman reported that it intended to release 1500 people (6% of its work force) just ahead of its third-quarter-reporting deadline in September.

The collapse of Lehman increased market turmoil, and brought more pressure to bear on other parts of the MBS market. Lehman had very large credit default swap contract positions with AIG. In fact, the extent of AIG's exposure was perhaps one of the main negative factors that came from Lehman's collapse. Almost immediately, the Federal Reserve felt itself forced to make a bridge loan to the insurance company. Ultimately, the government ended up taking on many of AIG's loses.

Also in September, a money market mutual fund (MMMF) was forced to inform its investors that because of its large losses on Lehman's commercial paper, it was not going to be able to pay investors off at par on their money market mutual fund accounts. This is called "breaking the buck," and it brought home to all of the investors who held money market mutual funds that their accounts, unlike those in commercial banks, were not insured. This led to fears that there would be a run on the MMMFs as investors sought to withdraw their funds first in order to avoid a loss, and in fact, large withdrawals did start to take place. In response, the Treasury stepped in and guaranteed the MMMFs, and the Fed intervened to buy commercial paper.

In October, Congress passed a bailout provision called the Troubled Asset Relief Program, or TARP, which authorizes Treasury to spend $700 billion to shore up the markets. The Federal Reserve also undertook major purchases of these assets through its so-called quantitative easing programs. It also dropped the Fed Funds Rate sharply and has kept it there for a very long stretch.

The extraordinary lengths to which the Federal Reserve went to stimulate the economy can be clearly seen in Figure 14.3. The figure shows the fed funds rate, which is the overnight rate in the inter-bank market. This rate is a very conventional target of monetary policy, and the Fed brought it down sharply

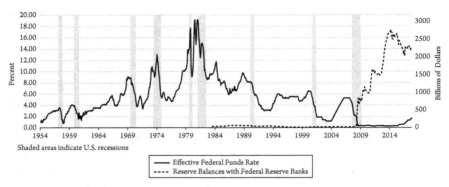

Figure 14.3 Federal Reserve Actions in the Great Recession.
SOURCE: FRED. Data Source: Board of Governors of the Federal Reserve System (U.S.).

and kept it at a very low level for a very extended period of time. By looking at the fed funds rate over the entire post-WWII period, one can clearly see that this policy response stands out. The shaded regions in the figure indicate periods of recession, and one can see that the Fed Funds rate invariably drops, and often drops fairly sharply, during these periods. However, it was never as low, nor held down as long, as in the Great Recession.

Figure 14.3 also shows the banking system's reserves. The Fed normally responds to a recession by expanding reserves as part of its actions to lower the fed funds rate and provide liquidity to the banking system. During the Great Recession, the Fed engaged in a variety of activities, including open market operations, in which it bought up securities from the banks in exchange for reserves in order to greatly expand the level of liquid assets on the banks' balance sheets. Both of these actions go far beyond the normal scope, and the expansion in reserves is far beyond anything we have seen previously. In fact, it is so dramatic that one cannot detect the normal response to the moderate recessions of this period.

The Fed's efforts did help to hold down the interest rates in the commercial paper market. Despite the Fed's efforts, the market for asset-backed commercial paper essentially collapsed.

The fallout for the investment banks was pretty devastating: Essentially every existing investment bank either went bankrupt or was bought out by a larger entity (Table 14.1).

2. THE MACROECONOMY

There have been two major economic downturns in the U.S.: one in the 20th century (the Great Depression of the 1930s) and one thus far in the 21st century (the Great Recession of 2008-9). As we can see from Figure 14.4, the level of real output falls sharply in 2008 and 2009, before starting to recover thereafter. One thing to note is that, historically, the sharper the decline, the sharper the recovery. This is not true here. Instead, output does not return to its peak until 2011. Moreover, the current output path looks to have shifted down relative to that prevailing before the recession. Finally, the growth rate of output from 2014 onward appears slower than what had prevailed before.

One major contributor to the fall in output and its slow recovery has been the behavior of labor participation. Figure 14.4 also shows the recent behavior

Table 14.1. FINAL TALLY FOR THE INVESTMENT BANKS

First Boston	brought by Credit Suisse	1998
Salomon Brothers	brought by Travelers Ins	1997
Donaldson Lufkin & Jenrette	bought by Credit Suisse	2000
PaineWebber	bought by UBS	2000
JPMorgan	bought by Chase	2000
A.G. Edwards	bought by Wachovia	2007
Bear Stearns	bought by JPMorgan Chase	2008
Goldman Sachs	became a financial holding com.	2008
Lehman Bros.	failed	2008
Merrill Lynch	bought by BoA	2008
Morgan Stanley	became a financial holding com.	2008

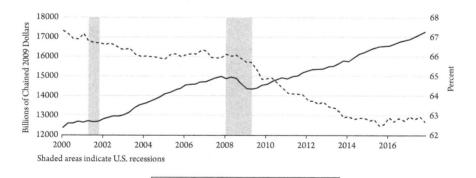

Shaded areas indicate U.S. recessions

——— Real Gross Domestic Product (left)
- - - - Civilian Labor Force Participation Rate(right)

Figure 14.4 Ouput and Labor Participation.
SOURCE: FRED. Data Source: BEA, BLS.

of this series.[3] Two long running trends were driving participation up until 2000. First, male participation was declining. However, this decline was offset by increasing female participation. Starting in 2000, female participation also stopped increasing. Prior to 2000 these forces had balanced and participation had been fairly constant throughout the 1990s.

Figure 14.4 shows how overall participation in the economy dropped sharply during the recession and continued dropping thereafter. This fall in participation rates is one reason why output fell. The fact that participation has continued to trend downward has also contributed to the recovery in the unemployment rate. In this case, however, the unemployment rate does not really capture the continuing weakness in the labor market.

3. THE AFTERMATH

It is worth pausing for a moment and considering the new lay of the land after the Great Recession and the policy responses it engendered. One of the most striking features was the extension of explicit or implicit insurance to many parts of the financial system. This include at a minimum the MMMFs and investment banks, and probably also other components of the "Shadow Banking system" (components of the financial system that behave in similar ways to standard commercial banks).

As we saw in our chapter on financial intermediation, extending deposit-type insurance either explicitly or implicitly will distort the pricing of risk at which these entities are borrowing. This will in turn subsidize their risk taking and incentivize them to continue to do so. Correcting these incentive distortions is not easy. We saw that simple capital controls are likely to prove inadequate; hence, it will probably prove necessary to expand regulatory oversight along with the extension of insurance coverage. Regulation creates its own inefficiencies so this is not something to untake lightly. It may be wise to ponder whether rolling back these insurance promises would be the more efficient course. But this would mean tolerating more collapses along the lines of Lehman Brothers. So this does not come for free either.

Another consideration is the effectiveness of the Federal Reserve's policies in response to the crises. The Fed undertook an extraordinary set of actions, but

3. Source for output data is U.S. Bureau of Economic Analysis, Real Gross Domestic Product [GDPC1], retrieved from FRED, Federal Reserve Bank of St. Louis; https://fred.stlouisfed.org/series/GDPC1. Source for participation rate data is U.S. Bureau of Labor Statistics, Civilian Labor Force Participation Rate [LNU01300000], retrieved from FRED, Federal Reserve Bank of St. Louis; https://fred.stlouisfed.org/series/LNU01300000

to what effect? The Fed's actions seemed to have headed off a major meltdown in the financial markets during the very height of the financial crisis. However, did the low funds rate and the incredible expansion in the reserves really end up doing much?

In Figure 14.5 are plotted the inflation rate and the Corporate Bond yield on Aaa rates bonds.[4] Two things stand out. First, there was no increase in inflation. This is surprising, and testifies to the extent to which banks simply choose to sit on the extra reserves the Fed gave them. Increasing the inflation rate would have been a natural way to reallocate losses, especially on mortgages, between borrowers and the lenders. This is something that one would have normally expected to see in the past. But, in the modern era central bankers are much more phobic about inflation, and at the same time seem to have a much harder time engineering it.

Second, the Fed's actions seem to have lowered low-risk private interest rate. The Corporate Bond rate fell over time, while the rate of financial commercial paper, where the Fed intervened very aggressively right away, dropped sharply. Despite this, the Fed's stimulus was not particularly effective in spurring the

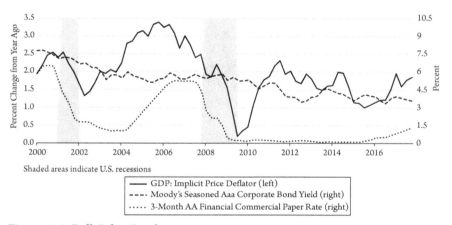

Shaded areas indicate U.S. recessions

> —— GDP: Implicit Price Deflator (left)
> ---- Moody's Seasoned Aaa Corporate Bond Yield (right)
> ····· 3-Month AA Financial Commercial Paper Rate (right)

Figure 14.5 Fed's Policy Results.
SOURCE: FRED. Data Source: BEA, Board of Governors, Moody's.

4. The source for the inflation measure is U.S. Bureau of Economic Analysis, Gross Domestic Product: Implicit Price Deflator [GDPDEF], retrieved from FRED, Federal Reserve Bank of St. Louis; https://fred.stlouisfed.org/series/GDPDEF, April 22, 2018. The source for the corporate bond measure is Moody?s, Moody's Seasoned Aaa Corporate Bond Yield [AAA], retrieved from FRED, Federal Reserve Bank of St. Louis; https://fred.stlouisfed.org/series/AAA, April 22, 2018. The source for the commercial paper measure is Board of Governors of the Federal Reserve System (US), 3-Month AA Financial Commercial Paper Rate [DCPF3M], retrieved from FRED, Federal Reserve Bank of St. Louis; https://fred.stlouisfed.org/series/DCPF3M, April 22, 2018.

economy. One might have expected banks to lend at great rates and that this would lead to more investment. However, this does not seem to have occurred.

Third, there was a concerted attempt to increase home ownership. While homeownership provides an important source of savings, especially retirement savings, it also increases household's mortgage borrowing. The financial exposure that resulted from this seems to have contributed to the fragility of the financial system. The financial risks this involves may not be well suited to lower income households. For both these reasons it might be wise to rethink this policy.

PART SIX

Deficits, Debt, Inflation, and Default

Since forever, sovereign decisions have had a particularly heavy impact on financial markets. The government's choices are often dictated by the gap between its revenues and its desired expenditures. This gap can lead to aggressive financing decisions like hyperinflation, heavy borrowing, or even default. In ancient times shocks to spending through wars played a prominent role. In modern times, spending needs through various commitments move more slowly, but the impact can be just as massive. This next part covers a wide range of issues that are tied to public finance and their impact on financial markets.

15

Debt, Spending, and Inflation

1. A BIT OF PUBLIC FINANCE HISTORY AND FACTS

Historically, public finance has turned out to be an extremely exciting topic as governments have struggled to spend as much as they want to without undertaking the other actions to finance that go with that spending, like high taxes or high inflation. Instead they have often ended up with large debts that have led to crises.

Several things have driven these expenditures historically. The first is wars. Wars can lead to sudden and extreme spikes in government spending. Typically, this sudden increase is financed by a combination of debt, tax increases, and money printing. A classic example of this is the United Kingdom's long history of fighting wars. During the 1700s and 1800s, war would lead the U.K. government's spending to jump from 10% of output to 20%, or even 30%, of output. Spending at this level was quite a feat, since early tax systems were quite primitive. Part of the U.K.'s success was finding a way to finance these wars, since no finance meant no army, a situation that would naturally lead to wars that are quickly lost.

Alexander Hamilton is famous for many things, but one of them is how he dealt with the accumulated Revolutionary War debt when he was Secretary of the Treasury under George Washington. The various states had accumulated very large debts fighting the War for Independence. In many cases, they could not credibly expect to pay these debts off. Hamilton chose to have the federal government take responsibility for paying off these debts and to pay them off in full, even though many of these IOUs were trading at only a fraction of their face value. He did this to ensure that the U.S. would be in a good position to finance future wars.[1]

In addition to wars, another factor that has driven expenditures is grand spending plans. This dates back to the pharaohs in Egypt and the building of the pyramids. The various kings of France were also famous for their spending. This spending, and the need to finance it, ultimately led to the French Revolution and the overthrow of the monarchy. However, all spending plans are not ill-advised. President Eisenhower led the creation of the Federal Highway System. Its construction began with the Federal Aid Highway Act of 1956.

Sometimes periods of large fiscal expenditures have ended with *hyperinflations*, persistent periods of very high inflation. By one definition, a hyperinflation starts when the monthly inflation rate exceeds 50% and ends in the first month in which the rate drops below this level. In ancient times, with minted coins, hyper-inflations were essentially impossible, but in the "modern" era of fiat monies, the ability to dramatically expand the money supply, with its resulting dramatic increase in inflation, has made it possible. Hyperinflations commonly arise right after or during wars, when the combination of large government expenditures and the disruptions due to the war or its aftermath limits revenues. Some of the classic hyperinflations include the post-WWI hyperinflations in Weimar Germany, Hungary, and Poland. The Weimar hyperinflation was triggered in large part by the need to pay reparatations to the Allied powers after WWI.[2] A recent example of a country with a hyperinflation is Venezuela, where consumer price inflation rose from 28% in 2010, to 255% in 2016. An even more extreme example is Zimbabwe, where the inflation rate went from 19% in 1991 to 24,000% in 2004.

Sometimes periods of large fiscal expenditures have led to countries repudi-ating their debts, or only paying off a fraction of what was owed. Reinhart and Rogoff (2009) discuss the history of debt repayment difficulties. One of their examples is Spain, which managed to default 7 times in the 19th century.[3]

In the modern era, government commitments to the welfare of their citizens, including old age support, medical care, income support pensions, and education, have become a major driver of expenditures. Governments seem particularly prone to making themselves popular by promising big "entitlements" down the

---

1. See George J. Hall and Thomas J. Sargent, "Fiscal Discriminations in Three Wars." *Journal of Monetary Economics* 61 (2014): 148–166.

2. John Maynard Keynes wrote a famous book, *The Economic Consequences of the Peace,* which argued that the lack of fairness and generosity of the Paris Peace Conference of 1919 would hinder the postwar recovery in Europe.

3. Carmen M. Reinhart and Kenneth S. Rogoff, *This Time Is Different: Eight Centuries of Financial Folly,* Princeton University Press, 2009.

Figure 15.1. Government Spending as % of Output.
SOURCE: IMF Fiscal Affairs Departmental Data. Data Source: Mauro et al (2015)
OurWorldInData.org/public-spending/.

road. But these entitlements may not be feasible. In that case, something has
to give.

In Figure 15.1. government spending as a share of output is plotted for several
major countries. The share of output devoted to fighting wars skyrockets during
the world wars, especially in the U.K. One can also see how government spending
has trended upward between the late 1800s and the late 1900s and early 2000s.
This reflects the larger role governments now play. These higher levels of government spending require efficient tax and financing systems to make them workable.
Even with efficient systems, financing high levels of government spending is a
difficult enterprise. High taxes can reduce output. At the same time, taxation is
necessary to generate revenue. On top of all this, spending is often popular but
taxation is not. When the level of spending is not consistent with the level of tax
revenues, some sort of adjustment is necessary.

2. FISCAL FACTS FOR THE U.S.

In this chapter we study the impact of monetary decisions on the government's
budget constraint. This, in turn, sheds light on the government's incentive to
inflate the price level because printing money and generating inflation turns out
to be one way that government can cope with the budgetary pressure generated
by its expenditures. Everything builds off of the government's budget constraint,
which here we are requiring to hold. That's a fancy way of saying that the government cannot directly default on its debts.

The government's budget constraint can be written as

$$q_t B_t + M_t - M_{t-1} + P_t T_t = B_{t-1} + P_t G_t + Tr_t,$$

where

- $q_t B_t$ is the revenue from selling pure discount bonds
- $M_t - M_{t-1}$ is the revenue from money creation
- $P_t T_t$ are tax revenues
- B_{t-1} are the bonds coming due
- $P_t G_t$ is government expenditure on goods and services
- Tr_t are government transfers

We turn next to some basic facts about the fiscal position of the U.S. The Economic Report of the President is a nice source for this information. We report the data in Table 15.1 in terms of the percentage of output since everything is growing over time.[4] Note that our debt variable is total outstanding debt, which includes that owed to the Social Security Administration (among other government agencies). Debt in the hands of the public is considerably lower. For example, it was 75.4 in 2017.

Table 15.1. FISCAL FACTS FOR THE U.S. (% OF GDP)

Years	1970	1980	1990	2000	2005	2010	2017
Receipts	18.4	18.5	17.4	19.9	16.7	14.4	17.1
Outlays	18.6	21.1	21.2	17.6	19.2	23.1	20.5
Deficit	−0.3	−2.6	−2.7	2.3	−2.5	−8.6	−3.4
Total Debt	36.3	32.5	51.5	55.4	61.3	91.5	104.1

From Table 15.1 we can see that from 1980 to 2000, receipts were roughly 18–20% of GDP, and expenditures were roughly 19-20% of GDP. Since 2000, expenditures have gone up somewhat, while receipts have fallen substantially. The total outstanding debt was around 30% of GDP during the post-WWII period up until the Reagan tax cuts of 1980 and 1986. Since then, it has risen fairly steadily except for the Clinton boom years of the 1990s. Since 2000, the debt-to-GDP ratio has climbed sharply from around 50% of GDP to over 100% of GDP.

One thing that has helped the U.S. during this period is that interest rates have been quite low. The 3-month T-bill averaged .06% in 2011, while the 3-year bond averaged 0.75%, and the 10-year bond averaged 2.78%.

If we look at expenditures, roughly 25% of total expenditures go to Social Security, another roughly 25% goes to Medicare and Medicaid, while roughly 15% goes to expenditures related to national defense. This leaves only 35% for all of the other expenditures of the U.S. federal government. The future commitments

---

4. The data source is the Federal Reserve Bank of St. Louis and the U.S. Office of Management and Budget; the data were retrieved from FRED, Federal Reserve Bank of St. Louis.

to so-called entitlements spending, primarily Social Security and Medicare, are expected to greatly expand the deficit in the future.[5] Much of this expansion is due to the aging of the population, which lowers the number of workers and taxpayers relative to entitlement recipients. In 1950, the percentage of older dependents to working-age population was 12.6%. Since then this percentage has risen fairly steadily, outside of a dip between 1993 and 2005, and stands at 22.8% in 2016.[6] Currently, the trust funds that cover many of our most important entitlement programs are solvent. Revenue plus interest in the Social Security and Medicare funds is greater than current expenditures. However, this is not expected to continue. These funds are forecast to run out of money in the fairly near term. A natural question is: How can this be? A retirement account, for example, is supposed to run out when you die. But since there are always new entrants, shouldn't these funds stay solvent forever? The answer is yes IF the amount that each generation receives does not exceed what they contribute or the number of young people supporting the fund grows fast enough or output itself grows fast enough. However, none of these conditions is currently being met.[7]

5. U.S. Treasury's "A Citizens Guide to the Fiscal Year 2015 Financial Report of the United States Government."

6. World Bank, "Age Dependency Ratio: Older Dependents to Working-Age Population for the United States," retrieved from FRED, Federal Reserve Bank of St. Louis.

7. http://www.ssa.gov/oact/trsum/index.html

16

Modeling Government Debt and Inflation

In the data we frequently see high inflation rates in countries with large debt or deficit levels We are going to construct a simple model to try to understand this relationship. Then we are going to use this model and various modifications of it to generate some basic insights about the connection between fiscal issues and inflation.

To begin, let's go back to the government's budget constraint, which we can write as

$$q_t B_t + M_t - M_{t-1} + P_t T_t = B_{t-1} + P_t G_t$$

On the left-hand side are the sources of government income: net real taxes T_t, new bond issuances B_t, and the change in money balances outstanding. For simplicity we will assume that all of the debt the government issues is in the form of one-period pure discount bonds, and that q_t is the selling price of a bond that promises to pay one nominal unit in period $t + 1$. On the right-hand side are the uses of government income: government real spending (including transfers) G_t, and the cost of retiring the bonds coming due B_{t-1}. Because government spending and net taxes are real, we must multiply them by the price level so that all of the elements of the budget constraint are in the same units.

The gross nominal interest rate is defined as

$$1 + R_{t+1} = \frac{1}{q_t},$$

and the gross real interest rate is defined as

$$1 + r_{t+1} = \frac{1 + R_{t+1}}{1 + \pi_{t+1}} = \frac{1}{q_t} \frac{P_t}{P_{t+1}},$$

where π_{t+1} is the inflation rate between t and $t+1$. We are going to conduct some fiscal experiments to see how a government can respond to budgetary pressure and what that leads to.

1. EXPERIMENT 1

What happens when the government causes the inflation rate to change? Start from the budget constraint

$$q_t B_t + M_t - M_{t-1} + P_t T_t = B_{t-1} + P_t G_t.$$

Let's focus first on what happens to the value of money. If real money demand is a constant at $\bar{M}$, then

$$\frac{M_{t+1}}{P_{t+1}} = \frac{M_t}{P_t} \Rightarrow \frac{M_{t+1}}{M_t} = \frac{P_{t+1}}{P_t} = 1 + \pi$$

and hence

$$\frac{M_{t+1} - M_t}{P_{t+1}} = \frac{\pi M_t}{(1 + \pi)P_t} = \frac{\pi}{1 + \pi}\bar{M},$$

and they earn *seigniorage*, which is the revenue from creating more currency in circulation.

The amount of seigniorage would seem to be bounded only by the real value of the money supply since revenue is

$$\frac{\pi}{1 + \pi}\bar{M}.$$

But this assumes that the real value of money isn't affected by the change in inflation. We'll come back to this.

Next, let's focus on what happens to the real value of the debt. To do this, fix real borrowing at $q_t B_t / P_t = \bar{D}$.

Case 1: If we assume that this change is completely unexpected and q is a constant, then

$$B_t / P_{t+1} = \bar{D} P_t / (q P_{t+1}),$$

and the real value of the debt falls in proportion to the change in P_{t+1}/P_t. This would seem to be a huge windfall for the government.

Case 2: If we assume that the real interest rate is roughly constant and tied to the discount rate in household preferences, then $r_t = r$ and the nominal interest rate is being driven by inflation since

$$q_t = \frac{1}{1+r}\frac{P_t}{P_{t+1}}.$$

Then

$$B_t/P_{t+1} = \bar{D}P_t/(q_t P_{t+1}) = \bar{D}(1+r),$$

and there is no change. This corresponds to a case in which inflation is completely anticipated and we have therefore assumed that it has no effect on the real interest rate that lenders demand.

1.1. IMPACT DEPENDS ON EXPECTATIONS (OR LACK THEREOF)

Naturally, people will catch on over time. As they do so, the new debt the government issues will reflect this reality. But the existing debt is still something the government can go after. This leads to the next experiment, in which we put in some numbers to see what they imply.

Sticking with Case 1, and starting from a baseline of 0 inflation, how large does the inflation rate have to become to reduce the debt by, say, half? This turns out to depend crucially on the maturity of the debt:

- If the debt is 10-year bonds, the annual inflation rate is $(1+\pi)^{-10} = .5$ or $\pi = .07$.
- If the debt is 1-year bonds, the annual inflation rate is $(1+\pi)^{-1} = .5$ or $\pi = 1$.
- If the debt is 3-month bonds, the annual inflation rate is $(1+\pi)^{-1/4} = .5$ or $\pi = 15$.

So the shorter the maturity of the debt, the more extreme the necessary inflation rate. Since our models generally imply that high inflation rates are costly, we can see how the maturity distribution of the outstanding debt becomes an important factor in whether the government wants to try to inflate a bunch of its debt away.

Still sticking with Case 1, imagine that the highest inflation rate the government could tolerate was 25%. What would happen? With 10-year bonds, that is fine, since $\pi = .07$. With 1-year bonds, the most the government can do is inflate away $1/1.25$, but then what? Does everyone now realize that the government is inflating and change their expectations accordingly? With 3-month bonds the results are even more extreme, since $1.25^{-1/4} = 0.9457$. And, if expectations adjust, that is all you get.

What about the impact of inflation on other revenues? Traditionally, taxes are determined in the prior year and collected at the beginning of the new year. But then taxes are determined using P_{t-1} and collected at time t, hence revenues can fall in real terms by as much as P_{t+1}/P_t.

2. EXPERIMENT 2

We can interpret Experiment 1 as showing the gains from surprise inflation. Next we want to consider the gains from sustained inflation. Start from the government's budget constraint

$$q_t B_t + M_t - M_{t-1} + P_t T_t = B_{t-1} + P_t G_t,$$

and assume that real government spending and net taxes are constant; $G_t = G$ and $T_t = T$. Given this, we can rearrange the government's budget constraint as

$$\frac{q_t B_t - B_{t-1}}{P_t} + \frac{M_t - M_{t-1}}{P_t} = [G - T],$$

where the government is choosing how to finance its budget deficit/surplus through either expanding the real value of the debt or creating revenue through real money growth.

Next, assume that the government's primary real deficit, $G - T$, is a constant fraction of real output, Y, which we denote by d. Assume also that the government's debt policy seeks to keep the government's debt as a constant fraction of output, so $B_t/P_t Y$ is constant over time, which we denote by b. This implies that

$$\left[\frac{q_t P_{t+1}}{P_t} - 1\right] bY + \frac{M_t - M_{t-1}}{P_t} = dY.$$

Finally, assume that the real interest rate is constant at r, as in Case 2. Then, the nominal interest rate is being driven by inflation since

$$q_t = \frac{1}{1+r}\frac{P_t}{P_{t+1}}.$$

Plugging this relationship for q_t back into the government's budget constraint yields

$$\left(d + \frac{r}{1+r}b\right)Y = \frac{M_t - M_{t-1}}{P_t}$$
$$= \frac{M_t}{P_t} - \frac{P_{t-1}}{P_t}\frac{M_{t-1}}{P_{t-1}},$$

where M_t/P_t is the real money supply. This relationship shows how the revenue from inflation must offset the impact of the real deficit and the real interest payments on the debt.

To close the model, we need only specify how changes in the money supply end up affecting the price level. To do this, we need to assume a specific form for the aggregate money demand function. A standard form in the literature is the so-called Cagan model demand function,

$$\log\left(\frac{M_t}{P_t}\right) = b + \log C - \gamma R_{t+1},$$

where γ is the "semi-elasticity" of money. C here is consumption, which we can think of as being proportionate to output Y.

Using these assumptions, we get

$$\frac{M_t/P_t}{Y} = \exp\left\{\tilde{b} - \gamma\left[(1+r)\frac{P_{t+1}}{P_t} - 1\right]\right\},$$

where $\tilde{b}$ is the constant adjusted to take account of the relationship between C and Y. Putting this into our relationship above and assuming a constant inflation rate gives us

$$d + \frac{r}{1+r}b = \left[1 - \frac{1}{\rho}\right]\exp\left\{\tilde{b} - \gamma\left[(1+r)\rho - 1\right]\right\} \qquad (18)$$

where ρ is the growth rate in the price level, or

$$\rho = \frac{P_{t+1}}{P_t}.$$

Equation (18) indicates the basic trade-off we face. Raising ρ increases the money supply gap between $M_t - M_{t-1}$ which raises revenue through the term $1 - 1/\rho$. However, it also lowers real money demand through the nominal interest rate, which lowers revenue through the other term involving ρ in (18). At $\rho = 1$, which means no change in the money supply, revenue is zero. and it is easy to see that the derivative of the r.h.s. expression for ρ, taken at $\rho = 1$, is positive. But to see more requires us to put in some parameter values.

Next, we plot the r.h.s. of (18) taking $\tilde{b} = 1$ and $\gamma = .05$. The first number is just a normalization, while the second is important since it governs how sensitive money demand is to the nominal interest rate. The value we have chosen is fairly standard in the literature on money demand. What is interesting/surprising about this figure is that it suggests that the revenue-maximizing level of inflation is fairly low, around 1%.[1]

This raises a question: Why do we see such high levels? One answer might be that γ is much lower than we've assumed. Another is that γ might be much lower in the short run than in the long run. Hence, governments are tempted into high rates of inflation by very immediate concerns and then somehow find it hard to turn back and lower the inflation rate. To illustrate the impact of a lower semi-elasticity of money demand, Figure 16.1 also plots the level of seigniorage-to-ouput for $\gamma = 0.1$, which is a much lower value. This does raise revenue considerably and push the optimal level of inflation upward, to around 2–3%.

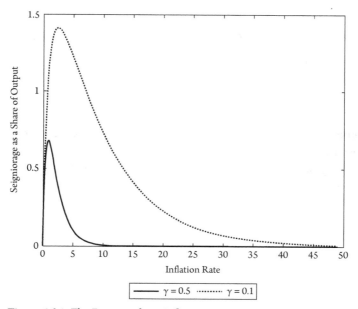

Figure 16.1 The Revenue from Inflation.

1. See Leonardo Auernheimer, "The Honest Government's Guide to the Revenue from the Creation of Money." *Journal of Political Economy* 82.3 (1974): 598–606.

Still, even under a fairly low semi-elasticity, the optimal level of inflation is quite low, especially relative to historical data on high-inflation episodes. Even more troublesome, the output share of seigniorage is essentially 0 for an inflation rate of 50%, which is the lower bound on a hyperinflation. This suggests that a final possibility is that we missed something key.

3. EXPERIMENT 3

Assume that the real interest rate and the real demand for money are constant and that the real value of the debt is $\bar{D}$. Imagine two different choices for inflation:

(1) Inflate away half the debt.
(2) Don't.

What happens when the government chooses a high or low inflation rate today? If it inflates away half of the real debt today, then

$$\frac{\pi}{1 + \pi}\bar{M} = \bar{D}/2.$$

If it doesn't, then the value of the debt tomorrow is $\bar{D}(1 + r)$, and lowering it to $\bar{D}/2$ through seigniorage means that

$$\frac{\pi}{1 + \pi}\bar{M} = \bar{D}(1 + r) - \bar{D}/2.$$

This implies a higher level of future inflation. Hence, if the government cuts taxes and doesn't inflate today, then future expectations could be much worse. This point was originally made by Sargent and Wallace in their classic article entitled "Some Unpleasant Monetarist Arithmetic."[2] It helps to explain why seemingly conservative behavior by a government that does not get its fiscal house in order can result in a dire future. As the debt gets worse, the presumption that eventually the government is going to have to run an even higher inflation rate gets stronger and stronger.

Example 9. Argentina experienced chronic hyperinflation during the period 1975–1990, as the government was forced over and over again to print money

2. Thomas J. Sargent and Neil Wallace. "Some Unpleasant Monetarist Arithmetic." *Monetarism in the United Kingdom.* Palgrave Macmillan, 1984, 15–41.

to finance its deficit. Starting in 1991, the government initiated a bold new policy as part of a fiscal reform. It pegged Argentinia's currency to the dollar and backed its currency with a large reserve of dollars. This is called a currency board. However, the fiscal reforms were incomplete and the government continued to run persistent deficits. These persistent deficits, combined with low inflation, served to drive the debt-to-output ratio ever higher during the 1990s. This was especially problematic in a country like Argentina with a poorly functioning tax system that limited the government's ability to raise revenue.

Despite 15 years of successfully pegging their currency, expectations that the board was unsustainable built up. The country experienced massive bank withdrawals in 2000, and the currency board collapsed. This example is interesting because just looking at the time series of the inflation rate and the exchange rate would imply that everyone should become more confident that the peg would be sustained. However, some "unpleasant monetarist arithmetic" was what actually took place.

4. EXPERIMENT 4

Assume that the real demand for money is constant and that the real value of the debt is $\bar{D}$. Assume that the price of the bond is given by

$$q_t = \frac{1}{1+r}E\left\{\frac{P_t}{P_{t+1}}\right\}.$$

For simplicity, assume that inflation could turn out to be either high or low.

What happens if inflation expectations are low? Then q_t is high, and the government can issue a smaller amount of debt at t to finance $\bar{D}$

$$B_t = \bar{D}/q^h.$$

As a result, the pressure on the government's budget constraint at $t + 1$ is lower, and the government may find it advantageous to, in fact, have a low rate of inflation.

What happens if inflation expectations are high? Then q_t is low, and the government must issue a larger amount of debt at t to finance $\bar{D}$

$$B_t = \bar{D}/q^l.$$

As a result, the pressure on the government's budget constraint at $t + 1$ is higher, and the government may find it advantageous to, in fact, have a high rate of inflation.

How big is the feedback effect of inflation expectations on the government's budget constraint? Assume that $q^h/q^l = 1.1$—so we're considering a 0% inflation rate vs. a 10% rate. If $\bar{D} = 0$, then the impact on the future budget constraint is 0. If $\bar{D}/Y = 1.0$, then the future impact is $1/g$ vs. $1.1/g$, where g is the growth rate of output. So, the effect is to raise the real cost of paying off the debt by 10%, and this cost will be mitigated by growth.

4.1. Lessons to Come Away with

(1) Expectations of high inflation will raise borrowing costs and make the future burden of the debt higher. This can then motivate the government to inflate away the debt. Hence, expectations can have real effects.

(2) This feedback channel opens up the possibility of multiple possible equilibrium outcomes, with the high cost of borrowing/high inflation outcome generated by bad expectations and a low cost of borrowing/ low inflation outcome generated by good expectations.

(3) Growth helps to make things better. So rapidly growing countries can sustain a higher debt burden. But when growth slows down, they're in real trouble. This is what happened, for example, in Italy, where growth has been low or zero for a decade.

(4) The ability to raise revenue is also key here. If tax avoidance is high or the political willingness to tax is low, then the debt burden that will trigger a high rate of inflation will be lower.

5. THE BARRO-GORDON MODEL OF INFLATION

A common way of thinking about the impact of inflation on output is through the *expectations-augmented Phillips curve*. To keep things easy, we are going to work with a simple reduced-form version of that model (known as the Barro-Gordon model) that has been used a lot in the literature. In this reduced-form relationship,

$$\pi_t - \pi_t^e = -\gamma \left(u_t - u_t^n \right),$$

where π_t^e is expected inflation, u_t is unemployment and u_t^n is the natural rate of unemployment. If we rearrange this equation, we get

$$u_t = u_t^n - \alpha(\pi_t - \pi_t^e), \text{ where } \alpha = 1/\gamma.$$

This implies that the government can affect unemployment and hence output through inflation surprises. Surprise inflation is thought to lower real wages and thereby stimulate employment and output.

The policymaker is thought to care about both inflation and unemployment. He is assumed not to like either inflation or unemployment to deviate from certain levels which are thought to be something of a necessary evil; that is, the cost of going below these levels is too high relative to the benefit. Here too we will follow the literature and assume that the policymaker's preferences are given by

$$-\left\{a\left(u_t - \bar{u}\right)^2 + b\left(\pi_t - \bar{\pi}\right)^2\right\}.$$

Here $\bar{\pi}$ is the target level of inflation, say, 2%, and small deviations are not costly, but large deviations in inflation in either direction are. The policymaker would also like unemployment to be close to the target level $\bar{u}$, so the economy isn't depressed, but also isn't overheating—which is thought to lead to a boom-bust cycle.

Fixing the household's inflation expectations, the policymaker's optimal choice of inflation is a solution to

$$\min_{\pi}\left\{a\left[u_t^n - \alpha(\pi_t - \pi_t^e) - \bar{u}\right]^2 + b\left(\pi_t - \bar{\pi}\right)^2\right\}.$$

The optimal policy choice is given by

$$-2a\alpha\left[u_t^n - \alpha(\pi_t - \pi_t^e) - \bar{u}\right] + 2b\left(\pi_t - \bar{\pi}\right) = 0.$$

Or

$$a\alpha\left[u_t^n - \alpha(\pi_t - \pi_t^e) - \bar{u}\right] = b\left(\pi_t - \bar{\pi}\right),$$

which equates the gain from inflation surprises to the cost of having inflation that differs from its target.

With this optimality condition

$$a\alpha\left[u_t^n - \alpha(\pi_t - \pi_t^e) - \bar{u}\right] = b\left(\pi_t - \bar{\pi}\right),$$

and it implies that the policymaker will seek to have surprisingly high inflation whenever $u_t^n > \bar{u}$ and surprisingly low inflation whenever the reverse is true.

But what happens when the public figures this out over time? If the public comes to anticipate the policymaker's behavior then

$$\pi_t^e = \pi_t.$$

But in this case there is no benefit to having inflation differ from $\bar{\pi}$. Since the payoff is

$$-\left\{ a \left[u_t^n - \alpha(\pi_t - \pi_t^e) - \bar{u} \right]^2 + b \left(\pi_t - \bar{\pi} \right)^2 \right\}.$$

So, the policymaker should just set $\pi_t = \bar{\pi}$. That is, the Fed should focus on price stability and not try to stabilize the economy using monetary policy.

But is setting $\pi_t = \bar{\pi}$ "optimal"? Return to our first-order condition

$$a\alpha \left[u_t^n - \alpha(\pi_t - \pi_t^e) - \bar{u} \right] = b \left(\pi_t - \bar{\pi} \right),$$

and note that if $\pi_t = \bar{\pi}$, then the marginal cost of a bit more inflation is 0, while the benefit of a surprise is positive if $u_t^n \neq \bar{u}$. So, the policymaker will find it "optimal" to try to surprise the public.

How do we resolve the strategic tensions here?

(1) The public wants to anticipate the policymaker's behavior correctly and set $\pi_t^e = \pi_t$.
(2) The policymaker wants to surprise households to achieve its unemployment target as long as it is not too costly to do so.

Conjecture that $\pi_t^e = \pi_t$, and let's try to determine a level of π_t that would be optimal for the policymaker under these conditions. If $\pi_t^e = \pi_t$ then the optimal choice condition of the policymaker becomes

$$a\alpha \left[u_t^n - \bar{u} \right] = b \left(\pi_t - \bar{\pi} \right),$$

so

$$\left(\pi_t - \bar{\pi} \right) = \frac{a\alpha}{b} \left[u_t^n - \bar{u} \right],$$

and we get systematic deviations in the inflation rate from its target even though this is useless because everyone anticipates the policymaker's behavior. These deviations will be large if $\bar{u}$ is far from the natural rate.

The Barro-Gordon model is thought to provide a nice answer to the question: "Why do we see persistent excessive inflation when the optimal level is probably close to zero or even negative?"[3]

6. BARRO-GORDON AND DEBT

The Barro-Gordon model does rationalize some inflation, but at the end of the day, the gains from inflation to raise money from printing money are small and the gains from reducing unemployment are also likely to be small once the public catches on. Why doesn't the government just do away with this? One answer might be that there are some other large gains from inflation that we have so far ignored. The gains from inflating away part of the debt are likely to be far larger than that from seigniorage or even reducing unemployment.

Consider a variant of our model in which the government cares about the real value of the debt. Assume that the price of the bond is given by

$$q_t = \frac{1}{1+r} E\left\{\frac{P_t}{P_{t+1}}\right\}.$$

If the real amount we need to borrow today is D_t, then the following relationship determines B_t, the number of bonds we need to issue today,

$$q_t B_t = P_t D_t.$$

This in turn implies a real debt tomorrow of

$$\frac{B_t}{P_{t+1}} = \frac{P_t}{P_{t+1}} D_t (1+r) \frac{1}{E\{P_t/P_{t+1}\}}.$$

Having a positive value of the debt may be optimal since government debt plays an important liquidity role. So, if we care about the log-deviation in the debt relative to its target share of output, then

$$\left[\ln\left(\frac{B_t}{P_{t+1}}\right) - \ln\left(d(1+g)Y_t\right)\right]^2,$$

where d gives the target share.

3. Robert J. Barro and David B. Gordon, "A Positive Theory of Monetary Policy in a Natural Rate Model." *Journal of Political Economy* 91.4 (1983): 589–610.

Substituting in using our relationship for the real debt tomorrow, and taking account of the growth in output between periods t and $t + 1$ leads to

$$\left[\ln \left(\frac{P_t}{P_{t+1}} D_t (1 + r) \frac{1}{E\{P_t/P_{t+1}\}} \right) - \ln \left((1 + g) Y_t \right) \right]^2$$

$$= \left[\begin{array}{l} \ln \left(\frac{P_t}{P_{t+1}} \right) + \ln (D_t) + \ln(1 + r) + \ln \left(\frac{1}{E\{P_t/P_{t+1}\}} \right) \\ \quad - \ln(1 + g) - \ln (Y_t) \end{array} \right]^2$$

$$\simeq \left[\pi_t^e - \pi_t + r - g + \ln(D_t/dY_t) \right]^2,$$

where the last approximate equality follows from the fact that $\ln(1 + x) \simeq x$ for x small. Note here that π_t is actual inflation and π_t^e is expected inflation.

So, assume the policymaker's preferences are given by

$$\min_{\pi} \left\{ a \left[\pi_t^e - \pi_t + r - g + \ln(D_t/dY_t) \right]^2 + b \left(\pi_t - \bar{\pi} \right)^2 \right\}.$$

where $\bar{B}$ is the target level of the debt. Then the policymaker's first-order condition is

$$a \left[\pi_t^e - \pi_t + r - g + \ln(D_t/dY_t) \right] = b \left(\pi_t - \bar{\pi} \right)$$

If we again argue that $\pi_t^e = \pi_t$, this condition becomes

$$a \left[r - g + \ln(D_t/dY_t) \right] = b \left(\pi_t - \bar{\pi} \right).$$

This condition says that we should expect higher inflation than the target when

(1) The level of debt D_t is large relative to the target dY_t.
(2) The real rate of interest is high relative to the growth rate.

These two results are very consistent with what we see in the data. For example, higher debt levels are associated with higher inflation levels. The second result is very consistent with what happened during the Volcker "disinflation." Paul Volcker was the chairman of the Federal Reserve between 1979 and 1987. The 1970s had been a period of high inflation, and Volcker is famous for very aggressively seeking to end this by raising the fed funds rate very sharply and lowering the rate of growth of the monetary base. This ultimately led to the sustained low inflation rates we have had since, but in the short term it drove up the risk-free interest rate and led to a recession in the U.S. For many developing countries, the high interest rates led to an increase in the debt-to-output levels and this in turn caused them to raise inflation rates.

17

Debt, Default, and Interest Rates

There is a long and colorful history of kings and governments defaulting on their debts. One major reason for defaulting on the outstanding debt is that it cannot be inflated away. This is true when the debt is denominated in gold or a foreign currency.

1. LATIN AMERICAN DEBT CRISES

The Latin American Debt Crisis is a name given to the events that unfolded during the 1980s in Latin America. A variety of countries in the region had borrowed fairly heavily in the preceding two decades. The sharp rise in oil prices at several points during the 1970s had contributed to current account imbalances for the oil importers in this region. At the same time, for others the rise in oil prices had led to a consumption and investment spree. Between 1975 and 1983, the region's external debt went from $75 billion to $315 billion, which meant that the debt to output ratio stood at 50%. The rise in interest rates in the U.S. in 1979 to try and reduce inflation (as part of the Volcker disinflation efforts) also contributed to Latin America's woes, as did the resulting U.S. economic downturn.

The decade of the 1980s was to play out very negatively in Latin America. A number of countries temporarily defaulted on their debts before eventually making some sort of arrangement with their creditors. We turn to discussing two countries from the region in detail to understand what went on.

1.1. Argentina

Argentina has a long tradition of struggling to match its government receipts with its expenditures. This problem became especially severe in the 1980s as many countries borrowed to offset the impact of high energy prices on their current accounts. At the end of the 1980s, Argentina reached the crisis point.

Its very high debt-to-GDP ratio put enormous pressure on the government budget. This led the government to begin printing money at a very fast rate to meet its spending needs. Figure 17.1 shows the paths of inflation and real output per capita.[1] The high inflation rate wiped out some of the public debt, but could not wipe it all out since much of it was dollar denominated. In 1983 the dollar-denominated debt was about 40% of output, and this debt grew substantially. In February 1989, the austral fell 64% against the dollar and the World Bank froze lending to Argentina. The combination of inflation, debt overhang, and uncertainty led to a decline in real GDP, which also lowered tax receipts.

Debt was restructured through a distressed exchange offering whereby the bondholders received haircuts of approximately 70%. Argentina also instituted a currency board, which pegged the Argentine peso to the U.S. dollar between 1991 and 2002 in an attempt to eliminate hyperinflation and stimulate economic growth. However, Argentina never resolved its fiscal problems and the external debt-to-GDP ratio climbed back up. The International Monetary Fund (IMF), however, kept lending money to Argentina and postponing its payment schedules. Massive tax evasion and money laundering explained a large part of the evaporation of funds toward offshore banks.

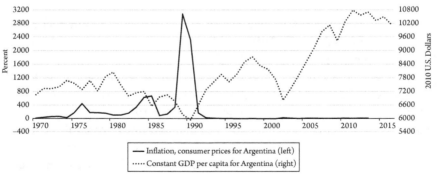

Figure 17.1 Argentina: Inflation and Output.
SOURCE: FRED. Data Source: World Bank.

1. World Bank, "Inflation, consumer prices for Argentina." World Bank, "Constant GDP per Capita for Argentina. Both retrieved from FRED, Federal Reserve Bank of St. Louis.

Late in the 1990s Argentina was hit with a large recession that lowered revenues and made its debt problems more severe. Spreads on Argentinean bonds over U.S. Treasuries went from 10% in December 2000 to almost 50% a year later. Because rates on foreign borrowing were prohibitively high, the government switched to borrowing from domestic banks: The share of government debt in bank assets rose from 15.5% to 21.5%. But this made it harder to inflate away the debt. In October 2001, public discontent with the economic conditions was expressed in the nationwide election when over 20% of all voters chose to enter so-called anger votes, returning blank or defaced ballots rather than indicate support for any candidate.

The government attempted to get out of the crisis through a voluntary debt exchange, which would avoid a default. However, to induce participation, it agreed to a 17% interest rate on this debt, which reduced its payments over the next 4 years by only $12.6 billion. The first exchange was made in June 2001. When that proved insufficient, a second exchange was tried in November. The crisis intensified when, on December 5, 2001, the IMF refused to release a US$1.3 billion tranche of its loan, citing the failure of the Argentinean government to reach previously agreed-upon budget deficit targets, and demanded further budget cuts, amounting to 10% of the federal budget. On December 4, Argentinean bond yields stood at 34% over U.S. Treasury bonds, and, by December 11, the spread had jumped to 42%.

Fearing the worst, by the end of November 2001 people began withdrawing large sums of money from their bank accounts, turning pesos into dollars and sending them abroad, causing a run on the banks. On December 2, 2001 the government enacted a set of measures, informally known as the *corralito*, that effectively froze all bank accounts for 12 months, allowing for only minor sums of cash, initially announced to be just $250 a week, to be withdrawn. In January 2002 the government ended the fixed exchange rate of the peso to the dollar. When default was declared in 2002, foreign investment fled the country, and capital flows toward Argentina ceased almost completely.

An agreement was eventually reached in 2005 where 76% of the defaulted bonds were replaced by others, of a much lower nominal value (25–35% of the original) and at longer terms.

1.2. Mexico

The decade of the 1990s looked to be a bright one for Mexico. It had recovered from the Latin American debt crises of the 1980s and the "lost decade" in which growth was negligible. Inflation seemed under control. Following a series of liberalizing reforms, investment funds poured into Mexico in the early 1990s. On top of this, Mexico had entered into a major trade deal with the U.S. The North American Free Trade Agreement (NAFTA) took effect in 1994 and would reduce trade barriers between the two countries to a new low. There were a couple of dark clouds on the horizon, but at the time, they did not seem that alarming. The influx of foreign investment also served to finance a very large current account deficit. These outcomes are depicted in Figure 17.2.

The Mexican exchange rate system featured a crawling peg in which government intervention kept the exchange rate within a narrow band. The top of the band was supposed to rise gradually, generating a gradual depreciation against the dollar. However, the real exchange rate, which we can define as $P/(P^*E)$, where P is the domestic price level, P^* is the foreign price level, and E is the exchange rate, was rising fairly sharply. This is referred to as a *real appreciation* of the peso. This real appreciation meant that the real price of Mexican goods was rising relative to the U.S., damaging exports, which contributed to the current account deficits.

Investor confidence collapsed in 1994 after a rebellion in the south and the assassination of the ruling party's presidential candidate. Capital began to exit rapidly. The central bank intervened to support the peso and the government repeatedly raised rates. As a result, the Mexican central bank lost close to $11 billion in reserves during a four-week period. This is a large loss given that the central bank had started with a bit under $30 billion in reserves in February 1994.

The Mexican government borrowed using both domestically denominated debt, called *Cetes*, and foreign-indexed debt, called *Tesobonos*. The fact that Tesobonos were foreign indexed meant that operationally they worked like foreign-denominated debt. Before the crises in late 1994, about 75% of government debt was domestically denominated. By May the rate on one-month government domestically denominated debt had risen to 16.4%, from 9.5% just

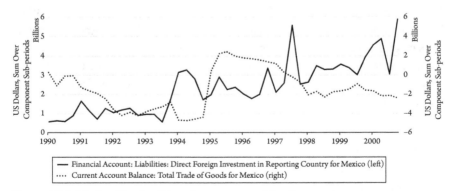

Figure 17.2 Mexico: Foreign Direct Investment and the Current Account.
SOURCE: FRED. Data Source: Organization for Economic Co-operation and Development.

3 months earlier. In response to this, the government switched to financing itself using foreign-denominated debt. This foreign-denominated debt could not be inflated away, which helped to promote investor confidence in it.

By November 1994, the Mexican government was primarily financing itself using 90 day Tesobonos. Domestically denominated debt was only 25% of total debt, while dollar-indexed debt was 70% of total debt. This change in the composition of the debt reduced the cost of debt service significantly because the interest rate on this debt was substantially below the rate on domestic debt. However, this change in composition also tied the government's hands, since it could not devalue (and use inflation) as a means of lowering the real value of its outstanding debts.

Another feature of the change in the composition of the government's debt was that the average maturity was now fairly short; the government was auctioning off Tesobonos in weekly auctions. As the maturity shrank and the dependence on the Tesobono grew, and the amount being auctioned off each week rose sharply.

The pressure on the government increased as its reserves fell further. This led the government to devalue the peso, which took the form of a sharp increase in the top of the crawling peg. The initial response to the devaluation was positive. The Tesobono auction following the devaluation was fairly successful, with $416 million in bonds sold at an 8.61% interest rate, only a 38 basis points increase. The Cetes auction the next day had an average yield of 16.22%, only a 142 basis points increase from the prior week. However, one troubling aspect was that the government had intended to auction off $600 million in Tesobonos.

The pressure on government reserves continued as people continued exchanging pesos for dollars. The central bank lost $4.5 billion in reserves in a single day, and reserves fell below $6 billion. This led the government to abandon its attempts to peg the currency on December 22. The response by the markets was swift and negative. The secondary market interest rate on Cetes rose to 24.5% and the peso fell sharply (40%) against the dollar.

The Tesobono auctions did not go well either. At the December 27 auction, where the government sought to auction $416 million in bonds, only $28 million was sold at an average yield of 10.23%. The next day's Cetes auction also did not go well, with bids well below the amount offered, and the yield jumped way up to 31.41%. This drying up of financial access for the Mexican government exacerbated investor concern over the $10 billion in Tesobono debt maturing in the first quarter of 1995.

By January 1995 the Mexican government was clearly in a state of crisis and, unless there was a massive shift in investor confidence, was going to be forced to default on many of its maturing debt claims. The U.S. initially organized an $18 billion dollar line of credit to aid the Mexicans on January 2. But this failed to stem the problem. The amount of Tesobonos sold in the first two auctions in January were quite small, while the yield rose to close to 20%. In February, the U.S. approved a $20 billion loan to Mexico on favorable terms with delayed repayment. The financial crisis passed and Mexico eventually repaid the U.S.[2]

2. THE EU CRISIS

At the end of 2010, investors became nervous about several European countries with substantial budget deficits, large debt levels, and slowing economic growth. This was especially true when a large amount of the debt was in foreign hands, as in Greece and Portugal. The result was a sharp increase in credit spreads on government bonds and risk insurance on CDS relative to safer countries like Germany.

Each European country took a different route to get into the crisis: Greece was Europe's fastest growing country, but it also ran large deficits. Then the economic slowdown hit its shipping and tourism industries very hard; this in turn led its debt-to-GDP ratio to grow rapidly. Ireland also ended up with a large debt-to-GDP ratio, but this was not because of government over-spending; rather it was because of the government's insurance of Irish banks that speculated and lost on the local real estate bubble. Portugal's problem has been blamed on a large government sector and excessive public employment. Italy had a small deficit but a large public debt and the decades-long slowdown in growth had made this debt burden seem too large. However, Italy's debt has a long maturity and is largely domestically held. In the next section we focus on Greece since it has attracted so much attention from the international financial community.

2.1. Greece

Greece joined the EU in 1981, ushering in a period of sustained strong growth; see Figure 17.3. The beginning of the end came in 2006 when growth started to slow. Eventually the situation turned very negative, and the level of GDP dropped sharply. By 2014, all of the growth from 2000 had been erased. One of the major sources of the economic decline was a sharp drop in the employment rate; this can also be seen in Figure 17.3. Employment dropped by more than 10 percentage points, a huge fall.[3]

2. For more on the Mexican crisis, see J. Whitt, "The Mexican Peso Crisis," in the Federal Reserve Bank of Richmond's *Economic Review*, vol. 81, no. 1, 1996.

3. Sources for figure are the University of Groningen and the University of California, Davis, Real GDP at Constant National Prices for Greece [RGDPNAGRA666NRUG]. Organization for

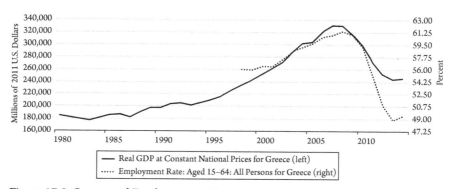

Figure 17.3 Output and Employment in Greece.
SOURCE: FRED. Data Source: OECD, University of Gronigen.

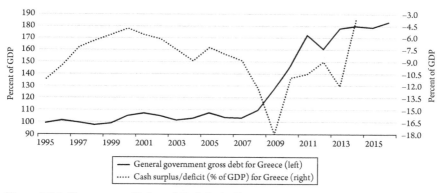

Figure 17.4 Government Debt and Deficits in Greece.
SOURCE: FRED. Data Source: International Monetary Fund, World Bank.

In Figure 17.4, one can see how the economic decline led to a worsening of the government's fiscal situation. The government's cash surplus, which is a measure of the excess of revenue over expenditures, was negative to begin with, reflecting the deficits the government ran during the growth years. However, the downturn led the country to drop sharply into the red.[4] The Greek government (in response to pressure from the ECB [European Central Bank] and European Commission) did reduce the extent of the negative numbers after 2009, but it's worth noting here how large the budget as a whole was during this period. In response to the fall in output and the large deficits, the debt-to-output ratio rose sharply from its

Economic Co-operation and Development, Employment Rate: Aged 15–64: All Persons for Greece [LREM64TTGRQ156S]. Retrieved from FRED, Federal Reserve Bank of St. Louis.

4. Note that this measure seems to be preferred over the standard official measure—the primary surplus—because "exceptional" expenditure charge-offs were allowed here.

already very high level. The truth is that it takes a large amount of fiscal rectitude to pay off debt-to-output ratios of 150%.[5] However, a recovery in employment and output would go a long way toward fixing the fiscal situation.

If we look at the fundamental sources of government expenditure pressure, we see that Greece has a very generous pension system with a fairly early retirement age. At the same time, life expectancy has risen, the fertility rate has fallen, so the share of the elderly in the population has risen. This implies that honoring these pension promises will be a substantial burden for the government going forward.

The debt problem was compounded by nervousness in the bond markets and a sharp increase in the yields that investors required to buy Greek debt. This is illustrated in Figure 17.5, where long-term bond yields are plotted for both Greece and Germany.[6]

Because both countries' bonds are denominated in euros, the difference in yields should just reflect the difference in the extent of default risk and the premia attached to this difference. One thing that is striking in the figure is how close the yields were in the two countries before the crisis, and how the gap widened during the crisis. The difference in yields alone may not fully reflect Greece's

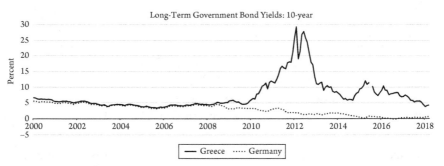

Figure 17.5 Bond Yields: Greece vs. Germany.
SOURCE: FRED. Data Source: Organization for Economic Co-operation and Development.

---

5. Sources are International Monetary Fund, General government gross debt for Greece [GGGDTAGRC188N], Eurostat, Gross Domestic Product for Greece [CPMNACSCAB1GQEL], and World Bank, Cash surplus/deficit (% of GDP) for Greece [CASHBLGRA188A]. Retrieved from FRED, Federal Reserve Bank of St. Louis.

6. Organization for Economic Co-operation and Development, Long-Term Government Bond Yields: 10-year: Main (Including Benchmark) for Greece [IRLTLT01GRM156N], and Organization for Economic Co-operation and Development, Long-Term Government Bond Yields: 10-year: Main (Including Benchmark) for Germany [IRLTLT01DEM156N]. Retrieved from FRED, Federal Reserve Bank of St. Louis.

credit difficulties. In October 2009 Greece experienced the first of a series of ratings downgrades. As a result, Greece found it increasingly difficult to borrow from private creditors and turned to official sources.

The Greek government came up with its first austerity package in February 2010, followed shortly (in March) by a second austerity package. There was a further series of austerity packages, culminating in the seventh austerity package in July 2013. In April, Greece and the EU leaders agreed to the first bailout package, for 110 billion euros over three years.

By June 2011 Moody's had reduced Greece's rating to Caa, and Standard & Poors (S&P) had reduced it to their lowest rating. In October 2011 investors in Greek debt agreed to a write-down of 50%. In June 2015 Greece missed a payment to the IMF. This put Greece at least temporarily in default to the IMF. The list of countries that have defaulted on IMF loans is very small: Cuba, Nicaragua, Vietnam, and so on.

3. MODELING DEFAULT

In this section I develop a simple model of sovereign default which we can use to think through the various episodes that have just been discussed.[7]

3.1. Consequences of Defaulting

In the corporate world, debt contracts are enforced by courts. A corporation can be sued and the courts can force it to hand over its assets, restructure its debts, or shut down and liquidate its remaining assets. For a government, there is no analog to bankruptcy court, and enforcing claims is more problematic:

(1) Few sovereign assets are located in foreign countries and a sovereign state cannot commit to hand over its assets.

(2) There are legal principles, called *sovereign immunity*, which claim that sovereigns cannot be sued in foreign courts without their consent.

---

7. A much more sophisticated infinite horizon model with quantitative applications can be found in M. Aguiar, S. Chatterjee, H. Cole and Z. Stangebye, "Quantitative Models of Sovereign Debt Crises," in *Handbook of Macroeconomics,* 2016, vol. 2. Another source is M. Augiar, "Sovereign Debt," *Handbook of International Economics,* 2014, vol. 4.

•

3.1.1. Sovereign Immunity

During the 19th century sovereigns were protected by absolute sovereign immunity which held that sovereigns could not be sued in foreign courts without their consent. After WWII a more limited view of sovereign immunity took hold in which the sovereign can be sued for commercial activity. (The U.S. advanced this view to potentially control Soviet economic activity within its borders.) Bond issuance and payments are considered commercial activity. Moreover, sovereign bonds now typically include waivers of sovereign immunity. Central bank assets—including international reserves—are typically immune to this waiver. However, changes in the law since the 1970s have made it easier for holdout creditors to receive judgment claims.

3.2. Costs of Default

The costs of default are thought to include

(1) loss of access to credit markets;
(2) various trade disruptions coming from creditors' ability to seize payments and a loss of access to trade credit;
(3) drops in output due to trade disruption, the need to adjust the government's fiscal stance, and use overall uncertainty with respect to future government behavior; and
(4) possibly an impact on the domestic banking system and domestic bond market.

4. MODEL OF SOVEREIGN BORROWING AND DEFAULT

The government's budget constraint can be written as

$$q_t B_t + M_t - M_{t-1} + P_t T_t = \delta_t B_{t-1} + P_t G_t + Tr_t,$$

- $q_t B_t$ is the revenue from selling pure discount bonds
- $M_t - M_{t-1}$ is the revenue from money creation
- $P_t T_t$ are tax revenues
- B_{t-1} are the bonds coming due
- $P_t G_t$ is government expenditure on goods and services
- Tr_t are government transfers

4.1. Default Decision

Since repayment is, in some sense, optional with sovereign debt, the government must weigh whether to fully repay and the various ways it could choose not repay. The choices are:

(1) fully repay;
(2) try to inflate the debt away;
(3) try to negotiate down its payments; or
(4) default, and possibly negotiate the extent of repayment down the road.

Here we focus on options 1 and 4.

Assume that there are two periods, $t = 1, 2$ and the government must decide whether to repay its debts in each period. Assume that if it fails to repay, then the country's output will fall by a fraction γ henceforth and that it will lose access to credit markets. (We could modify our model by not having the fall of γ last forever, but instead just for a couple of years.)

The country's output is stochastic, with $Y_t \in Y$ and the probability is $\Pi(Y_1)$ in the first period and $\Pi(Y_2|Y_1)$ in the second. Assume also that the government cannot adjust the tax rate τ very readily, so we will take it to be fixed.

Strategic models are often solved by backward induction, and that is what we are going to do here. The steps are:

(1) Compute the optimal default rule in $t = 2$,
   • first assuming no prior default,
   • then assuming prior default
(2) Compute the second period payoff and bond pricing function
   • Compute the payoff when default both has and has not has already occurred.
   • Compute the bond pricing function both when default has and has not has already occurred.
(3) Compute optimal $t = 1$ behavior and bond pricing if we want to default in $t = 1$.

4.1.1. PERIOD 2 DEFAULT DECISION - NEVER DEFAULTED BEFORE
In the second period, the government's revenue is

$$\tau Y_2 \text{ if it doesn't default, and}$$
$$\tau \gamma Y_2 \text{ if it does.}$$

The government budget constraint then implies that

$$G_2 = \tau Y_2 - B_2 \text{ if it doesn't default, and}$$
$$G_2 = \tau \gamma Y_2 \text{ if it does}$$

and private consumption is

$$C_2 = (1 - \tau)Y_2 \text{ if it doesn't default, and}$$
$$C_2 = (1 - \tau)\gamma Y_2 \text{ if it does.}$$

If we assume that the government's payoff in period 2 depends upon both government spending and private consumption,

$$V(G_2) + U(C_2),$$

then the government should default if the payoff from doing so is greater than repaying, or

$$V(\tau \gamma Y_2) + U((1 - \tau)\gamma Y_2) \geq V(\tau Y_2 - B_2) + U((1 - \tau)Y_2).$$

Clearly, the government should never default if $(1 - \gamma)\tau Y_2 > B_2$. Moreover, the benefit to defaulting is increasing in B_2 and decreasing in Y_2. There will exist a cut off level of debt $B_2(Y_2)$ such that the government will default if $B_2 > B_2(Y_2)$, and repay otherwise.

To get a better sense of things, I have plotted a "typical" case in Figure 17.6. In the figure we have plotted a line that shows the combinations of Y_2 and B_2 at which the government is just indifferent between defaulting and not. We assume that when the government is indifferent it chooses to repay. So $\delta = 1$ along the line. δ is also equal to 1 at all points below the line, and $\delta = 0$ at all points above the line.

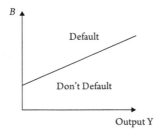

Figure 17.6 Default Set.

4.1.2. PERIOD 2 DEFAULT DECISION: ALREADY DEFAULTED

Since the government has already defaulted, its second period revenue is $\tau\gamma Y_2$, irrespective of whether it defaults or not today. But then its consumption is

$$G_2 = \tau\gamma Y_2 - B_2 \text{ if it doesn't default, and}$$
$$G_2 = \tau\gamma Y_2 \text{ if it does}$$

and private consumption is $C_2 = (1-\tau)\gamma Y_2$ whether it defaults or not.

So, the government should always default if $B_2 > 0$.

4.1.3. THE SECOND PERIOD PAYOFF

The second period payoff to the government (assuming it did not default in the first period) is given by

$$W(B_2, Y_2) =$$
$$\delta(B_2, Y_2)\left[V(\tau Y_2 - B_2) + U((1-\tau)Y_2)\right]$$
$$+ (1 - \delta(B_2, Y_2))\left[V(\tau\gamma Y_2) + U((1-\tau)\gamma Y_2)\right].$$

This payoff will be decreasing in B_2 and increasing in Y_2.

Note that the option of defaulting is acting like partial insurance for the government, since it prevents both government and private consumption from falling too far if Y_2 is small relative to B_2.

4.1.4. THE LENDING DECISION

We will assume that there are a large number of competitive lenders who buy the government's first period debt. We assume that debt issuance happens *after* the first period default decision, so these lenders need to know about default only in $t = 2$.

Let $\delta(B_2, Y_2)$ denote the government's default decision, where

$$\delta(B_2, Y_2) = 1 \text{ if } B_2 \leq B_2(Y_2), \text{ and}$$
$$\delta(B_2, Y_2) = 0 \text{ otherwise.}$$

In Figure 17.6 we have graphed a version of the default rule $\delta(B_2, Y_2)$ with the second period debt level on the y-axis and the second period output level on the x-axis. Along the line, the country is just indifferent between defaulting and not, while below the line, the level debt level has fallen relative to the indifferent level, and hence the country now prefers to repay, while above the line the reverse is true. The set of outcomes above the line is called the *default set*, and those below are called the *repayment set*. The lenders will take these two sets as given. The borrower will choose its debt level B_2 in the first period. Given this, the probability that the lenders will be repaid is the probability of getting an outcome level at or above the cut-off for the repayment set. Since this output level is increasing in the debt level, the likelihood of repayment is decreasing, because it will take a more fortunate outcome to induce the government to repay.

If lenders are risk neutral and have a discount rate of R^{-1} the price of a government bond today is

$$q = \frac{1}{R} \sum_{Y_2} \delta(B_2, Y_2) \Pi(Y_2 | Y_1). \tag{19}$$

This price is the probability of repayment times the lenders' discount factor. At this price, the lenders just break even in expectation. Of course ex post they either enjoy a high return when the government repays or a complete loss when the government defaults. The high return is supposed to compensate them for the ex ante risk of default.

The price of government debt in (19) will depend on the amount the government borrows through δ. The realization of the period 2 output level Y_2 implicitly impacts on the determination of q through both through δ and the probability of Y_2. But q does not depend upon Y_2 directly since it is not known in period. The price can depend upon period 1 output, Y_1 to the extent that it affects the probabilities w.r.t. Y_2 tomorrow. This dependence is direct since Y_1 is known in period 1. The price q will be declining in B_2. Since a high output level Y_2 will lead the government to choose not to default, if a higher Y_1 increases the probability of a high Y_2 tomorrow, then q will be increasing in Y_1. (If the reverse is true, then it will be decreasing in Y_1.) And, if Y_2 is independent of Y_1, it will not depend on current output, only current borrowing. To reflect all these possibillities, denote this price by $q(B_2, Y_1)$.

The fact that the price that it gets for its debt will fall when increasing its issuance leads to a higher likelihood of default is an important component of sovereign borrowing. In this respect sovereign borrowing is like the problem of a monopolist who understands that the more she tries to sell, the lower the price of her good. The government here is a monopolist too, in that while there may be other debt products in the marketplace, their debt is special in that their default decision directly affects its payoff.

4.1.5. THE LENDING DECISION—ONE KEY CAVEAT

If the lenders anticipate that the government is going to default in period 1 then, as we noted earlier, the government will default for sure tomorrow. This implies that $\delta(B_2, Y_2) = 0$ for all possible Y_2 draws, and hence

$q = 0$ if government will default in $t = 1$.

In Figure 17.7 I have graphed the price schedule for both the case in which the country had not defaulted in the prior period (solid line) and the case when it had (dotted line). The price schedule when it had not previously defaulted starts at the level implied by the risk-free discount rate $1/R$, and stays at this level so long as the debt level is low enough that the probability of default is 0. This corresponds to being below the point where the default indifference line hits the y axis in figure 17.7. As the debt rises above this intersection point, then the country will optimally choose to default at the lowest output level. Now default will occur with positive probability, and the price schedule turns down. With higher debt, the likelihood of default is higher still and the price schedule keeps going down, until it hits a price of 0, at which point default is occurring for sure. This corresponds to such a high debt level that the country is defaulting in Figure 17.7. For all debt levels above this point the price is 0. In the prior default price schedule, the price is 0 for any positive amount of debt issuance.

A key aspect of the price schedules the country faces is that they depend upon the country's prior default and current borrowing decisions. This is something the country will optimally choose to internalize in deciding how much debt to issue.

4.1.6. BORROWING DECISION

The payoff to the government if it does not default in period 1 is given by

$$\max_{B_2} V(\tau Y_1 - B_1 + q(B_2, Y_1)B_2) + U((1 - \tau)Y_1)$$
$$+ \beta E\{W(B_2, Y_2)|Y_1\},$$

where the government is optimizing over B_2. Note that if it chooses too large a value of B_2 then $\delta_2 = 0$ for sure and $q = 0$. Hence, there is a natural cap on the

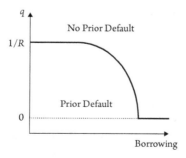

Figure 17.7 Price Schedules: Regular and Prior Default.

amount it can borrow. Today's income affects the payoff both directly and through the expectations about Y_2.

4.1.7. DEFAULT DECISION

Countries normally borrow in order to help repay debt that is coming due. This opens up the possibility of borrowing and then defaulting. What limits this is that debt is normally coming due throughout the year, and the government holds regular debt auctions to roll over the debt piece-by-piece. To account for this in an annual model, we will assume that when a country defaults, it only gets a fraction γ of the new debt that will be issued that year.

4.1.8. THE FIRST PERIOD DEFAULT DECISION

We have already computed the payoff to not defaulting, given that the government chooses the optimal level of borrowing,

$$\max_{B_2} V(\tau Y_1 - B_1 + q(B_2, Y_1)B_2) + U((1-\tau)Y_1)$$
$$+ \beta E\{W(B_2, Y_2)|Y_1\}.$$

In this problem, the government will be trading off the benefits of smoothing government consumption in the face of revenue shocks, and the potential increase in the costs of borrowing.

The payoff if the government defaults is given by

$$V(\tau\gamma Y_1 + \gamma q(B_2, Y_1)B_2) + U((1-\tau)\gamma Y_1)$$
$$+ \beta E\{V(\tau\gamma Y_2) + U((1-\tau)\gamma Y_2)\}.$$

The government will choose to default or not in period 1, depending upon which payoff is larger.

The model we have constructed features something like a *solvency-based default*. This occurs when the amount the government has coming due is simply too big for it to ever possibly repay. This is what happened in Grenada after it was hit by a hurricane.

Even if the government can repay, it may choose to default instead. These *defaults of choice* will generally be triggered by low output realizations. This is because the cost of defaulting in terms of lost output $(1-\gamma)Y$ is increasing in Y, while the amount to be repaid is independent of Y.

In addition, an increase in the likelihood of a default decreases the current price of the new government debt, which, in turn, makes default more attractive. So there is a natural feedback loop that makes the government not want to default for high output levels and want to default for low ones.

Defaults of choice are much more common than defaults of solvency. Argentina is an example of defaults of choice.

The model also allows for *liquidity crisis* types of default, in a manner somewhat similar to the Diamond-Dybvig model of banks. To see this, assume that no one would lend to the country in period 1 for fear that the government would default on these new loans. Then, the government would have to suddenly repay all of the outstanding debt coming due.

This changes our payoffs from not defaulting to

$$V(\tau Y_1 - B_1) + U((1-\tau)Y_1)$$
$$+ \beta E\{W(0, Y_2)|Y_1\},$$

and from defaulting to

$$V(\tau\gamma Y_1) + U((1-\tau)\gamma Y_1) + \beta E\{V(\tau\gamma Y_2) + U((1-\tau)\gamma Y_2)\}.$$

The sudden need to drastically cut government consumption in order to repay the country's debts can make defaulting either more attractive or simply necessary. This can be true even when the country would have repaid under the standard equilibrium we considered first. Such a liquidity crisis outcome can potentially explain contagion effects and outcomes like the Mexican debt crisis.

There are two potential price schedules in the case of a liquidity crisis. The first corresponds to the case in which the debt level is high enough that the country would optimally choose to default today in the event of a crisis. This price schedule looks like the prior-default price schedule in Figure 17.7. The other price schedule corresponds to the case in which the government would not default today even if it could not borrow. In this case, the government can credibly say it will not default today, and hence, its price schedule looks like the regular no-prior-default schedule in Figure 17.7.

When the country's debt level is high enough and its output level is low enough that a crisis is possible, we refer to the country as being "in the crisis zone." By this we mean that fundamentals are such that a crisis can occur, but not necessarily that it will occur. Whether a crisis occurs depends upon which of the two possible equilibrium outcomes will be selected, something very hard to say much about concretely.[8]

8. For more on sovereign debt and sovereign debt crises, a good source is Aguiar and Amador's "Sovereign Debt: A Review," which was published in the *Handbook of International Economics*, vol. 4, 2014. See also the entry "Self-Fulfilling Crises" in Wikipedia.

4.2. Default Worries and Economic Activity

Thus far, we have taken output of the country to be exogenous, but there is an important interaction here. What if agents expect the economy to be less productive if the country defaults? This can be especially important with respect to the incentives to invest.

To see why this is the case, consider the payoff to a firm from investing in an extra unit of capital. Assume that it takes the following fairly standard form

$$F_K(K, L)$$

if the government does not default and

$$\gamma F_K(K, L)$$

where $\gamma < 1$, if it does default. This reduction in the return is coming from the fall in overall productivity that one expects to see following a default. Then, the expected payoff today is given by

$$\frac{1}{R} \sum_{Y_2} \left[\begin{array}{c} \delta(B_2, Y_2)\, [F_K(K, L)] \\ +(1 - \delta(B_2, Y_2))\, [\gamma F_K(K, L)] \end{array} \right] \Pi(Y_2 | Y_1).$$

Note that the higher the probability of default, the lower the expected return on investing in more capital. Thus, concerns about future sovereign default can lower investment today and output tomorrow. This in turn can make it more likely that the government will end up defaulting.

So-called sudden stops refer to cases in which a country is growing rapidly while experiencing large amounts of capital inflows. Often, these inflows mean that either there is a lot of private borrowing going through the banking system, or government borrowing, or both. Often the price of nontradeable goods like houses and wages can rise sharply. At some point fears about a possible default seem to kick in and this all can reverse sharply. This sharp reversal is the sudden stop, and it can lead to defaults and financial crises. The simple extension that we have just considered shows how fears of default can lead to a sudden reduction in investment. This sudden reduction in investment is an important element of these sudden stops.[9]

9. See Guillermo A. Calvo, "Capital Flows and Capital-Market Crises: The Simple Economics of Sudden Stops" *Journal of Applied Economics*, (1998), vol. 1, no. 1 (November) for more on sudden stops.

4.3. Default and Maturity

The maturity structure of the government's debt can have an important impact on the government incentives with respect to its policy choices. Remember that the longer the maturity, the easier it is to inflate away the outstanding debt. With 10- or 20-year-old debt, a mild inflation will do the job of inflating half or more of the debt away. As a result of this, many countries find borrowing using long term debt very expensive, especially during any kind of crisis period. This can lead them to shorten the maturity structure of their debt. But this shortening can have an important impact on their incentives to default.

To discuss this, consider a simple two-period model: Assume output is constant at Y; that the government has an outstanding debt balance of B; and that the gross interest rate is 1.

Case 1: Assume the government has $B/2$ units of debt coming due today and $B/2$ units tomorrow and is planning to pay off its debt each period.

- Then, its payoff from repaying looks like

$$[V(\tau Y - B/2) + U((1 - \tau)Y)] [1 + \beta].$$

- This payoff is independent of whether anyone would lend to the country in the first period so no lending is being planned.

Case 2: Assume that the government has B units coming due today and is planning on paying off half of its debt and rolling over the other half.

- Then, its payoff from repaying, given that it can roll over at a gross interest rate of 1, is

$$[V(\tau Y - B/2) + U((1 - \tau)Y)] [1 + \beta].$$

- But if there is a liquidity crisis and no one will lend to the country in the first period, this payoff becomes

$$V(\tau Y - B) + \beta V(\tau Y) + U((1 - \tau)Y) [1 + \beta]$$

The sudden need to pay off all of the maturing debt can make defaulting much more attractive. Something like this is what happened in Mexico.

4.4. International Rescue and Incentive Problems

In the old days, bondholders were largely on their own. One counter example to this is when the British intervened in Egypt in the 1880s in part to protect British bondholders. During the 19th century, Egypt was formally part of the Ottoman Empire and the ruling dynasty in Egypt had borrowed and spent large sums on various infrastructure projects. These projects were at least partially intended to bolster military control of the country, and the government itself was quite corrupt. Perhaps as a result of all this, the expenditures did not end up translating into a large increase in output. This made the country's economic situation poor, and the paying off the debt to European lenders difficult. When various militant actors in the government, in particular the military, threatened to overthrow the Khedive (who was ruling the country), the Europeans intervened. In the end, Europeans took over the running of many aspects of the country (including the Treasury), the debt was forgiven, and the Europeans took control of the Suez Canal in return.[10]

Things have changed a lot since those colonial days. Now, there are international agencies like the IMF that can rush to the rescue. But this leads to the following question for the bondholders: Can we get some of our money back from the IMF? Often, the initial phase of an IMF intervention includes loans that help the government roll over its debt on more favorable terms. This typically leads to private lenders being paid off and private loans being replaced by official loans from the IMF and the World Bank, among other non-private entities. The IMF can also help the country negotiate the terms of its outstanding liabilities, often leading to a reduction in the amount that the country has to pay, and lengthening the horizon over which it can make these payments.

If British investors in Egyptian bonds during the 19th century anticipated that the British government would intervene to protect their interests, then they also realized that they were more likely to be paid off. Hence, they were more eager to lend to Egypt than to a government in which the British government was less interested and hence less likely to intervene. In a similar manner, if investors believe that the IMF will come in and bail out the country, at least for a while, the magnitude of the investors' losses in the event of a crisis will be smaller.

To see how this works, assume that investors think this bailout will reduce their losses by 50% in the event of a default. Then, their bond price function for government debt changes from (19) to

---

10. See the discussion in Wikipedia under "History of Egypt under the British" for more information on this period. For more amusing reading about this period, see the Mamur Zapt detective novels by Michael Pearce.

$$q = \frac{1}{R} \sum_{Y_2} [\delta(B_2, Y_2) + (1 - \delta(B_2, Y_2))/2] \, \Pi(Y_2|Y_1),$$

This reduces the price reduction from default risk. In effect, default is being subsidized by the IMF. This subsidy then encourages governments to take these risks that can raise the likelihood of default because lenders are now willing to lend to them on better terms than before if they do so. The moral hazard aspect of IMF interventions has been a topic of concern for a long time. It was also an important issue for the EU and was the reason for requirements on fiscal discipline within the EU that sought to limit deficit spending.

PART SEVEN

Reviews

18

Math Reviews

The course is concerned with using models to think about how the world works and the optimal government response in terms of monetary and fiscal policy. We will assume that individuals are rational, which we will take to mean that they have a well-defined payoff function that they are seeking to maximize. This will imply that we are making extensive use of basic optimization theory. In addition, we will have to think carefully about how these individuals make their optimal choices in the face of uncertainty. As a result, we will also be using basic probability theory extensively. In this section, we provide a short review of this material.

For more information on optimization theory, a great place to start is Avinash Dixit's *Optimization in Economic Theory* (either the first or second edition) from Oxford University Press.

1. OPTIMIZATION REVIEW

Our models features individuals and agents who seek to maximize their payoff. The payoff is a ranking of the set of possible outcomes from best to worst. Constraints then determine which elements of the overall set of possible choices are feasible for the agent. Their problem is to pick the best element in the set of feasible choices. We will represent preferences over outcomes with a function. This function will tell us the numerical value associated with different outcomes and the ranking is implied by these values. For example, the payoff or utility from a consumption vector c is given by the function $U(c)$ which maps from the space of possible consumptions, C, to the real line. A higher value such as $U(c_1) > U(c_2)$ means that c_1 is preferred to c_2.

For another example, assume that the individual cares about consumption and labor effort, with more consumption making him better off and more labor effort making him worse off. Then the utility function U will map from the set of possible consumptions, C and the set of possible labor efforts, L, to the set of possible payoffs which will be elements of the real line, R. We denote this by $U : C \times L \to R$. Because consumption is a good thing the marginal impact of an increase in c will be positive while an increase in l will be negative.

All of the possible consumption c and labor effort l choices, which we denote by $(c, l) \in C \times L$, will not necessarily be feasible. We construct the set of feasible choices by imposing a constraint. A typical constraint would be a budget constraint

$$c \leq w * l.$$

The set of feasible choices would then be given by $\{(c, l) \in C \times L : c \leq w * l\}$.

For another example of a constraint, assume that there were two types of consumption, A consumption and B consumption, which we denote by c_a and c_b. Then a budget constraint over these two types of consumption would be

$$p_a c_a + p_b c_b \leq y.$$

Non-linear constraints often arise in production economies. For example, assume that output is produced with labor l and capital k, and that this output can be used either for consumption c or next period's capital k'. Then a typical non-linear budget constraint would be

$$f(k, l) \geq c + k'.$$

We will characterize (i.e., describe) the optimal actions of our agents, households, firms, and so on, by solving their optimization problem. This optimization will typically consist of an objective function, a choice set, and a constraint that limits the choice set further. For example: (i) maximize U by choosing values of c and l that satisfy the budget constraint, or (ii) maximize U by choosing values of c_a and c_b that satisfy the budget constraint.

We will assume that these functions are nice in the following sense. First, they will in general be continuous and smooth. A *smooth function* is one that changes continuously, which will mean that such a function is differentiable (more on this later).

With respect to preferences, we will assume the functions are concave so that positive amounts of all goods are preferred to consuming simply one good or the other. A function U is said to be *concave* if for any two consumption points (c_a, c_b) and $(\bar{c}_a, \bar{c}_b)$ and any λ between 0 and 1, where we define the consumption point $(c_a^\lambda, c_b^\lambda)$ by

$$c_a^\lambda = \lambda c_a + (1 - \lambda)\bar{c}_a$$
$$c_b^\lambda = \lambda c_b + (1 - \lambda)\bar{c}_b$$

then,

$$U(c_a^\lambda, c_b^\lambda) > \lambda U(c_a, c_b) + (1 - \lambda)U(\bar{c}_a, \bar{c}_b).$$

Note that this does not imply that equal amounts of the two goods are preferred. In fact, the individual may have a distinct preference for one or the other of the two goods. However, completely extreme consumption bundles are not desirable. Here are two examples of concave functions:

1.

$$U(c_a, c_b) = c_a^{1/2} + c_b^{1/2}$$

2.

$$U(c_a, c_b) = \log(c_a) + \log(c_b)$$

Before turning to optimization we need one other key definition. A set G is said to be *convex* if c and $c' \in G$, then $\lambda c + (1 - \lambda)c' \in G$ for any $\lambda \in [0, 1]$.

We turn next to optimization. Assume that c is a vector, F is a concave function, and the set of feasible choices G is convex. Then, if we are not at an optimum, we can always improve locally by moving toward the optimum. To see this, assume that $F(c') > F(c)$, and both c' and c are in G. Then for any $\lambda \in [0, 1]$, the fact that G is convex implies $\lambda c + (1 - \lambda)c' \in G$ if $c', c \in G$. And since F is concave $F(\lambda c + (1 - \lambda)c') > F(c)$. Hence, we can always find a local improvement (i.e., λ close to 1) that is feasible if we are not at the global max. Also, by the same logic, a local max is also a global max. This is why we often make these assumptions.

A one-dimensional choice problem is one in which the choice variable, say, x, is a scalar, and the choice problem is

$$\max_x F(x).$$

If F is a concave function, then there is one optimal choice, though it could be at the extremes. Concave functions are hump shaped and have only a single hump.

The top of the hill is flat and concave. This is true even in the multi-dimensional context. To use this fact, we next define tangency and derivatives.

The *slope* of a line between two points x and y is:

$$\text{slope} = \frac{F(y) - F(x)}{y - x}.$$

A *tangent line* meets but does not pass through a curve or surface. If the surface is curved, this means that it will meet at a single point if a sufficiently small interval is considered. This occurs because the tangent line replicates the slope of the curve at the meeting point. Because the top of the hill is flat, local peaks (and troughs) have a tangent line with slope $= 0$.

The *derivative* is the slope of the line around the point x, or the slope between x and y as y approaches x:

$$\lim_{y \to x} \frac{F(y) - F(x)}{y - x}.$$

In other words, it is the slope of the tangent line at the point x.

Two key facts about derivatives are:

(1) The derivative of the sum of two functions is the sum of the derivatives:

$$\lim_{y \to x} \frac{\left[F(y) + G(y)\right] - \left[F(x) + G(x)\right]}{y - x}$$

$$= \lim_{y \to x} \frac{\left[F(y) - F(x)\right] + \left[G(y) - G(x)\right]}{y - x}$$

(2) The derivative of composite functions $F(G(x))$ is given by the product of their derivatives or

$$F'(G(x))G'(x).$$

To understand this second fact, assume that these functions are linear

$$F(G) = A + B * G,$$
$$G(x) = C + D * x,$$

then

$$\frac{F(G(x+h)) - F(G(x))}{h} = \frac{B * D * [x+h] - B * D * x}{h}$$

$$= B * D$$

Figuring out the derivatives of functions typically boils down to knowing some key derivatives and then using them to build up to the derivative of the function in question. To see how this is done, we work out a key example.

Example 10. The derivative of x^2 is the solution to

$$\lim_{h \to 0} \frac{(x+h)^2 - x^2}{h} = \frac{x^2 + 2xh + h^2 - x^2}{h}$$

$$= \lim_{h \to 0} (2x + h) = 2x.$$

Here are some examples of derivatives we will use:

1: The derivative of $x^{1/2}$ is

$$\frac{1}{2x^{1/2}}.$$

2: The derivative of x^α is

$$\alpha x^{\alpha-1}.$$

3: The derivative of $\log(x)$ is

$$\frac{1}{x}.$$

4: The derivative of $-e^{-\alpha x}$ is

$$\alpha e^{-\alpha x}.$$

5: The derivative of a^x is

$$a^x * \ln(a).$$

2. PROBABILITY THEORY REVIEW

Probability is a way of expressing the likelihood that an event either will occur or has occurred. The probability of an event A is represented by a real number in the range from 0 to 1 and written as $\Pr(A)$. An impossible event has a probability of 0, and a certain event has a probability of 1. However, the converses are not always true: probability 0 events are not always impossible, nor are probability 1 events certain. There is a rather subtle distinction between "certain" and "probability 1."

The opposite or complement of an event A is the event [not A] or A^C ; its probability is given by $\Pr(A^C) = 1 - \Pr(A)$. As an example, the chance of not rolling a six on a six-sided die is $1 - (\text{chance of rolling a six}) = 1 - 1/6 = 5/6$.

If both the events A and B occur on a single performance of an experiment this is called the *intersection* or *joint probability* of A and B, denoted as $\Pr(A \cap B)$. If two events A and B are independent, then the joint probability is $\Pr(A \cap B) = \Pr(A)\Pr(B)$. For example, if two coins are flipped, the chance of both being heads is $1/2 \times 1/2 = 1/4$.

The probability of events A or B occurring is denoted by $\Pr(A \cup B)$. If the events are mutually exclusive, then $\Pr(A \cup B) = \Pr(A) + \Pr(B)$. However, if they are not mutually exclusive, then we are in essence double counting the probability of the event that both A and B occur, and hence $\Pr(A \cup B) = \Pr(A) + \Pr(B) - \Pr(A \cup B)$.

Conditional probability is the probability of some event A, given the occurrence of some other event B. Conditional probability is written $\Pr(A|B)$, and is read "the probability of A, given B." It is defined by

$$\Pr(A|B) = \frac{\Pr(A \cap B)}{\Pr(B)}.$$

For example, the likelihood of rolling a 2 on a six-sided die is $1/6$. However, the conditional probability of rolling a 2 given that the value of the die was less than or equal to 3 is

$$\frac{1/6}{3/6} = \frac{1}{3}.$$

If we use the conditional probability result, we can derive Bayes' rule. To do that, start by noting that

$$\Pr(A|B)\Pr(B) = \Pr(A \cap B) = \Pr(B|A)\Pr(A).$$

This then implies that

$$\Pr(A|B) = \frac{\Pr(B|A)\Pr(A)}{\Pr(B)},$$

which gives us a simple way of computing one conditional probability from the knowledge of the other. This formula is used a lot in statistical updating.

A random variable is a way of assigning a real number to each possible event. For example, the temperature tomorrow at noon. The set of events is all of the possible things that can happen tomorrow, and for each of those events, we have a temperature reading. A random variable has an associated *probability density*, which gives the probability of a particular value, and a *probability distribution*, which gives the probability that the random variable is less than or equal to some value. Let x denote a random variable and $G(x)$ its distribution. Then, $G(\bar{x}) = \Pr\{x \le \bar{x}\}$ and its density is $g(x) = dG(x)/dx$ if x is continuous, and is equal to $G(x_j) - G(x_{j-1})$, where x_{j-1} is the next lower value of x. The *expected value* is almost surely (i.e., with probability 1) the limit of the sample mean as sample size grows to infinity. Note that this is not the most likely value and may even be impossible—like having 2.5 children. We denote the expected value of x by $E\{x\}$, and it is given by

$$E\{x\} = \int_x xg(x)dx$$

if x is continuous, or

$$E\{x\} = \sum_x xg(x)$$

if it is discrete. The conditional expectation of a random variable is the expected value of x given that it takes on the value in the set A only. This is given by

$$E\{x|A\} = \sum_x x\Pr(x|A) = \sum_{x\in A} x\frac{g(x)}{\sum_{x\in A} g(x)}.$$

For example, the mean of a six-sided die is

$$\frac{1+2+3+4+5+6}{6} = 3.5$$

and the conditional mean given that the roll of the die was less than or equal to 3 is

$$[1+2+3]\frac{\frac{1}{6}}{\frac{1}{6}\times 3} = \frac{1+2+3}{3} = 2.$$

adverse selection 159
Alexander Hamilton 200
American International Group
    (AIG) 186, 191
Argentina 211, 219
    corralito 219
Argentina debt crises 218
asset prices
    Beta representation 77
    price of risk 81
    Sharpe ratio 78
asset-backed securities 183

bank reserves 192
banking
    deposit insurance 177
    lender of last resort 177
bankruptcy 7
banks
    bank run 172, 176
    bank suspensions 169
    Banking Act of 1933 169
    capital requirements 179
    commercial banks 156
    Emergency Banking Relief Act 169
    Federal Reserve Act 169
    investment bank 156
    loan commitments 182
    rollover crisis 176
    standby letters of credit 182
    suspensions 172

Barings of London 156
barter 121
Bear Stearns 182, 191
Bitcoin
    Coinbase 140
    hash function 142
    ledger block 141
    miner 141
    Mt. Gox 140
    wallet 140
bonds
    bearer bonds 156
    bill of exchange 155
    coupon bond 29
    deferred coupon 31
    discount bond 29
    discounting 155
    eurobond 127
    par 31
    Tontine 31
    yield 32
broker 14
broker-dealer 14, 15
Building and Loan Associations 10

capital markets 11
collateral 37, 162
collateral call 162
competitive bid 18
consols 11
credit rationing 159

cryptocurrencies 139
currency
    appreciation 127
    depreciation 127
currency board 211
currency carry trade 135
cypher
    Caesar cypher 144
    key 143

dealer 14
dealer bank 16
debt bondage 8
    Nexum 8
debt contract
    Robert Townsend 162
default penalties 7
derivatives 11
    credit default swaps 186
    forward contract 12, 85
    futures contract 12, 85
    letter de faire 85
    options contract 12
    put 87
    swap contract 12
discriminating price auction 18

Egypt
    British intervention 236
    Khedive 236
encryption
    digital signatures 149
    RSA 149
equity premium 57
exchange rate
    Forex 126
exchange rate regime
    Bretton Woods 129
    fixed 127
    floating 127
    Gold standard 128
exchange trading 14

Fannie Mae 169, 189, 191
Fed funds rate 192
FICO score 189

Forex 127
forward rate puzzle 134
Freddie Mac 169, 189, 191

Glass-Steagall Act 169
government budget constraint 205
government spending 201
Great Depression 169, 177
    bank holiday 177
    bank runs 177
Great Recession 188
Greece 225
Greek debt crisis 222

hash function 151
hyperinflations 200

I.M.F. 225
IMF 236
insurance 7
interest rate parity 133
interest rates 28
    compounding 29
investment banks 182
    commercial paper 182
    leverage ratios 182
    proprietary trading 182
iterated expectations 33

J.P. Morgan Chase 162
JP Morgan Chase 191

labor participation rate 194
Lehman Brothers 162, 182, 191
limit order 15
Lloyd's of London 7

market order 15
Medicaid 203
Medicare 203
Medici of Florence 156
Mexico
    Cetes 222
    Tesobonos 222
Mexico debt crises 220
Modigliani-Miller theorem 108

modulus 146
money market mutual funds
        190, 191
money markets 11
monitoring 162
Moody's 225
Morgan Stanley 182
mortgage-backed securities
        186
mortgages 189
    adjustable rate 176
    alt-prime 189
    interest rate sensitivity
        176
    MBS 189
    prime 189
    subprime 189

non-competitive bid 18

OTC market 190
over-the-counter trading 14

Paul Volcker 216
President Roosevelt 169
primary markets 10
private information 162
proof-of-work 151

random walk 91
repo 16
repurchase agreements 182

Revolutionary War debt 200
Rothschilds of London 156

Savings and Loan Associations 180
    crisis 180
    Keating Five 180
secondary markets 10
secured debt 37
seigniorage 205
Social Security 203
sovereign immunity 226
Standard and Poors 225
stocks
    price-dividend ratio 48
    price-earnings ratio 48
stop order 15
sudden stops 234

tranching 183

U.S. government deficit 202
U.S. government expenditures
        202
U.S. government receipts 202
underwriting 7
uniform price auction 18

velocity model 117
velocity of money 122

yield curve 56
    inverted 57

Printed in the USA
CPSIA information can be obtained
at www.ICGtesting.com
CBHW050919280724
12254CB00004BA/63

9 780190 941703